Restructuring of Enterprises

A Practical Approach

About the Author

Prof. Jayashankar is a global management educationist and practitioner. As Dean of the UN Centre ICPE in Ljubljana, Slovenia he launched the first International post experience management programme in Eastern Europe for policy-makers and executives. He was a Diplomat and Industrial Advisor to the Republic of Slovenia in its nascent nationhood. The exposure to transition economies around that period resulted in the development of comprehensive restructuring programmes for Multilateral agencies like the Asian Development Bank, UNDP, World Bank and the Commonwealth Secretariat. As a Professor and Consultant to the Maastricht School of Management, The Netherlands from 1992, he has participated in its global outreach teaching, training, and consulting activities for diverse countries including Uganda, Tanzania, Kenya, Rwanda, Malawi, Zambia, Ghana, Kuwait, Saudi Arabia, Yemen, Egypt, Australia, Indonesia, Singapore, Vietnam, Mongolia, Peoples Republic of China, Thailand, Kyrgyztan, Kazakhstan, Poland, Ukraine, Malta, Cyprus, Costa Rica, Peru and Suriname.

Earlier, Prof. Jayashankar till the mid-eighties had taught in University of Delhi and Institutes of Management having obtained his Doctoral degree from the Faculty of Management Studies, Delhi University. He was subsequently appointed by The Indian Government as Director, Planning and Management services for the Goa Port and Head of Education and Training for CMC Ltd., leading to a significant contribution to the advent of computers and information technology in the country at that critical juncture.

Prof. Jayashankar (*www.profjayashankar.com*) can be contacted at shankar@msm.nl

Restructuring of Enterprises

A PRACTICAL APPROACH

R. JAYASHANKAR
Professor and International Consultant

CONCEPT PUBLISHING COMPANY PVT. LTD.
NEW DELHI-110059

ISBN-13: 978-93-5125-193-4

First Published 2016

Published and Printed by

Concept Since 1974

Concept Publishing Company Pvt. Ltd.
A/15-16, Commercial Block, Mohan Garden,
New Delhi-110059 (INDIA)
Phones : 25351460, 25351794, *Fax* : 091-11-25357109
Email : publishing@conceptpub.com
Website: www.conceptpub.com

Editorial Office: H-13, Bali Nagar, New Delhi-110 015, India.

Cataloging in Publication Data—DK Courtesy: D.K. Agencies (P) Ltd. <docinfo@dkagencies.com>

Jayashankar, R., 1954- author.
Restructuring of enterprises : a practical approach / R. Jayashankar.
pages cm
Includes bibliographical references.
ISBN 9789351251934

1. Corporate reorganizations. 2. Privatization. 3. Economic conversion. 4. Government business enterprises. I. Title.

HD58.8.J39 2016 DDC 658.406 23

Foreword

The first industrial revolution began in the late 18th century, with the automation of the textile industry. The earlier periods of 20th century, ushered in the age of mass production which heralded the second industrial revolution. Now a third revolution is under way as manufacturing is being rocked by the advent of digital technology. Governments, private and public sector players are carrying out restructuring in some form or the other.

The book on Restructuring of Enterprises: A Practical Approach, emphasizes the methodological "how to do it" aspects of restructuring enterprises rather than the "what to do" approach usually emphasized in conventional subjects. Thus, it should prove useful both to the experienced manager who is interested in enhancing the value proposition to the enterprises and to management students for whom the methodological focus can serve to complement the important "what to do" decision-making skills that can be developed through simulations of real world situations.

My association with Prof. Jayashankar goes a long way as colleagues in the Maastricht School of Management (MSM) since the beginning of the 90's. We shared a common interest in the subject of enterprise restructuring as well as a connection to Eastern Europe owing to my roots in Macedonia and the author's career in Slovenia. As the adage goes 'MSM is located in Europe, but present in the world'-MSM, thus enlightened our global perspective about enterprise restructuring. I sincerely hope that the book will be an indispensable ready reckoner for restructuring of enterprises worldwide.

Prof. Dragan A. Nikolik, Ph.D
Emeritus Professor of Management
Information Systems
Maastricht School of Management
The Netherlands

Foreword

[illegible]

[illegible] ... business simulations [illegible] ...

[illegible]

Preface

Global thought leaders have constantly debated on ways to bring about a massive transformation in developed and developing economies during the World Economic Forum, WTO negotiations and G8 summits. The onus is not only on politicians, economists and academics to achieve long-term economic and social sustainability. Both public and private sector enterprises have a key role to play in contributing to an economic turnaround through effective restructuring strategies.

Restructuring at the enterprise level requires a systematic framework to address issues of adaptation to diverse microeconomic, sectoral, national and international contexts. Managers are required to use skills and expertise of different business functions together to develop and implement a restructuring strategy. There is also a need for a framework, applicable to both public and private enterprises, which helps identify critical constraints, and also serves as a planning tool to implement enterprise restructuring measures.

Where does the discipline of restructuring stand in this evolutionary process? Suffice to say that the delayed maturity of the subject of restructuring can be primarily attributed to the requirement of managers to use skills and expertise of different business functions together to conceive and implement a restructuring strategy. While there is no dearth of literature on specialized topics like mergers and acquisitions, business valuation, the need of the hour is a practical and applied approach to restructuring based on best practices of both researchers and practitioners. Quite apart from any text available today, this book is unique in the sense, that it provides an integrated, holistic, multidisciplinary and practical guidelines for restructuring of enterprises.

The ideas in this book are based on hard won experience and knowledge acquired over a period of time across the globe. My tryst with restructuring began way back in the late eighties and early 90's, which was a time of dramatic changes with the disintegration of the Soviet Union, the fall of the Berlin wall and the emergence of new republics. A restructuring and privatization project carried out for the Asian Development Bank in Mongolia by the Maastricht School of Management (MSM), The Netherlands, aroused my consciousness about the complexities involved in the process. Subsequently, I was engaged in a series of workshops, consultancy, advisory activities for the China Institute for Reform and Development, Haikou, East and South African Management Institute in Arusha, Tanzania, Private Sector Federation, Rwanda, Maltese Management Association, Valetta, CENTRUM catolica Graduate Business School, Peru, FHR Lima Po Institute of Social Studies, Suriname, Regional Information Technology Institute (RITI) Egypt, to name a few. I had immensely benefited from the execution of projects on behalf of the Commonwealth Secretariat, the World Bank, and the United Nations Development Programme. After having steered Corporate Restructuring courses at the Master's level and workshops for restructuring and privatization officials from different continents at MSM, since the 1990's, I have been inspired to integrate theory with best practice to advance the field of corporate restructuring. These officials from diverse countries were facing restructuring problems and crisis points. All of them wanted more success in their restructuring efforts. This book would be of immense help with all of those situations and would facilitate the preparation of an action plan for the restructuring process in an innovative way.

The book comprises of two parts. Part-I of the book deals with concepts and frameworks related to restructuring of enterprises. Chapter 1 commences with an overview of the fundamental concepts of restructuring. The basic integrated framework for restructuring and privatization would enable a proper appreciation of the different issues to be dealt with in the subsequent chapters. The next one on Diagnosis of organizations provides a comprehensive approach for assessing the viability of an enterprise and a checklist for understanding the causes and symptoms of decline, which are the basic prerequisites for devising appropriate restructuring strategies. Business Valuation forms an integral component of organizational diagnosis. Accordingly, Chapter 3 gives a detailed treatment of the methodologies of business valuation and discusses the manner of institutionalizing the process of valuation. Chapter 4 deals with change of ownership structure and discusses the different strategies of privatization. The restructuring case of one of the largest enterprises from Suriname is illustrated. An exhaustive treatment of the different restructuring strategies is provided citing actual examples in chapter 5, without much over emphasis on issues like mergers and acquisitions.

Part-II begins with a chapter on country experiences on restructuring of enterprises. The chosen countries are Slovenia (Europe), Peru (Latin America), Tanzania and Ghana (Africa), Bhutan and Sri Lanka (Asia). A description of the history of the restructuring process, the role of the multilateral agencies and national restructuring agencies, major restructuring examples, and pitfalls in the restructuring process are provided for each country. Chapter 7, provides the framework for developing a viable Action Plan for restructuring. The process of restructuring the Health sector in Philippines and the restructuring of the Uganda Commercial Bank are illustrated by using the proposed framework for developing an Action Plan. The dual nature of the audience to which the book is focused—practicing managers and students—is addressed through the incorporation of cases and review questions in Chapter 8. The cases would stimulate the managers to apply the ideas to their own situation. The Review questions are intended to serve the more traditional purpose of chapter review and the elaboration and expansion of restructuring methodologies.

The strength of this book is largely attributed to the collective wisdom, work and experiences of multi-lateral agencies, restructuring and privatization agencies and officials, policy makers and workshop participants. I owe an intellectual debt to all those institutions and individuals.

R. Jayashankar

Contents

PART-I

1
Restructuring
An Integrated Framework

There has been an unprecedented move on the part of different countries worldwide, to revive their economies, industries and enterprises through restructuring in one form or the other. The primary objective of the restructuring action is to attain a greater level of performance or to survive when the existing structure becomes dysfunctional.

During the last three decades or so, the shift towards a market oriented system has brought about a profound new economic thinking and action in many transitional economies. Transitional economies refer to countries moving from a centrally planned system to a market oriented system. Restructuring, reorganization, reinventing, reorientation, transformation, turnaround, re-engineering, privatization became the frequently used terms in developed, developing and transitional economies. There is no denying the fact that industrial change ultimately occurs at the enterprise level. However, enterprise restructuring cannot be seen in isolation without reference to the particular sector the enterprise is in, or the environment within which it functions. Also policies oriented towards economy wide reforms and institution buildings have not directly addressed the problems of industrialisation.

In the coming days, the impact of Restructuring and other reform measures for enterprises is going to be widespread. For economies moving towards marketisation, a major role now devolves on private initiative in the process of industrialization.

In many cases there is a lack of clear-cut industrial strategies, especially for Public enterprises/parastatals/State owned enterprises, and it is proposed that a strategic management approach as applied to the process of adjustment can help to define more effective approaches and more efficient means of action. Accordingly this chapter, provides an insight into the concepts of restructuring and other reform options and demonstrates the usage of an integrated strategic approach for enterprise restructuring and privatization for developed, developing and transitional economies.

Reform Options

Restructuring is carried out in service and manufacturing enterprises from both private and public, government sectors of different countries. The options, open to a Government for reforming public/state owned/parastatals forms the basis for a finer understanding of the concept of restructuring.

There are three basic options for reforming a state owned enterprise. This would include Restructuring, Privatisation, and Liquidation.

Restructuring

The term enterprise restructuring signifies certain actions initiated at the level of the enterprise, to minimize the gaps between current performance and the performance required for the enterprise to be nationally and internationally competitive. Gaps arise for variety of reasons and this would include factor prices, technology, organisation, marketing and a variety of other factors. The numerous technological advancements related to new product development and design, engineering, manufacturing, marketing, and distribution have resulted in enterprises reaping new competitive advantages over rivals, mainly with regard to the efficiency of providing products and services. Conversely, companies that have failed to incorporate these advancements have lost the ability to compete effectively, resulting in losses in market share and profit margin. Thus, enterprises to minimise the gap, take recourse to a number of actions, which collectively is known as restructuring. The range of actions may include reducing assets, labour, costs, reorganisation of the Balance sheet, etc. which are detailed in the subsequent paragraphs. These actions are initiated to turn an organisation around whether its facing a declining market share, tough industry conditions or erosion of its basic competitiveness in the market.

While turnaround refers to terminally sick companies, restructuring refers to appropriate actions or measures to prevent a company from reaching such a stage of sickness. Also the combination of selling noncore business and reducing employment is referred to as downsizing.

Restructuring can also pertain to a sector wide view of the industrial process and this would involve adjustments in the compositions of the subsectors of the industry. Sectoral level restructuring brings about a change in the production structure and new arrangements across enterprises At the level of the whole economy, restructuring may pertain to long-term response to market trends, adhering to technological changes, and revamping of the macroeconomic policies. The concept of restructuring, used to signify an economy wide view is important and is of utmost concern to those involved in formulating overall industrial and development strategy for both developed and developing countries. World Bank's lending facilities, coupled with policy prescriptions are primarily oriented towards bringing about long-term macro-economic stability in the member countries.

Privatisation

Privatisation signifies a transaction that diminishes either a Government's ownership in, or control over a State owned enterprise and results in the liquidation and sale of its assets. In many transitional economies, the formal private sector is weak, so that privatization not only entails transferring firms from the public to the private sector but also from the formal to the informal sector. Though there exists financial and socio-political justifications for privatization, the primary objective of a change in ownership from public to private hands is purely economic. The economic reason is to increase the efficiency with which the enterprise's resources are used.

For example, the primary role of the World Bank in privatization was to assist in promoting a policy environment in which ownership change will produce efficiency gains that expand production and employment and enhance welfare over the long run. Privatisation thus entails a change of ownership structure from Government to private hands, and thus can be considered as an organizational form of restructuring. Thus, from the point of view of a state owned enterprise, restructuring is a broader term and privatization is a subset of the same.

Liquidation

Liquidation or winding up involves closing down the operations of sick or non-viable enterprises, selling the assets, realizing cash and paying off the liabilities. Many Governments are reluctant to initiate a process of liquidation. The weak capacity of courts and enforcements of judgements makes liquidation an exception rather than the rule. Also the lack of exit of sick companies inhibit the entry of new enterprises and the expansion of existing viable ones. Thus, the perpetuation of sick enterprises subsequently obstructs the transfer of resources to more viable enterprises.

Factors Affecting Enterprise Performance

Restructuring experiences of different economies reveal that the bias towards macro-economic stabilization has not resulted in substantial benefits. For example, the aims and instruments of the structural adjustment loans and sectoral loans of the World Bank have been predominantly macro-economic. To accelerate the process of indusrialisation in transitional economies, financial, human and technical resources should be mobilised, besides expanding their markets. This would call for a redefinition of the role of the State. Excessive regulations by the State have hampered the expansion of industries. The State performs the crucial role of a facilitator, mobilising all the actors together and arbitrating between divergent interests. The Strategic Management approach, as applied to the process of adjustment require that the performance of an enterprise will have to be analysed as the outcome of an interplay of factors at four distinct levels.

(a) *Global/International factors (Mega)*: The international factors, which have a bearing on the performance of an enterprise, encompass the global interest rates, exchange rates, strategic alliances, terms of trade, debt and the international trading rules. These international issues exert pressure for macro-economic adjustment.

(b) *National factors (Macro)*: A host of policies pursued by the Government like the exchange rate, fiscal and credit policies influence the enterprise performance. Also competition policies including import liberalization, free trade regime for exports, licensing subsidies, entry-exit barriers, taxes, price controls would invariably affect the performance of an enterprise. Domestic factor prices, Infrastructure, and institutional proactive services are of equal importance.

(c) *Sectoral factors (Meso)*: In the reform process one of the important decisions to be taken is with respect to the sectors, which need restructuring effort. The sector under consideration may be either a major subsector, a promising subsector or a strong key player in the economy. A major subsector is one which contributes a major share towards industrial output, exports and employments. A promising subsector may be regarded as one whose firms have a very small gap between performance and performance required for global compctitiveness. The sectoral restructuring is a prerequisite for an enterprise to be restructured.

(d) *Factors at the enterprise level (Micro)*: At the level of the enterprise, plethora of factors affects the performance. This may include factors like poor management, inadequate financial control, adverse movements in commodity prices, lack of marketing effort, high cost structure, and lack of strategic planning.

Strategic Planning in Transitional Economies

At this stage it will be useful to link the above mentioned factors to the overall strategic planning process in enterprises. In most transitional economies, planning was one of the key elements in the economic system during the time when these economies were centrally planned. In a market-oriented economy, the planning process is highly decentralised and is the prerogative of individual enterprises. Also in these economies, which were once centrally planned, enterprises were by and large inhibited from playing an economic role of their own. As opposed to this, market economies are governed by the fact that the best way to maximize the wealth for enterprises is to promote competition with each other and that resources can be allocated in an optimal manner, through the forces of supply and demand.

Towards this endeavour a Strategic management approach is likely to play a dominant role in enterprises of transitional economies. Strategic planning, formulation and implementation would provide a convenient interface between the basic corporate philosophy and the detailed needs of operative planning which focuses on specific functional areas like marketing, production, finance and personnel.

External and Internal Analysis

An analysis of the International and national factors affecting the enterprise performance would lend an insight into external opportunities and threats. Besides, the factors mentioned in the preceding paragraph, thorough analysis of the general setting in which the enterprise is operating would include factors like the state of the economy, the political and legislative setting, the technological setting, the socio-cultural setting. For example, in understanding the state of the economy, factors like the propensity to consume, and invest, energy prices etc will have to be considered. The legislations enacted at the central and local levels, corporate tax legislation, regulations and legislation on tariffs, form an important component of the political and legislative settings. For enterprises in transitional economies, major technological changes, would result in improved opportunities. Similarly factors associated with socio-cultural settings would include work ethic and leisure patterns, age structure, and changes in values and lifestyles. Such an analysis of a broader context is purely external and yields essentially the opportunities and the threats in store for the enterprise. As suggested earlier, the sectoral and the enterprise factors (the meso and micro) lend an insight into the strengths and weaknesses. It should however be noted that an enterprise's strengths and weaknesses are relative and would largely depend on the competitors. It will be useful to deduce the strengths and the weaknesses through an in-depth analysis of the resources and an analysis of the competitors. While analyzing the enterprise's resources, key factors, which determine the success of the existing operation, will have to be considered. Also an assessment of the factors, which need to be improved for the enterprise to be more competitive, can be inferred through such an analysis. Factors pertaining to products, costs, finance, marketing, personnel need to be considered as suggested in the checklist, given in Table 1.1. Analysis of the competitors would warrant certain assumptions. However, information about competitors can be from both internal and external sources of information.

Strategic Options

Having familiarized with the context in which the enterprise carries out its activities, the strategy needed to achieve an ideal combination between the strengths and weaknesses and the opportunities and the threats posed by the market should be analysed. For enterprises in transitional economies, it is worth considering three broad strategies. These are the Cost advantage strategy, Market niche strategy and Product identity strategy.

Cost Advantage Strategy

The basic objective of cost advantage strategy is to sell cheaper products than the competitors. Thus the cost advantage strategy is applicable to

Table 1.1: Check List for Analysis of Resources

• Resources	• Indicators
• Products	• Market share, Quality, Price • Productivity
• Production Potential	• Extent of automation • Life of plant • Method of Production
• Marketing	• Sales/Marketing organization • After sales service, warranties
• Research & Development	• Patents and licenses • Size of Budget, Support from government • Staff and laboratories
• Finance	• Profitability • Liquidity • Solvency • Assets and Liabilities structure • Cash flow
• Costs	• Direct costs • Overheads • Procurement Costs • Production Costs • Selling and distribution costs • Inventory costs • Personnel costs
• Personnel	• Attitude and Morale • Productivity and Turnover • Number and Quality of Personnel
• Location	• Nearness to market for finished goods and raw materials • Infrastructure
• Management	• Motivation and Management Style • Strategic alliances • Corporate image

standardized goods. In traditional economies, enterprises will have to strive to maintain the cost leadership strategy, by fulfilling certain basic conditions. These are:

(a) Rationalising production methods and processes.
(b) Existence of sufficient capacity.
(c) Optimising inventories, research, sales and marketing activities.
(d) Appropriate control measures for fixed and variable costs.
(e) Concentration on big markets.

Of course this strategy does entail some risks. By focusing on few big customers, there is always a risk, if just one of the customers takes recourse to other suppliers or changes his requirements.

In many cases this strategy has been complemented by the strategy of market leadership. An enterprise, which focuses on high volume of production, is in a position to cut unit costs through standardization.

Product Identity

The basic ingredient of this strategy is to inculcate certain unique features for the product of the enterprise, so that it is quite distinct from those of the competitors.

This may be achieved through a better design, warranty clause or a better after sales service.

Requirements: If the objective is to enhance the quality of the product, then cost, and subsequently price will play a dominant role in the implementation of this strategy.

Prerequisites

(a) The enterprise will have to adopt state of the art technologies.
(b) Substantial investment is required for better product design, image and advertising.
(c) Good back up of after sales service.

It must be appreciated that for imparting a distinct identity for the product, the price component will be higher. However, the price must not be so much higher, so as to enable the competitor to derive an advantage by attracting the customers. Other risks associated with this strategy include a certain design becoming obsolete, or competitors also resorting to similar enhancements in design and image for their products.

Market Niche Strategy

This strategy is focused at a certain segment of the market or a particular group of customers. The market must be one, which can be compartmentalized into different segments. There must be a definite group of customers under each segment. The enterprise should have detailed knowledge of the expectation of the customers in terms of their attitude, styles, preferences, etc. A situation should not arise wherein the enterprise while concentrating on a specific market niche, neglects others.

Feasibility of the Chosen Option

Before opting for a specific strategy, it is to be ensured whether the chosen strategy fits in with the overall profile of the enterprise. For example, pursuing a cost leadership strategy, and reaping the benefits of economics of scale would require sufficient warehouse capacity. However at the same time, production cost should be low, so that there is a price advantage. The feasibility of the proposed strategy in terms of its implementation, in the context of any legal restructuring, being initiated in transition economies should not be lost sight of. Strategic planning has to do with formulation of long-term objectives.

Operative planning is concerned with short-term objectives, for specific functional areas like procurement, production, marketing and finance. As operative planning is concerned with details, strict discipline and control is called for. A detailed Business plan should ideally incorporate all the salient features of both Strategic Planning and the Operative Planning.

Organisational Diagnosis

There is a felt need in transitional economies to have a sound framework to diagnose the enterprises for their categorisation in terms of their strategic importance and their viability or otherwise. The proposed integrated framework to Restructuring and Privatization, suggests that the starting point for the analysis is the classification of the enterprises into two broad types, namely strategic and non-strategic.

Strategic *Vs* Non-strategic

The enterprise restructuring process ideally should begin with a comprehensive evaluation of the enterprises to identify those that are strategic, viable and those that are not. The Privatisation/Restructuring agencies in most Governments have a system of classifying enterprises as either strategic or non-strategic. Depending on the importance accorded by the respective agencies of the Government for different attributes, a ranking scheme as suggested in Table 1.2, may be adopted for the said purpose.

Table 1.2: Ranking Scheme

Factors/Attributes	*Ranking*		
Impact on Economy/Share of industrial output	High	Medium	Low
Export potential	High	Medium	Low
Import substitution	High	Medium	Low
Competitive advantage	High	Medium	Low
Employment generation	High	Medium	Low
Extent of gap in performance (Local vs International)	High	Medium	Low
Policy constraints	High	Medium	Low
Issues across sectors	High	Medium	Low

Viable *Vs* Non-Viable

The second step in the proposed integrated approach warrants a determination of the viability of an enterprise. The process is initiated through an assessment of the financial performance of the enterprise. In most transitional economies, under the previous command system, the main party interested in the enterprise accounts was the Government. Only essential financial and costing information was the requirement and the Government wanted to ensure that the assets and liabilities were being adequately controlled. Hence, an assessment of the viability of the enterprise, invariably would involve re drafting the financial statements as per the Standard International accounting practices. Under the market oriented system if the shareholders, creditors, management and other interested parties in the transition economies are to derive meaningful information, the financial statements need to be recasted based on cardinal principles of accounting and International accounting practices.

Independent auditors may be required to review the adequacy of the financial statements. An important component of the organisational diagnosis is a corporate financial analysis covering the enterprise's debt situation and in particular the Government's exposure with respect to capital structure and past financial performance. It may be pointed out that relying solely on commercial factors an enterprise may be viable in the short run, but may not be viable in the long run. Similarly an intervention of the Government may be called for at the Sectoral level, for an enterprise to be viable in the long-run. Thus non-economic factors also need to be considered, and the holistic approach for diagnosing an enterprise can be thought of as encompassing: (a) An understanding of the causes and symptoms of decline, (b) Business plan, and (c) Business valuation.

Causes and Symptoms of Decline

In the process of analyzing an enterprise's decline or inefficient performance, it will be relevant to distinguish between the causes and symptoms of failure. Symptoms provide possible clues as to what might be wrong, but do not provide a clear cut guideline for initiating necessary corrective remedial action.

Causes of Decline

Poor Management

Ineffective management and inept handling of vital managerial issues is an important cause of decline in most enterprises. The basic objective of restructuring and privatization is to institutionalize enterprise governance, accountability and autonomy as the underpinning of effective performances by enterprises in a market economy. However, this is not clearly understood by the managers, employees, government bureaucrats and the shareholders. Ineffective board of directors and lack of management depth compound the problem of poor management in most enterprises.

Inadequate Financial Control

Inadequate financial control implies that cash flow forecasts, costing systems and budgetary control are either totally absent or inadequate. In most enterprises in transition economies the typical problem is one of inadequate systems rather than no systems at all. Poorly designed management accounting systems and lack of understanding of the usage of such systems, generate poorly presented information. Also effective control is hampered because of a weak organization structure.

Competition

Competition may pertain to either a product or price competition. Responding to market needs does not necessiate following the market trends. The enterprise simply may not have the resources to develop any competitive advantage as technology or consumer needs change.

High Cost Structure

Enterprises in transforming economies are not in a position to compete on price, as their cost structure is too high. Cost disadvantage may be the result of improper management style, organization structure or control of raw material supply by outside parties. With the high propensity of bad management in turnaround situations of transition economies, operating inefficiencies is also a major cause of decline.

Lack of Marketing Effort

Lack of marketing effort would imply—(a) a poorly motivated sales force, (b) lack of market research, (c) weak new product development function, (d) ineffective advertising, and (e) absence of focus on key customers and major products

Symptoms of Decline

The commonly used indicators for an insight into the symptoms are the financial indicators, though for enterprises in traditional economies, a number of non-financial indicators will have to be taken into account like, decreasing profitability, increase in debt, lack of planning, declining market share, and improper accounting practices.

A detailed account of the causes and symptoms of decline, which forms an important component of organizational diagnosis, is dealt with in the next chapter.

Business Valuation

In times of economic restructuring the process of business valuation is of great significance and forms a very important component of the organizational diagnosis.

The process of business valuation is more than just determining the enterprise's market value. Especially for enterprises in traditional economies, if the process and reporting of business valuation is done properly it can be ensured that: (a) enterprise restructuring will be smooth, (b) enterprises can be prepared for survival in competitive markets, and

(c) Public support can be built for the new system. The objective of valuation is not to grind numbers through valuation models. One can readily develop computer models to do this. The objective is to elucidate the interaction between financial valuation and the concepts of business economics and strategic planning.

Thus an assessment of viability can be done through an organizational diagnosis, which would involve: (a) An understanding of the causes and symptoms of decline, (b) Business valuation, and (c) Business plan. Categorising an enterprise as either viable or non-viable in a clear-cut manner may pose a problem sometimes, though the same is extremely useful for initiating the appropriate restructuring measures. However, due consideration should be given to other relevant aspects such as long-term viability and the linkages between the sector and the enterprise. The methodologies of valuation and other aspects of valuation report are dealt with in Chapter 3.

Restructuring or Turnaround Strategies

The major causes of decline have a profound effect on deciding which strategies are required to effect a successful turnaround operation. There is a considerable degree of difference in the turnaround strategies adopted by enterprises that are successful and those that are unsuccessful in achieving the desired results with the restructuring operations. The turnaround strategies employed in different situations that are successful and those that are not, lies in the quality of implementation. Restructuring strategies, can be broadly categorized into following types:

Strategic Restructuring

Strategic restructuring involves articulating a mission statement, and development of a business plan, as outlined in the earlier Section.

Organisational Restructuring

Most restructuring situations require strengthening of the existing board or the chief executive officer, as the single most important factor leading to decline is poor management. Divisionalisation and decentralization are appropriate turnaround strategies, though organizational change below the top management level is usually avoided in the early days of the restructuring period. Training should also complement organisational change.

Asset Reduction Strategies

Asset reduction strategies are the most widely used strategies in a turnaround situation. This interalia includes the following.

Divesting Operating Units

The concerned operating units of the enterprise may be incurring huge operating losses or may be unproductive. Hence it will be useful to reduce the asset base of the enterprise by selling such operating units to private parties.

Divesting Specific Assets

Assets that are surplus with respect to the future requirements of the business may be sold off.

Sale and Leaseback of Assets

When large amounts of capital are tied up in fixed assets, cash may be realized for some of its assets through a sale and leaseback arrangement.

Reducing Working Capital

Cost Reduction Strategies

The cost reduction strategies would include:

Reducing Material Costs

Material costs can be reduced through: (a) Improved buying practices, (b) Better utilization of materials, and (c) Efficient inventory management.

Reducing Unit Labour Costs

Reduction of labour cost is possible through: (a) Manufacturing overheads, (b) Administration overheads, and (c) Selling and distribution overheads.

Financial Restructuring

Financial restructuring is the key to success of the reform process in transitional economies. For the sake of brevity, financial restructuring can be thought of as encompassing: (a) Asset reduction strategies, (b) Cost reduction strategies, and (c) Debt restructuring.

Revenue Generating Strategies

In turnaround situations, three revenue-generating strategies are commonly used. These include:

- Marketing Improvement Strategy
- Product Market Orientation
- Growth through Acquisition

Mergers and acquisitions are a prominent feature during turnaround situations. This may involve acquiring enterprises in areas of business closely related, or it may involve diversification into unrelated areas. The programmeme must be well planned and acquisitions should not be usually attempted until well into the recovery phase.

Labour Redundancy Programmes

Employees are rendered redundant and this is a highly sensitive issue and has implications throughout the environment in which the enterprise operates. The prevailing economic climate and political mood are important factors determining the redundancy programmes.

Management will have to develop an implementation plan suitable for its own situation. The decision to implement such a programme is easy to make on analytical grounds, however the implementation can be a complex process as well as time consuming.

Legal Restructuring

Legal restructuring may range from simple amendments in the articles of association to the dissolution of an enterprise and transfer of its assets and liabilities to a new corporate entity. When shares are to be offered to a private purchaser or to the general public, a number of specific legal steps may be required to convert the enterprise into a joint stock corporation or a public limited company.

Physical Restructuring

Physical restructuring involves fresh investment in rehabilitation, modernization or expansion of the existing facilities in the enterprise. It is useful to distinguish between financial, legal and organizational restructuring on the one hand and physical restructuring on the other. The first three types of restructuring may be absolutely essential to privatize an enterprise while the last is best left to future owners.

Chapter 5, presents in detail the various restructuring/turnaround strategies.

Appropriate Privatization Strategies

A brief description of the various privatization methods, as is relevant for the integrated framework follows:

Sell Shares to the Public

Under this method shares are offered to the public, through the stock exchange. Thus the distribution of shares is wide and there is openness and transparency in the privatization process.

Sell to Employees (Buy Outs)

The term employees are meant to include people employed at all levels in an enterprise, from company president to an assembly worker. Variety of plans have been developed to facilitate the purchase of shares by employees:

- Workers could receive shares at a discount
- Workers would be able to pay in installments
- Workers could participate in profit sharing with the sharing to be utilized for stock purchases.
- Employee Stock Ownership Plans (ESOPs) are plans to help convert employees into shareholders

Sell to Preidentified Investors

Under this method shares are sold to existing national business groups or foreign business groups. Established enterprises have the necessary technical, managerial, expertise and the financial resources. If they are the buyers, a State owned enterprise can be restructured more easily

Sale of Assets

Assets can be sold on an open competitive bidding or carried out through an auctioning process. The assets can also be sold as a result of direct negotiation with a pre identified party. The is a very useful method for downsizing an enterprise.

New Private Investment

Physical restructuring measures require capital increase in the enterprise and this can be made feasible by offering equity ownership to the private sector. This is a very useful method for undercapitalized enterprises, and the privatization process can be brought about in a gradual manner.

Fragmentation into Units

This method is concerned with splitting up of a large enterprise into several separate units. Each unit may be privatized, using a distinct method, thus maximizing the overall efficacy of the privatization process.

Leasing and Management Contract

The methods of leasing and management contract do not signify full-fledged privatization. Rather these are intermediate methods, which can eventually bring about privatization of State owned enterprises. Under leasing State remains the owner of the property, but the operation of the business is leased out to a private party. Under Management contract, private sector management, technology is provided to the enterprise, on the basis of a contract. Both the methods are useful in implementing the turnaround strategies, and bringing the enterprise to an acceptable level of profitability.

Distribution of Coupons to All Citizens

This is relatively a new method, which evolved out of necessity, when transitional economies were confronted with the challenge to privatise State owned enterprises. The idea is to issue coupon to every citizen, which could be exchanged for shares in any enterprise. This is a better method than allocating shares in a specific enterprise directly to the citizen, as a person might receive shares of an enterprise in which he or she has no interest. Thus to transfer the ownership of enterprises from public to private hands, mass privatization is the quickest method available. If such privatization brings with it more effective management, then such a mass privatization will lead to better performance. Privatisation strategies and the implementation issues are dealt with in Chapter 6.

Integrated Strategic Framework for Enterprise Restructuring and Privatization

The Integrated Strategic approach for Restructuring and Privatization, suggests appropriate steps to be adopted at different stages of the reform process of enterprises in transitional economies. Given the increasing trend towards privatization in most transitional economies, the scheme also prescribes the appropriate techniques of privatization, according to the classification and status of the enterprises. The issue of restructuring before or after privatization has been confronting many enterprises in reforming economies. If restructuring is done before privatization, the slimmed down enterprises will be attractive enough to find a buyer, though attempts to restructure have been quite limited, in the past.

Strategic Viable

For Strategic enterprises, which are viable, the restructuring action, which is being suggested, is only a Strategic restructuring. Strategic restructuring involves the development of a Business plan. The outcome of such an exercise will be a redefined mission for the enterprise, and a comprehensive business plan. It will be prudent, in such cases for the State/Government to retain control of such enterprises. However, if the policy of the Government is to necessarily privatise State owned enterprises, the technique, which is recommended, is issue of shares to the public through the stock exchange. This would ensure transparency and openness in the privatization of strategic enterprises. The public also would be motivated to buy shares of strategic, viable enterprises.

Table 1.3: Integrated Strategic Framework for Restructuring and Privatization

Classification	*Status*	*Size*	*Restructuring Action*	*Outcome*	*Decision*	*Techniques*
Strategic	Viable	All	Strategic/Business Plan	Mission	Government	
				Strategic Plan	Privatise	Sales of Shares to Public
Strategic	Non-Viable	All	Turnaround Programme	(a) Sustainable recovery		Sales of Shares to Public
				(b) Mere survival (unexciting profit)	Privatise	Sale of assets Buy outs
				(c) Short-term survival	Privatise	Sale of assets
				(d) Failed turnaround	Liquidate	Buy outs
Non-Strategic	Viable	Medium/Small	Strategic/Business Plan	Mission	Privatise	Buy outs
				Strategic Plan		Sale of assets
		Large	Strategic/Business Plan	Mission	Privatise	Sales of Shares to Public
				Strategic Plan		New private investment
Non-Strategic	Non-Viable	All	No Action		Liquidate	

Strategic Non-Viable

The framework suggests a major restructuring effort for Strategic, non-viable enterprises. This would involve implementation of turnaround programmes in a systematic manner. The turnaround programmes include strategies with respect to: (a) Asset reduction, (b) Cost reduction, (c) Revenue generation, and (d) Labour redundancy programmes, discussed earlier. Some comments on the likely outcomes for Strategic and non-viable category of enterprises, which would have undergone major restructuring, are relevant. It is not that, all crisis-restructuring situations are recoverable. As is the case with strategy formulation problems, the issue is fundamentally one of matching the enterprise's resources against the environment in which the enterprise is operating, in order to determine a viable future direction for the enterprise. The chances of recovery depend on the combined effect of the factors influencing the development of a sound recovery strategy. Thus there is a range of likely outcomes, from complete and suitable recovery through mere survival and at the extreme end, failed recovery.

As depicted in the framework, the four outcomes are as follows:

Sustainable Recovery/Good Profit

This category of enterprises would be successful in implementing the turnaround strategies, in such a way that the enterprise make above average profits in the long run. It is clear that for such enterprises, which become viable as a result of the turnaround strategies, there are two courses of action open to the Government. Either the Government retains control of the enterprise, or privatizes the same. Thus the appropriate technique for privatization is the sale of shares to the public through the stock exchange.

Mere Survival/Unexciting Profit

For enterprises belonging to this category, though survival is feasible, sustainable recovery may not be possible. It is recommended that such enterprises, be privatized through sale of assets or a management employee buy out schemes.

Short-term Survival/Eventual Failure

Enterprises belonging to this category would have succeeded in improving the profit situation in the short run, but are unable to develop any sustainable competitive advantage. The idea is to privatise such enterprises through sale of assets or buy out schemes.

Failed Turn Arounds

Enterprises under this category cannot exist as viable independent enterprise even in the short run, inspite of comprehensive restructuring efforts. Such enterprises need to be liquidated though many Governments are reluctant to initiate such a measure.

A perusal of the framework would suggest that for Strategic—Non-viable enterprises, successful restructuring efforts involve, a similar approach like that of strategic-viable enterprises. This would imply that either, the State/Government retains the enterprise or depending on the policies being pursued by the Government, the enterprise is privatized.

If a strategic non-viable enterprise, as a result of restructuring efforts makes unexciting profits, or is unable to develop any sustainable competitive advantage (second or third situations), the logical choice would be to privatise through the sale of assets or buy out schemes. A failed turnaround calls for liquidation of the enterprise, which would result in sale of assets and payment of liabilities to the extent possible.

Non-Strategic Viable (Medium and Small)

Medium and small sized enterprises, which are Non-strategic and viable, require the development of only a business plan, resulting in a redefined mission and a detailed strategic plan and sub plans. The Government would do well to privatise such enterprises by encouraging the existing management and the employees to buy out schemes.

Non-Strategic Viable (Large)

Enterprises which are large, Non-Strategic and viable may be privatized through sale of shares to the public in the stock exchange. Alternatively, the Government could consider diluting its equity in the enterprise by encouraging new private investment over a period of time.

Non-Strategic Non-Viable

Finally the framework suggests that enterprises which are non-strategic and which at the same time are non-viable, need to be liquidated.

Conclusion

Most economies in the world endeavour to make the rhetoric 'Market economy', a reality. It is well accepted that the primary objective of enterprise restructuring is to improve the performance of State owned enterprises, in order to prepare them for eventual privatization. Restructuring is also carried out in private enterprises to cut down costs and improve profitability. The peculiar circumstances prevailing in different economies will have to be examined. What can be done effectively in one situation, cannot be matched in another. It is hoped that an integrated strategic approach for enterprise restructuring and privatization, would aid in identifying critical constraints while at the same time act as a planning tool for both public and private enterprises.

2
Organizational Diagnosis

A thorough examination of the enterprise's financial operations, is a basic requirement, for determining the viability of the enterprise earmarked for restructuring. However, this activity should be preceded by conversion of the Financial Statements, as per standard accounting practices. Conversion of financial statement is required, because of the fact that in many countries, more so in transitional economies, the financial statements in enterprises are not set out according to standard international accounting practices. For example, the transition process in Eastern Europe started in the late eighties with the collapse of communism. After the breakdown of the centrally planned economies, the European transition countries have been trying to attract foreign investors. This would necessitate well functioning domestic capital markets that promote the transition process and economic growth. Accounting regulation that conforms to the demands of a market economy must also be developed. During the transition process investors have been worried about the quality of accounting information as well as the application of accounting regulation and control mechanisms that presumably will ensure that companies provide credible information. As of today some countries have completed the transition and are now market economies. Other countries are still struggling with the transition process and yet others have not entered the transition path. Thus, the understanding of accounting and the transition process has not lost its importance. It has implications for other emerging markets-markets which did not experience the same political and economic changes as the transition economies but also have underdeveloped capital markets. The financial statements need to be prepared, based on cardinal principles of accounting, if shareholders, creditors, management, and other interested parties are to derive useful information.

The Main Differences in Financial Statements

The following explanation shows how enterprises which do not set out financial statements according to standard accounting practices (here in after referred to as the non standardized system) can evolve a conversion mechanism, so that a realistic financial information can be provided. (standardized system)

Calculating Profit or Loss

Various accounting conventions are used to calculate whether a profit or loss has been made. The two most important ones are: The Accruals Basis-costs are included when incurred and not when paid for. Likewise income is included when invoiced and not when received. The aim being to match costs and income in similar periods. For example, dividends are shown in the period in which they are declared and not later when paid.

Prudence—losses are provided for when foreseen and not when they occur. For example, if a debtor who normally pays within 30 days has not paid for 60 days, a provision for doubtful debts is made, in case the debtor eventually does not pay. Likewise, if purchase have been in a foreign currency, the amount owing is converted at the year end rate and not at the original rate.

Costing and Financial Statements

The non-standardized system, includes all production costs in the cost of production and several statements provide Government with other cost data. In the standardized system, costing details are kept separate from financial accounting—it is usually regarded as highly confidential.

Accounts Presentation

There is no standard form of presentation of accounts in the standardized system although the Balance Sheet and Profit and Loss Account attached are common. A significant difference is the use of supporting schedules to provide detail—the Balance Sheet detailing totals only.

Fixed Assets

Under the non-standardized system, the accounts show the book value (or cost) of the fixed assets. The depreciation, schedules of additions and disposals and the calculation of the depreciation are shown seperately.

Depreciation rates are standard and announced from time to time by the Government.

Under the standardized system, the accounts show the Net Book Value which is the difference between the cost (or revalued amount) and the accumulated depreciation. Although, the Governments in the West and some other countries announce depreciation rates which are allowed for taxation purposes, each company is allowed to select rates which they consider are realistic for themselves—adjustments are later made for tax purposes.

The main steps in conversion include:

Categorization

It is common in non-standardized system for fixed assets to be grouped into ten or more categories. A smaller number is more common in the standardized system—groups having similar "lives" being categorized together. If a company has one item which is a substantial percentage of the total assets, it is often shown separately.

Asset or Expense

Enterprises should adopt a clear policy over what it will charge against profits in the Profit and Loss Account and what it will include in Fixed Assets to depreciate over a period. For example, small items should not be capitalised, such as calculators and a lower limit for capital is often set. Likewise, repairs should be charged to the Profit and Loss unless they are substantial and are in effect a replacement of an existing asset.

Productive or Non-productive Assets

This division is not maintained in the standardised accounting and all assets are categorised as productive—usually because non-productive assets are too small to be worth identifying separately.

Depreciating the Assets

Fixed assets are either depreciated on a diminshing balance method or by fixed annual installments. The former is generally applied to all assets except land and buildings as it is thought to reflect the actual situation more closely—namely that the value of an asset depreciates more quickly in the first few years. Typical rates used are:

Vehicles	25 per cent of written down value
Plant	20 per cent of written down value
Furniture	20 per cent of written down value
Buildings	1 per cent of cost (writing the building off over 100 years by equal annual amounts)

The reducing balance and fixed instalment methods can be illustrated by taking an asset costing $ 10,000 and depreciating at 20 per cent pa and at 1 per cent pa:

	$ Reducing Balance	*$ Fixed Instalment*
Cost	10,000	10,000
Year 1 @ 20%	(2,000) @ 1%	(100)
WDV	8,000	9,900
Year 2 @ 20%	(1,600) @ 1%	(99)
WDV	6,400	9,801
Year 3 @ 20%	(1,280) @ 1%	(98)
WDV	5,120 etc.	9,703 etc.

Sale of Fixed Assets

When fixed assets are sold, the resulting profit or loss from the sale, is included in the Profit and Loss Account.

Buildings or Other Fixed Assets in Progress

These are shown as a separate group in Western Accounts and are not depreciated until the asset is finished and in use.

Revaluations

The example shown does not include an asset revaluation. In theory the adjustment is straightforward. The revalued amount replaces the Net Book Value and the difference between the Net Book Value and the Revalued Assets is credited to a Revaluation Reserve.

Current Assets and Liabilities

Presentation in the Balance Sheet

In the Western accounts, current assets and liabilities are shown in total only and details shown in a Note to the accounts. This highlights the most important figure—the Net Current assets or Liabilities, which gives an indication of the liquidity of the company.

Basically an item is "current" when it is due or payable within a year. This is a general rule which is only strictly applied to loans—long-term loans being shown separately.

Current Assets

Debtors

All amounts due to the company are generally grouped under one heading. Sometimes Trade and Other debtors are separated so that the age of the Trade debtors can be calculated by referring to the Sales figure. Other debtors would include prepayments, staff debts etc.

The major difference between Western accounting and the improper one is that a provision is made in Western accounting for doubtful debts. This is to recognise that there is risk attached to any sale on credit, but if a debtor has taken longer to pay than was allowed, there is cause for concern. The older the debt the higher the provision.

A doubtful debt provision is calculated commonly by producing an aged list of debtors and applying a percentage to the age-groups. For example, if a company allows all its customers 30 days credit and the aged debtors list revealed:

	Total	*30 days*	*60 days*	*90 days*	*Over 1 year*
$	120,000	100,000	10,000	8,000	2,000

The company might calculate its provision by taking 20 per cent of debts over 60 days, 50 per cent for those over 90 days and 100 per cent for those over a year old. Many companies will have to analyse the accounts of large customers to ascertain which invoices have been paid.

Provision for Doubtful Debts:

		$
20 per cent * 10,000	=	2,000
50 per cent * 8,000	=	4,000
100 per cent * 2,000	=	2,000
		8,000

This amount would be charged in the Profit and Loss Account and reduce the balance of debtors in the Balance Sheet.

Stocks

Under Western accounting the figure for stocks is usually based on a physical count of stocks which are then valued. Stocks are counted at least once a year, usually at the year end. Provision is made against "slow moving" stocks and those which the company may never use, due to technical obsolescence. This could be 5-10 per cent of the total but is better related to a physical list and an examination of each stock category.

Cash

This should present no problems.

Current Liabilities

Creditors

When suppliers have to be paid in foreign currency, and the value of the currency is changing, the amount to be included in the accounts is the amount payable in foreign currency converted to local currency at the date of the accounts. The difference is charged to the Profit and Loss Account as Difference on Exchange.

Taxation

The estimated tax liability for the period of the accounts should be treated as a liability added to amounts outstanding from earlier periods.

Bank Overdraft

Amounts repayable within one year should be indicated here.

Dividends

When a company has declared a dividend it is a liability and should be shown in the accounts.

Long-term Loans

These are usually shown as a deduction from assets.

Shareholders' Fund

The major differences between the two accounting systems occur in the treatment of the Shareholders' Funds. In Western accounting the Shareholders' Funds comprise the Share Capital and Accumulated Profits, less Losses (Reserves). The total of Shareholders' Funds are represented by the Net assets.

The conversion involves grouping the balances on the Charter Fund, the Social and Economic Development Fund, and any other funds, deducting the Share Capital, and the balance are the Reserves to which the annual profit is added. There are no deductions against Reserves, such as the expenses which are currently debited to the Social and Economic Fund.

Both Funds disappear and are replaced by Reserves.

Also, no entries relating to Fixed Assets are made to the Reserves. Dividends declared, tax payable and the profits brought forward from the previous period are shown separately.

The Profit and Loss Account

The Profit and Loss Account is designed to show the results of a period and expenses should be matched against revenue—which does not occur if accounts are prepared on a cash basis. Most adjustments have been discussed.

Non-production Expenses

These form part of the expenses and can be shown separately if desired.

Selling Expenses

Selling and transport of finished goods are company expenses which must be charged against income in calculating the period's profit or loss.

Payments to Government

These are currently grouped together—in Western accounting they are not shown separately, and taxes, with the exception of the tax on profits, form part of the cost of the item to which they relate. i.e. Wages will include the payroll tax, the cost of an asset will include import duty etc.

Balance Sheet

Tugrik 000's	*Note*	*31/12/2003*
FIXED ASSETS	1	195,729
CURRENT ASSETS		
Debtors	2	11,390
Stocks	3	36,571
Cash	4	94,082
		142,043
CURRENT LIABILITIES		
Trade Creditors	5	51,306
Other Creditors	5	1,321
Taxation	6	16,865
		69,492
Net Current Assets		72,551
Less: Long-Term Loan	7	(20,500)
Net Assets		247,780
SHARE CAPITAL	8	212,155
RESERVES	9	35,625
Shareholders Funds		247,780

Profit and Loss Account

Tugrik '000's	*31/12/2003*
Gross Sales	223,908
Net Sundry Income	2,608
Cost of sales	226,516

Tugrik '000's	*31/12/2003*
Manufacturing:	
Sub-contractors	41,750
Raw materials	39,430
Fuel	23,314
Spare parts	5,243
Wages	14,864
Transport hire	5,008
Other	12,357
	141,966
Administration:	
Business travel	520
Communications	747
Rent of land	761
Building repairs	2,017
Electricity	623
Heating	999
Water	1,246
	6,913
Financials:	
Doubtful debt prov	1,100
Loss on Exchange	4,514
Depreciation	7,330
Profit – Sale of FA	2,000
	14,944
Total Expenses	163,823
Net profit	62,693
Taxation	(28,719)
Profit After Tax	33,974
Dividend Paid	(472)
Retained Profit	33,974
Reserves B/F	2,123
Reserves C/F	35,625

NOTE 2
DEBTORS

	31/12/2003
Other property	20
Trade Debtors	8,552
Due from indiv.	98
Other debtors	3,820
Less: Provision for Doubtful debts	(1,100)
	11,390

NOTE 3
STOCKS

	31/12/2002
Raw materials	29,313
Bags	157
Stationery	262
Other	299
Fuel:	336
Hard	
Petrol	893
Other	667
Spares:	
Tyres and Sp.pt	1,794
Equipment	16
Animals	948
Consumables	
In store	1,372
In progress	514
	36,571

NOTE 4
CASH'

	31/12/2003
Local	13
Foreign	82
Bank local	421
Bank foreign	93,566
	94,082

NOTE 5
CREDITORS

	31/12/2003
Trade	
Other:	51,306
Insurance	906
Dues	43
Tax – payroll	372
	1,321

NOTE 6
TAXATION

	31/12/2003
Profit for Tax	62,693
Tax Agreed	28,719
Tax Paid	(11,854)
Outstanding	16,865

One creditor for T 2,000 was for imports.

The goods were purchased in dollars when the exchange rate was T 200 = $1. i.e. $10000 * T200 = T2m. Tugrik is the Mongolian currency

The rate at 31/12/2003 was T 300 = $1. Hence, $100000 * T300 = T3m.

This amount has been included and T1m. charged to Loss on Exchange.

NOTE 7: The long-term loan is repayable after five years.

NOTE 8 : The Share Capital comprises 2,121,550 shares of T 100 each.

NOTE 9 : RESERVES

The Reserves B/F (brought forward) comprise:

Charter Fund	210,000
Social and Economic Development Fund	4,278
	214,278
Share Capital	(212,155)
Balance = Reserves	2,123

Steps in the Diagnosis Process

Once the conversion of the Statements is carried out, a detailed examination of the enterprise's financial operation needs to be carried out for determining the viability of the enterprise. The diagnosis should consist of a corporate financial analysis covering the enterprise's debt situation and in particular the State's exposure with respect thereto, capital structure and past financial performance. Independent auditors may be required to review the adequacy of financial statements. The status of the enterprise as viable or non-viable can be arrived at through a realistic diagnosis of commercial viability—cost, quality, organization, technology, and market characteristics. A thorough understanding of the causes and symptoms of decline will be very useful in this regard. It is pertinent to point out that relying purely on commercial factors may not always be the right yardstick. An enterprise which is viable in the short run may not be viable in the long run. Similarly intervention of the Government may be called for, at the Sectoral level, for an enterprise to be viable in the long run. Hence, an overall assessment needs to be done, to give due cognizance to non-economic factors. It is for this reason, a holistic approach is suggested to provide a better perspective of the viability of an enterprise. The diagnostics comprises of: (a) an analysis of the causes and symptoms of enterprise decline, (b) business plan, (c) business valuation.

Causes of Decline

It will be useful to understand how and why enterprises, in reforming economies, find themselves in a crisis situation. This also will be relevant for devising the turnaround strategies, as a result of restructuring efforts. When analysing an enterprise's decline or poor/inefficient performance we ought to distinguish between causes and symptoms of failure. Symptoms give hints as to what might be wrong with the enterprise, but they do not provide a clear cut guideline, for initiating necessary management action. Hence, it will be useful to understand the basic causes of enterprise's problems, to enable the sick enterprise's recovery. However, it should be kept in mind that the enterprise managers need more than just a checklist. How often the causes occur and under what conditions? Are the causes of decline the same in service businesses as in manufacturing businesses?

Poor Management

It is quite clear that the basic objective of privatization, viz. to institutionalize enterprise governance, accountability, and autonomy as the underpinning of effective performance by enterprises in a market economy is not clearly understood by the managers, employees, government bureaucrats, and the new shareholders. The major management defects in the composition and methods of operation of the management team, would encompass: (a) combined chairman and chief executive, (b) ineffective board of directors, (c) lack of management depth.

For effective corporate governance, the chief executive of an enterprise should have at least partial supervision and control. In many cases when the same person acts as a chairman and also a chief executive officer, the result is ineffective management. Also in many enterprise situations the Board may be ineffective in taking vital decisions or might cause a delay in the decision-making process. Sometimes, the Board meetings are not held at frequent intervals. Lack of management depth, arises from the fact that the basic managerial functions of planning, organization, direction, motivation, coordination and control functions are not carried out properly.

In some of the Eastern European countries, the system of governance in most enterprises is not effective, as the shareholders are too diverse. The management is accountable directly to shareholders rather than to a Board of Directors. The equivalent of the Board is the Control Council. The role of the Control Council is quite vague. The law only specifies that the role of the Control Council is to control the activities of the company.

Inadequate Financial Control and Financial Policy

Lack of adequate financial control, mainly arises from the fact that while financial statements may exist, they usually reveal an Alice in Wonderland accounting world, designed to reflect the needs and dreams of central planners rather than depict economic reality. Inadequate financial control might imply that, cash flow forecasts, costing systems, and budgetary control are either totally absent or inadequate. In larger enterprises in reforming economies, the problem typically is one of inadequate systems, rather than no systems at all. Common problems in most enterprises can be summed up as follows:

(a) Poorly designed management accounting systems and lack of understanding of the usage of such systems. The systems, generate poorly presented information. There is no understanding of the critical success factors by the top management. Critical success factors are those factors that are vital for the manager to be successful in accomplishing the objectives of the organization.
(b) Effective control is hindered by the organisational structure. The essence of a well designed organization structure is to aid management control. Over-centralisation would make control more difficult.
(c) With the shift towards marketisation, enterprises will be serving a range of consumers in different market segments. Most enterprises adopt a costing system, if any in which overheads are allocated to individual product lines on the basis of labour content, machine hours or total variable costs. This would imply that the cost of serving one customer is the same as serving next customer.

Competition

Competition, as a cause of decline refers to both product and price competition. Responding to market needs, does not necessarily warrant following the market trends. The enterprise may not have the resources to develop any competitive advantage as technology or consumer needs change.

Cost Structure

Turnaround situations are characterized by the inability of enterprises to compete on price because their cost structure is too high. The main sources of cost disadvantage that can cause an enterprise to charge higher prices than its competitors are as follows:

(a) Relative cost disadvantages due to the enterprise's inability to reap benefit of economies of scale and its inexperience as compared to competitors. The presence of economies of scale, yields a cost advantage to a larger firm. Economies of scale may arise as a result of division of labour, the indivisibility of technology, spreading of fixed costs over a larger volume etc. It is very important for management to analyse each element of the enterprise's cost structure separately to determine the particular relationships between unit costs and scale.

(b) Absolute cost disadvantages may arise because of ownership or control of raw material supply, by outside parties.

(c) Cost disadvantages may also arise due to management style and organizational structure. A hierarchical organization with poor communications typically leads to lower productivity at the plant operating level.

(d) Cost disadvantages due to operating inefficiencies can be primarily attributed to poor management. With the high propensity of bad management in turnaround situations, it is not surprising that operating inefficiency is the major cause of decline.

Market Demand

A drop in the total demand for a product, or even a change in the pattern of demand, to which the enterprise does not respond, can be an important factor for the enterprise decline.

Lack of Marketing Effort

Most enterprises that are in a period of profit decline are characterized by management and employee complacency at all levels in the organization. Lack of marketing effort would encompass:

- A poorly motivated sales force,
- Ineffective advertising,
- Efforts not targeted on key customers and major products,
- Lack of market research,
- Lack of promotional material,
- Weak new product development function.

Symptoms of Decline

The symptoms of decline are often easier to detect than causes of decline. The commonly used indicators for diagnosis are the financial indicators, though for enterprises in decline a number of non-financial indicators will have to be taken into account.

Decreasing Profitability

The enterprise is in decline if the profitability trend is lower in absolute terms. However, for enterprises in transition economies it will be meaningful to adjust for inflation and reveal the profit in real terms. Other measures of decreasing profitability are lower profitability as a percentage of sales and a declining rate of return on investment. Sales trend will be meaningful after adjusting for inflation.

Increase in Debt

An increase in the enterprise's debt to equity ratio is commonly accepted as an indicator of impending trouble.

Decrease in Liquidity

Enterprises often fail, because they run short of cash. Various measures of liquidity such as current ratio and acid test ratio are frequently used. However, for turnaround situations debtor days, creditor days, and inventory turnover are better indicators of liquidity.

Accounting Practices

Adoption of unacceptable accounting practices, delays in publishing and auditing of financial statements are often considered as a symptom of decline.

Rapid Management Turnover

A high degree of disagreement is indicated with the top management when the turnover is high.

Declining Market Share

A declining market share signifies that the enterprise is losing out to competitors. This conclusion might not be obvious, from sales analysis if there is inflation.

Lack of Planning/Strategic Thinking

Most enterprises in need of turnaround are characterized by gross lack of strategic thinking.

Predicting or Forecasting the Decline of Enterprise

Financial ratios based on current or past performance are quite often used to help predicting the future. However, it may be pointed out that the choice of ratios and the interpretation of the results are normally dependent on the judgement of the analysts. Past research studies conducted by different authorities suggest that ratios like cash flow/total debt, net income/total assets, total debts/total assets, current assets/current liabilities, yield useful results in predicting the decline of enterprise. Also the studies revealed that failed businesses were characterized by lower rates of return, higher levels of gearing, lower levels of coverage for the fixed interest payments and more variable return on shares. Most of these studies focused on univariate analysis, because it focuses on only one single ratio at any particular point of time. However, there are practical problems associated with univariate analysis. For example, past research has identified two ratios as being good predictors in identifying financial distress. When applied to a particular business one ratio will predict financial distress, whereas the other does not. Given these conflicting signals, it is extremely difficult for the decision maker to interpret the results.

The weaknesses of univariate analysis led researchers to develop models which involves a combination of ratios, so as to produce a single index, that can be interpreted more precisely. Multiple discriminant analysis is a statistical technique which can be deployed to draw a boundary line between those businesses which fail and those businesses which do not fail. The boundary line is known as the discriminant function. This can be illustrated with the help of an example. Suppose, in a commercial bank, a manager wants to segregate corporate loan applicants into those likely to default or not default. Time series data are available with respect to a group of firms which includes both companies that went bankrupt and companies that did not. For the sample firms, the current ratio and the debt/assets are analyzed, as given in columns 2 and 3 of Table 2.1. The x's in the Figure 2.1 represent firms that went bankrupt, while the dots represent firms that remained solvent. The purpose of discriminant analysis is to construct a boundary line through the graph such that, if the firm is to the left of the line, it is not likely to become insolvent. It is likely to go bankrupt if the firm happens to be on the right of the line. The boundary line is called the discriminant function and can be expressed as:

$$Z = a + b_1 \text{ (Current ratio)} + b_2 \text{ (Debt ratio)}$$

Z represents the z score, a is a constant term, b_1 and b_2 signify the effect of the current ratio and the debt ratio on the probability of a firm going bankrupt.

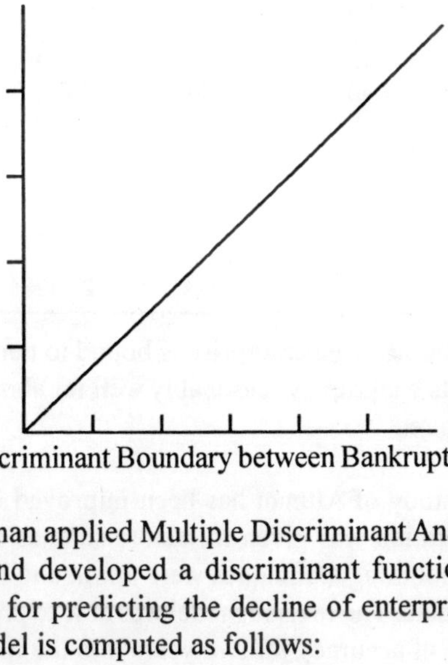

Fig. 2.1: Discriminant Boundary between Bankrupt and Solvent Firm

Edward Altman applied Multiple Discriminant Analysis to a sample of enterprises and developed a discriminant function that has been extensively used for predicting the decline of enterprises. The Z score for Altman's model is computed as follows:

Z = 0.012x1 + 0.014x2 + 0.033x3 + 0.006x4 + 0.999x5
X1 = Net working capital/Total assets
X2 = Retained earnings/Total assets
X3 = Earnings before interest and taxes/Total assets
X4 = Market value of common and preferred stock/Book value of debt
X5 = Sales/Total assets
X1, X2, X3, X4 are expressed as percentages rather than as decimals.
If z = 2.99 and more, the probability of bankruptcy is less.

Table 2.1: Current ratio and debt/assets

Firm Number	*Current Ratio*	*Debt/Assets Ratio*	*Did Firm Go Bankrupt*	*Z Score*	*Probability of Bankruptcy*
(1)	*(2)*	*(3)*	*(4)*	*(5)*	*(6)*
1	3.6	60%	No	-0.780	17.2%
2(A)	3.0	20	No	-2.451	0.8
3	3.0	60	No	-0.135	42.0
4	3.0	76	Yes	0.791	81.2
5	2.8	44	No	-0.847	15.5
6	2.6	56	Yes	0.062	51.5
7	2.6	68	Yes	0.757	80.2
8	2.4	40	Yes	-0.649	21.1
9	2.4	60	No	0.509	71.5
10	2.2	28	No	-1.129	9.6
11	2.0	40	No	-0.220	38.1
12	2.0	48	No	0.244	60.1
13	1.8	60	Yes	1.153	89.7
14	1.6	20	No	-0.948	13.1
15	1.6	44	Yes	0.441	68.8
16	1.2	44	Yes	0.871	83.5
17	1.0	24	No	-0.072	45.0
18	1.0	32	Yes	0.391	66.7
19(B)	1.0	60	Yes	2.012	97.9

If z = 1.81 and less, the enterprise is bound to decline. The model predicts bankruptcy reasonably well for about two years into the future.

The original study of Altman has been improved over a period of time. Due consideration was given to factors such as capitalized lease obligations and smoothing techniques were applied to level out random fluctuations in the data. The revised model was able to predict bankruptcy with a high degree of accuracy for two years into the future.

Multiple discriminant analysis has been used with a fair degree of success by credit analysts to determine default probabilities for individual consumer and corporate loan applicants. It is also used to provide useful insights into the feasibility of a reorganization plan filed under the Bankruptcy Act. Altman's model has been used by investment banking houses like Morgan Stanley to appraise the quality of junk bonds used to finance takeovers and leveraged buyouts.

Study by Rathinasamy (1985)

Rathinasamy selected a total of 31 companies to represent the failed sample and another 31 matched non-failed firms from the same industry and year of failure. 21 financial ratios were computed for each company and on the basis of the Univariate F-ratio, 11 ratios were significant at the 0.001 level. A stepwise procedure using the original list of variables resulted in a final discriminant function with 4 variables. Rathinasamy obtained the unstandardized discriminant function as:

$$Z = 0.2088971X1 + 1.389963X2 - 2.745602X3 + 0.9935117X4 - 5.889544$$

Where

X1 = Equity/Total Liabilities
X2 = Log 10 of Total Assets
X3 = Total Debt/Total Assets
X4 = Cash Flow/Current Liabilities
(Cash Flow = Net Profit before Tax + Depreciation)

Study by Sweeney (1994)

Sweeney matched 27 distress firms with healthy public-listed firms in the same industry with similar market capitalization size. These 27 matched-pairs were then divided into 2 sub-samples, with fourteen pairs in the in-sample and thirteen pairs in the holdout-sample.

A total of 20 financial ratios were aggregated with weights of 0.5, 0.3 and 0.2 assigned to the first, second and third year prior to distress respectively. Through Factor Analysis, 8 factors were extracted. When discriminant analysis via the direct approach was performed on the 8 ratios, 3 ratios were deleted. The remaining 5 ratios were found to be well-distributed amongst the key financial performance areas of liquidity, profitability, leverage and efficiency with the prediction model as follows:

$$Z = 0.0237X1 + 4.765X2 + 0.104X3 + 1.287X4 + 1.373X5$$

Where

X1 = Current Ratio
X2 = Total Equity/Total Assets
X3 = Cash/Current Liabilities
X4 = EBIT/Total Capital
X5 = Net Income/Sales
(All ratios are in absolute values, not percentages).

Conclusion

The *Z* score computation thus provides an insight into the zones of discrimination as given below:

$Z > 2.99$	"Safe Zones
$1.81 < Z < 2.99$	"Grey Zones"
$Z < 1.81$	"Distress Zones"

Healthy enterprises would fall under safe zones. Enterprises which are in the Grey zones would require restructuring efforts. Enterprises under the distress zones need to be either liquidated or would require comprehensive restructuring efforts.

3
Valuation of Business

The process of Business appraisal or valuation of business is of paramount importance in the process of Restructuring and privatization. Together with an understanding of the causes and symptoms of decline, and Business plan, the valuation process and reporting, forms an important component of the organizational diagnosis.

Legal Cases

The importance of business valuation from the point of view of economic restructuring can be well appreciated from two legal cases of the early nineties. Barbara Johnson, a Polish American was on the verge of buying a controlling interest in Lenin Shipyard in Gdansk, Poland. The Shipyard, being the birthplace of the Solidarity movement attracted lot of public attention. However, the deal fell through when Mrs Johnson's accountants realized that the shipyard was worth less than a tenth of what the Polish government was asking for. At about the same time, Hungar Hotels, a hotel chain, in Hungary was to be acquired by Swedish and Dutch investors. There was a public outcry over the low value that had been placed on the company and the deal was not concluded. Thus in the Polish case, the Government was quoting a higher price than the real value, while in the Hungar Hotel case, the real value was much higher than the price quoted by the Government. All these cases and many more just like them from other parts of the World point out the crucial role of business valuation in times of economic restructuring.

Importance of Valuation

Valuation is the process of arriving at an assessment of the total value of an enterprise or the value of the company's common/equity/ordinary stock. In countries with a vibrant stock market, security analysts employ a process of valuation to determine what individual stocks are worth or to understand, whether the market has under or overvalued them. Bankers and financial analysts use valuation to have a proper perspective about their clients and assist them to implement value creating strategies. Also they use valuation for facilitating mergers, acquisitions, divestitures and evolving business plans.

The process of valuing a company derives more benefit than merely determining the firm's value. If the valuation process and reporting are done meticulously, the company's transformation will be smoother. Also public support can be gathered for the new market system and the enterprise will be geared for survival in competitive markets.

The process of business valuation provides a factual appraisal of the future performance of a company. This is valuable for different stakeholders-owners, managers, employees customers, suppliers and the general public.

The process and reporting of valuation is an important component of the strategy formulation of a company. Managers are given an insight into their position in the market, opportunities for future growth, the external threats, internal strengths and weaknesses. Valuation report is usually discussed in the annual strategic plan meeting. The process of valuation, thus identifies alternative actions and determines the one, which would maximize the value of the company.

Interfirm comparison is facilitated, as the valuation report usually presents a study of financial data comparing the performance of a company to a sample of similar firms in the industry. The analysis would assist the managers to understand the deviations of their operations from market norms.

Valuation of enterprises is important to ensure transparency in the privatization process. A realistic valuation would eliminate the deals which should not be made and muster public support for those which are valid.

Proper valuations also have international implications and more realistic offers would be made to the enterprises. Positive negotiations with potential foreign investor is facilitated.

Business valuations are essential in cases when employees and management are buying a substantial portion of the company's stock. It affords the employees and management greater security in their decision to become owners and assume a risk, they had never before faced.

What is Value?

There are various connotations of value. For example, Book value is the value of assets and liabilities, as provided in the financial statement. Insurable value is the principal value for which the assets are insured. Salvage value is the value of the assets, if they are sold as a scrap. However, for the purpose of business valuation, the relevant value is what is known as the Fair Market value. Fair market value can be defined as the cash or cash equivalent at which property would change hands between a willing buyer and willing seller, neither party being compelled to buy or sell and both the parties being aware of the terms and conditions of the purchase and sale.

In the past, the financial community relied overwhelmingly on Relative Value approaches, with their focus on accounting-based indicators such as Price/Earnings ratios and earnings per share growth. Discounted Cash Flow (DCF) analysis is the most widely approach as it overcomes limitations of the other approaches.

Although most security analysts still use some Relative Valuation methods, they actually have come to rely more on dividend discount models which are somewhat similar to the DCF analysis. Nearly all major investment firms now use the DCF analysis, particularly in their mergers and acquisition analysis.

The move to the DCF model can best be understood by looking at the shortcomings of the accounting-based indicators. Recently, many companies which achieved impressive annual earnings per share (EPS), the growth rates have actually provided their shareholders only minimal or even negative rates of returns, as measured by dividends and share-price changes. The key limitations of the EPS and related accounting measures such as Return on Investment (RoI) and Return on Equity (RoE) are:

1. They are influenced by arbitrary but acceptable accounting conventions such as LIFO *vs*. FIFO inventory methods and various depreciation models.
2. They fail to consider:
   (a) levels of business and financial risk in different firms,
   (b) working capital and fixed capital investment needed for projected sales growth,
   (c) dividend policy, and
   (d) the time value of money where money received today is worth more than money received in the future because it can be reinvested to earn a return in the future.

Definion of Value

The price of all goods in a market economy, including that of an enterprise, is determined by supply and demand. However, a realistic price cannot be established without a functioning market. Valuation is one of the instruments, which can be used to create a market. The objective of the valuation process is to determine "fair market value". Fair market value is defined as the price at which business would be sold by a willing seller to willing buyer in an open and unrestricted market when neither is under compulsion to buy or to sell and both have reasonable knowledge of the relevant facts. It is important to emphasize that a fair market value is a valuation estimate by the valuer. The price ultimately obtained in negotiations between a buyer and a seller may be different and will reflect the particular objectives and circumstances of the buyer and seller. It is important to recognize that the endeavour should be to arrive at a range of values, and not an absolute value. The establishment of a range of values would facilitate a meaningful negotiation between the buyer and the seller.

Methods of Valuation

There are three basic methods of valuation which have been found to be extremely relevant for restructuring.

The Net Asset Method—Underlying Asset Value

The asset valuation approach usually involves appraising a business's assets to determine their liquidation or replacement value. While this may be appropriate for some non-renewable assets, two assumptions of this approach demand that caution be used when valuing a business. First, it assumes that the business will not be operational and that its economic value does not come from the cash flow generated. Second, it assumes that the value of the assets is the same whether the business is sold piecemeal or in its entirety, and that the value will be the same to all buyers. Logically, however, a floor to the valuation of the enterprise is set in this way. The selling firm or country should never accept less than this amount.

As the name suggests, the net asset method is based on an assessment of the enterprise's assets on a certain date. The net asset value is the sum of all assets at their net replacement value minus all liabilities. The method seeks to establish the amount, which would have to be spent to reestablish the enterprise in the present state. Thus, it is based on a Balance Sheet or a status report specially drawn up for the purpose. This implies that an enterprise's future development does not influence the net asset value directly as fixed and current assets vary depending on the assessment of the business prospects for the years to come. This simple method of valuation can be illustrated with the help of an example as shown below

Calculation of fair market value, as per the asset appraisal method.

XYZ limited Dec 31, 2011

Asset Type	*At Book Value*	*At Revised Value*
Current Assets	$ 2,900,000	$ 2,700,000
Fixed Assets		
—Plant, Property and equipment	$ 3,100,000	$ 3,800,000
Intangible Assets		
—Goodwill	$ 0	$ 3,500,000
Total Assets	$ 6,000,000	$ 10,000,000
Less Current Liabilities and Loans		$ 200,000
Fair Market Value of the Business		$ 98,000,000

The method however has to be used with a degree of caution, as there is a tendency on the part of enterprises, to include non-productive assets. This is especially true in the case of state owned/public enterprises in transitional economies. This limitation however can be overcome if this method is used in conjunction, with other methods described below for determining the range of values.

Market Comparison Method—The Relative Value

The market comparison method involves comparing the subject company to those of other similar ones whose stock is traded on the stock market. The key is a ratio of price to earnings, or the P/E ratio. The analysts finds P/E for similar companies in the same industry and then makes adjustments for several factors such as financial risk measured by traditional ratio analysis, Profitability ratio analysis, growth rates, size, and market position. The direction of each adjustment on the standard or market P/E is clear but the amount of each adjustment is subjective. The result of these adjustments is the P/E ratio, which, when multiplied times the earnings, produces the market value of the company.

This approach does not work well when the firm has negative or very low earnings at the time of analysis. Furthermore, the adjustments needed cannot be precisely verified. The comparisons with other firms are often qualitative and those which are quantifiable cannot be added together in one adjustment.

The method can be illustrated with the help of an example. As mentioned earlier the starting point is the computation of P/E ratio. The P/E ratio is calculated by dividing the market price of one stock by the earnings per share. Suppose, the market price of a stock is $ 20 and the earnings per share is $ 5, the P/E ratio is 4. This implies that the market values, each stock as equivalent to 4 times its earnings. The next step is to estimate the expected average profit for one year in future. The calculated price earning ratio is revised as discussed earlier. The fair market value can then be estimated by taking up the expected average profit and multiplying the same by the revised price earnings ratio. Suppose the expected average profit is $ 200,000 and the adjusted price earnings ratio is 5, the fair market value is $ 1000000.

The method presupposes the availability of stock market and industry data. Hence the method is not relevant in situations where there is paucity of data and in countries where the stock market is not vibrant.

The Earnings Capacity Method or the Discounted Cash Flow Approach

This method is popular among enterprises which purchase other firms in the industry. The key here is operational knowledge of how the businesses function. The purchasing company knows what income return on assets the target firm should be able to earn. The next step is to value the assets of the target to which the return on asset ratio is applied. Then the buyer capitalizes this income by the rate of return it demands from such investments. From this price the buyer subtracts any immediate capital outlay needed to run the target. The remainder is what the buyer is willing to pay for the existing company.

This method is based on an enterprise's future prospects. The earning capacity refers to the cash flow after deductions, aggregate assessed for a certain date, expected from continuing the business in future. The method is based on the underlying going concern concept.

The aggregate cash flow is projected separately for the current year and say three to five subsequent years and reduced by an individually established capitalization rate. Constant earnings are assumed for years further ahead and a constant discount made on these stable profits. The earnings capacity method, therefore, presupposes the preparation of a business plan, account projections and income statements for the years ahead.

Basic Steps

The basic steps to the earnings capacity method are as follows:

1. Analysis of future earnings, as well as review of the necessary capital expenditures to maintain future earnings and other items that affect the total cash flow available to investors.
2. Determination of an appropriate discount rate, to adjust for the fact that the prospect of receiving a certain amount money in the future is less attractive than the prospect of receiving the same amount of money immediately.
3. Calculation of the present value of all future cash flows, through the application of the discount rate. The total present value thus calculated is an estimate of the Fair Market Value of the invested capital of the business. Since, the capital includes both long-term debt and equity, the long-term debt must be deducted to arrive at the estimated value of equity.

Similar to the income approach to fixed assets, in the DCF method the value of a company is measured by estimating the expected future cash flows to the owner and then discounting those flows by the owner's required rate of return in order to determine the present value of the future cash stream. The economic rationale for the DCF analysis rests on three main points related to the importance of cash flows in equity valuation:

1. Shareholder returns come from dividends plus capital gains. Capital gains reflect the market's estimation of future dividends, which must be paid in cash or cash equivalents.
2. Financial claims of employees, creditors, and shareholders must also be met with cash or cash equivalents from the company's cash flow.
3. The key to the corporation's power to pay all financial claims lies in the combination of its cash generating ability and its ability

to attract outside capital. Cash generating capability is simply the company's competence at generating positive net cash flows. Attracting outside capital requires convincing potential lenders that the company's future cash generating capability will be adequate to pay its claims.

In applying the DCF analysis, the analyst must first determine the cash flow expected each year and then discount that cash flow back to the present using the appropriate discount rate which reflects the basic risk-return relationship in finance. In an investment of finite duration, the difference between the present value of the cash flows and the market value of the company is the residual value.

Cash Flow

The cash flow of a company is calculated each year using the following steps:

Net Income After Taxes
Plus
Depreciation and other non-cash expenses
Minus
Increases in Net Working Capital
Minus
Capital Expenditures
Plus
New Capital
Equals
Available Cash Flow

The analyst must project values for each of these factors. The historical performance of the company provides the starting point of this process. However, when a company is being evaluated as a potential purchase, the buyer must re-cast these data to reflect the changes in operations expected upon the change of ownership.

Proper adjustments to the existing financial data require specific knowledge of the industry. When a potential buyer ventures out of its field of experience serious errors can be made here. In such cases it is advisable for the buyer to engage a consultant who has significant direct experience in that sector to assist in making the projections.

Determining the proper discount rate can be even more difficult. This requires an analysis of the degree of risk the company poses for the investor or buyer. Here, risk means the degree of uncertainty of the future cash flows. The higher the risk, the higher the rate of return a rational investor will demand. The higher the rate of return, the higher the discount rate and therefore the lower the present value of future cash flows.

When there is a market price for a company's securities, the risk the overall market perceives can be discerned from the amount investors are willing to pay for the stock and bonds. We assume that the market, being the sum of all investor perceptions, is efficient or correct in its analysis, at least in the long run. Under these conditions we apply a form of the DCF model called the Gordon model to calculate the discount rate. Here the rate of return demanded by investors is the same as the cost of the equity capital for the company. The formula for the cost of capital, *k*, is:

$$k = Dl/Mpo + g$$

Where

k = the cost of equity capital or the discount rate

Dl = the dividend expected in the first or next year

Mpo = market price for the common stock

g = expected growth rate for dividends

All three variables needed to calculate the cost of equity capital or the discount rate are available from market data, the company's performance, and known financial analysis. For an entire company, we use cash flow instead of *Dl* or dividends.

For a company which is not traded on a market, we must use other methods. Two of these methods which build on the concept of risk premium will be discussed. In both cases we begin with the notion of a risk free investment and then add additional interest premiums to compensate for higher levels of risk.

In the first method, called relative risk premium, we compare the risk of the company being analyzed to those which do have securities traded on the market. Factors considered include all the items in traditional financial ratio analysis and many company specific points identified earlier. Once one or more "comparable" companies are located, the market supplies the relevant discount rate. The range of rates are shown below:

Type of Investment	*Approximate Rates of Return*
US Government Bond	8%

AA rated Corporate Bond	10%
B rated Corporate Bond	13%
AA rated common stock	13 – 15%
B rated common stock	16 – 17%
"Junk" Bonds	16 – 20%
Small, unrated common stock	20 – 24%
Start-up company stock	25 – 30%

The second method, called Capital Asset Pricing Model (CAPM), is based on a study of relative volatility of company returns on equity. Greater volatility of company's returns as compared to average return in the entire market is assumed to mean greater risk for the investor. Less volatility means less risk.

In this process, the degree of relative volatility of each company's return on equity, a statistic called Beta or Greek B, is calculated. This is done over a recent period, usually five years. A company whose return varied exactly the same as the overall market would have a Beta of 1.0. A company whose returns varied over this period twice the market rate of variation would have Beta of 2.0. The firm with half the market volatility gets a Beta of .5.

The Beta for each company is then used in the following formula to calculate the required rate of return or discount rate k as follows: $k = krf + B\,(km - krf)$, where

krf = the risk free rate of return
B = the Beta for the company being analyzed
km = the rate of return for the entire market

The beta is multiplied times the difference between the risk free rate of return and the market return and added as a premium to the risk free rate. It is assumed that the beta determined from past performance will reflect the expected volatility of a given company as compared to the market in the future.

Residual Value Stock prices suggest that the market frequently acknowledges management's ability to implement sustainable long-term competitive strategies which will create new value for shareholders. This is seen in the differences between the price of the stock and present value of dividends for some finite period, say 5 years. This addition to value is essential when analyzing companies which are not traded on markets but have significant growth potential. Key factors contributing to this future potential include: technological advantage, investment in and results from research and development, sustainability of competitive position in the market, and the willingness and ability of management and technical personnel to lead the competition.

To return to the DCF model, there are many variations which attempt to take into account changes in growth or super-normal growth potential. The Basic Gordon model can be reformulated to give us Market Price (MP) or value of company:

$$MP = \text{CASH FLOW}/k - g \text{ where}$$
$$k = \text{the discount rate or required rate of return}$$
$$g = \text{the expected growth rate of cash flow}$$

This presents a clear statement of value based on the three key variables, cash flow, discount rate, and the growth rate. This can be used to show the effect a change in each of these will have on the value of the firm.

It may be mentioned that there are number of valuation packages which have become popular amongst security analysts. Most of these packages identify six key factors they call value drivers. These are Sales Growth Rate, Operating Profit Margin, Tax Rate on Operating Profit, Fixed Capital Investment needed to support sales growth, Working Capital Investment needed to support sales growth, and the Cost of Capital. These variables, when determined, can quickly lead to the value calculation.

Discount Rate: As mentioned earlier, the discount rate determines the way in which projected Cash flows are given a capital value. It is chosen according to the rate of return which investors would look for an investment in the business. The higher the required rate of return, the higher the discount rate and lower the capitalised value ascribed to projected cash flows. If the investor pays this capitalised value for the cash flows, his required return will then be achieved provided the cash flows occur as projected. The discount rate, however needs adjustment to consider the risk profile of the business being valued. These risks include:

- The State of the economy—slow growth in GDP, increasing inflation, and sustainable convertible currency debt.
- There will inevitably be serious transition problems as the country moves toward a more market-oriented economy, compounded by years of under investment in the economic infrastructure of the country.

- The Currency convertibility and exchange rate fluctuations.
- The extent of vibrancy of the Stock Exchange.
- Preparation of Accounting information according to International Accounting Standards.
- Political situation prevailing in the country.

Thus the projected cash flow for the foreseeable future is discounted to the present values. The last year for which the cash flow can be projected is known as the Terminal or Residual year. The fair market value = Present value of future cash flows (upto the forecasted period) plus the present value of the terminal value.

Terminal Value = Terminal year cash flow/discount rate.

The calculation of terminal value which is based on the concept of annuity in perpetuity smoothens out aberrations if any in the number of years taken up for forecasting.

The procedure for arriving at range of values under the earnings capacity method is demonstrated in the Sample Valuation report:

Obtaining a Range of Values

It may be pertinent to understand that the basic purpose of valuation is to determine a range of values, and not an absolute value. The range will facilitate meaningful negotiations between the buyer and seller and minimize the chance of an impasse in the restructuring process. The manner of arriving at a range is illustrated below.

Situation 1 *(Figures in Million $)*

Asset appraisal method	5		
Market comparison method		3	
Discounted Cash flow method			4
FMV range	3 - 4		

Situation 2 *(Figures in Million $)*

Asset appraisal method	2		
Market comparison method		3	
Discounted Cash flow method			3.5
FMV range	2 – 3.5		

Transactions with Variable Pricing

In countries where the markets are well developed, a buyer and a seller may still have very different estimates for the value of a complex of business assets. If a transaction is to take place, some method must be devised to overcome the impasse. If the seller is supplying a sizable portion of the finance or credit for the proposed transaction, then the valuation impasse could be overcome using a method known as "variable pricing", "contingent pricing", or an "earn-out".

The general idea of variable pricing is to use information obtained in the future to revise the valuation that is the basis for the purchase-and-sale or lease agreement. Then the future payments are revised to reflect the new valuation and to reflect the payments already made. In the case of the sale of business assets, the future payments from the buyer to seller would be partly contingent on the actual profits made using the business assets, if the assets proved to be as profitable as estimated by the seller's desires. However, if moderate or low profits were generated using the assets, then the payments will be adjusted accordingly. Another example of variable pricing is a lease of retail space where the future lease payments are variable according to a formula based on the gross revenues obtained by the lease.

An *ex-ante* valuation is not an end-in-itself; it is only a means to get the transaction done. The variable pricing technique allows the deal to be done without starting with a definitive *ex-ante* valuation.

Variable pricing can be used when there is outside third-party finance, if shares in the buyer's new company have a market. The buyer obtains finance to pay the seller a low price all in one payment. But the buyer also gives the seller warrants or options to buy shares in the buyer's company at a low price. If the assets turn out to be rather profitable, the share price will increase and the seller can exercise the warrants by buying at the low option price and reselling at the higher market price.

Variable Pricing: An Example

Consider a simple example of an asset with an economic lifetime of three years with no scrap value. If the owner of the asset invests \$I at the beginning of the first year (say, for raw materials and other ancillary inputs), then the owner will receive the returns of \$R (1), \$R (2), and \$R (3) at the end of years 1, 2, and 3. These returns are net of maintenance and other operating costs. The asset would be valued at the present value of the initial investment and the returns discounted using an interest rate r appropriate for the risk.

$$PV = -I + R(1)/(1 + r) + R(2)/(1 + r)^2 + R(3)/(1 + r)^3.$$

In the idealized world of this example, the value of the asset would be PV since the seller would not accept less (the seller would receive PV by continuing to hold the asset) and the buyer would not pay more (since the buyer would only receive PV by owning the asset).

There are many ways payments could be arranged even when PV is the agreed upon price. For instance, the whole purchase price could be amortized in a number of equal payments, or part of the price could be paid upfront as a down payment with the remainder being amortized.

To keep the example simple, let us suppose that 50 per cent of PV will be paid as a down payment with the remainder being amortized. However, PV represents the seller's estimate of the value while the buyer is quite skeptical. The buyer insists that the future amortization payments be adjusted to incorporate the information provided by the actual returns obtained during the period.

If PV was the agreed upon price and the remaining 50 per cent of PV was to be paid for in two equal annual payments PMT at the end of the first and second years, then the amortization payment PMT could be calculated using standard formulas. If the interest rate used to calculate the amortization payments PMT is I (not necessarily the same as the discount rate r), then the formula is:

$$\text{PMT} = PV/(2 * \text{A}[2, i]),$$

Where the amortization factor A[2, i] is defined using the formula:

$$\text{A}[n, i] = 1/(1 + i) + 1/(1 + i)^2 + \ldots + 1/(1 + \text{i})^n.$$

The buyer however does not agree on the total price PV. One-half of PV has been paid as a downpayment so that much is guaranteed to the seller. The seller agrees that the remaining payments will be adjusted to use information about the early actual returns.

Suppose that $R'(1)$ is the actual return at the end of the first year. The projected future returns might be re-estimated in view of the first year return. For simplicity, we will keep the same future estimates so the new present value PV' would be calculated as:

$$PV' = -I + R'(1)/(1 + r) + R(2)/(1 + r)^2 + R(3)/(1 + r)^3.$$

If PV′ were the total price, then subtracting the down payment of PV/2 leaves PV′ – PV/2 to be amortized in two payments in the amount

$$PMT' = (PV' - PV/2)/A[2, i].$$

Hence, the amount PMT' is paid at the end of the first year.

At the end of the second year, new information becomes available, namely the actual returns R′(2) from the second year. To re-estimate the value, one could re-estimate the third year returns. One simple method is to take the average of the first two years' returns, or one could use a more complicated linear regression formula (if trends were important). We will use the simple average formula. The new and final estimate PV" for the value is

$$PV'' = -I + R'(1)/(1 + r) + R'(2)/(1 + r)^2 + (R'(1) + R'(2))/(2 * (1 + r)^3$$

To compute the second and last annual payment, we must first consider the present value already paid. In addition to the downpayment of PV/2, the buyer has paid PMT' at the end of the first year which has a per cent value (at time zero) of PMT′/(1 + i).

Hence, the present value to be paid for in the second payment is—

$$PV'' - PV/2 - PMT'/(1 + i)$$

So, the second and last payment is

$$PMT'' = (1 + i)^2\ [PV'' - PV/2 - PMT'/(1 + i)].$$

If the calculated payment was negative, then no payment would be made. The seller would have received the downpayment plus the variable payments up to that point. With a longer payment period, there could be a series of zero payments followed by positive payments as future returns again revised the value upward.

The general principles of a variable pricing scheme can be extracted from this simple example. As the actual returns become known during the amortization period, the future returns are re-estimated and the estimate of the total value of the asset is revised. Then the next payments are calculated taking into account all the payments made up to that point. All the formulas can be entered on an electronic spreadsheet so that each payment is calculated upon entering each new return.

The variable pricing scheme can be applied to any transaction where the valuation can be periodically revised by new information. The arrangement is also most applicable in the context of seller-supplied financing. A third-party financier would ordinarily not be interested in bearing the equity-like risk involved in the variable pricing arrangement.

Sample Valuation Report

Executive Summary

The purpose of this report is to present our valuation of the business of XYZ Flour Co Ltd. as of 31st December 2011. The management of XYZ Ltd has requested the preparation of this report to assist them in possible strategic alternatives.

As indicated in our proposal letter of 15th November 2009 we have determined a fair market value based on a combination of the discounted cash flow approach and the asset appraisal approach.

The discounted cash flow approach included a thorough analysis of the company's 2009 budget and based on our discussions with senior officials, the extrapolation of the revised budget out into the future. We then calculated the value of these future earnings using a discount rate which included both the expected rate of return for this industry and an additional risk premium for investments. The asset appraisal approach relied on the replacement value of assets, in order to develop an estimate of the value of the company. Consistent with the discounted cash flow approach, we also applied a range of discount factors to reflect the additional risk for investments in XYZ Ltd. The range used will no doubt, be narrowed in the process of discussions between the company and outside investors.

Based on a combination of these approaches, we have valued the entity of XYZ Flour Co: in the range of USD 2953440 to 4439847. This range of values is lower than the net asset value of the business of as shown in the Balance Sheet at 31st December 2009, after conversion of financial statements to an international format. The shortfall reflects the fact that XYZ currently faces significant difficulties in achieving satisfactory rates of return on the assets employed.

In arriving at this range of values, we have made several assumptions which have been supported through our discussions with senior company officials. Perhaps the most critical assumption is the exclusion of any benefits or costs that may arise from the possible restructuring operation. It is essential that our entire report be read in order to fully comprehend the methodology employed in our approach to the business valuation, and the impact of key assumptions on the range of values determined.

Introduction

In accordance with our proposal letter of October 2009, we present our valuation of the business of XYZ Ltd as of November 2009.

Use of this Report

This report was prepared for the management of XYZ Ltd and the State Privatization Commission to assist them in the evaluation of various strategic alternatives for restructuring and full privatization of XYZ Ltd. This report is not to be released to any third parties, including prospective investors without our prior written consent. If our valuation report is to be given to a prospective investor, it should be made clear to that party that it should not exclusively rely upon the report but obtain its own independent advice and carry out its own due diligence procedures. Our report does not address or reflect the interests or circumstances of a particular prospective investor, and furthermore we will accept no responsibility to any prospective investor in relation to a prospective investment in XYZ Flour Ltd., whether or not our valuation report influences that party's decision.

Definition of Value

In the course of this report, we discuss the process of valuation. The objective of our analysis will be to determine what we term "fair market value". Fair market value is defined as the price at which the business would be sold by a willing seller to a willing buyer in an open and unrestricted market when neither is under compulsion to buy or to sell and both have reasonable knowledge of the relevant facts.

It is important to emphasize that a fair market value is a valuation estimate by the valuer. The price ultimately obtained in negotiations between a buyer and a seller may be different and will reflect the particular objectives and circumstances of the buyer and seller.

History and Overview of the Business

Assessment of Strengths, Weaknesses, Opportunities and Threats

Strengths

1. Capacity to manufacture three kinds of flour.
2. Able to reap the benefits of the economy of scale.
3. Locational advantages.
4. Productivity of staff is very high and no problem of labour relations.
5. Good working traditions and concern for family welfare by the management.
6. Flour company, not much affected during the transition phase of the economy, although quite a few organizations are in deep trouble.
7. Transportation advantages with respect to the market for flour.
8. Strong cooperative ventures with other flour mills in Mongolia, and technical assistance through educated specialists.

Weaknesses

1. The machineries and equipments installed in 1975, have become obsolete and is due for replacement.
2. Non-availability of spare parts from Russia aggravates the problem.
3. High interest payments on loans borrowed from the bank, for purchase of wheat.
4. More adaptability to changing conditions is required. The organization is not flexible and dynamic.

Opportunities

1. Enough scope exists for manufacturing and marketing new products making use of existing resources and facilities.
2. New bread manufacturing equipment from Czechoslovakia to be installed in Ulan Baatar.
3. Animal feed export on the increase to countries like Russia and China.
4. Saving in cost of production of flour, by improving the quality.

Threats

1. Small and medium scale enterprises, manufacturing flour on the increase.
2. Imported flour from China and Russia, which even led to temporary stoppage of the milling operations during 2001.
3. International price of wheat of USD 307.5 per tonne does not compare favourably with the present average subsidized purchase price of USD 90 per tonne. Farmers may be forced to increase the price of wheat, thereby making wheat an expensive raw material for the existing flour mills.

Mission

The Director and the management felt that the mission of XYZ Flour Mill is to effect a drastic improvement in the market share from the existing 27 per cent, and to increase the profit by several times by manufacturing new products, with changes in the ownership structure of the company facilitating full ownership by the management and the employees.

Financial Condition of the Company

Our assessment of the financial condition of XYZ Ltd was based on the financial statements and analysis presented in our accounts conversion and business review reports and on further information and prospective financial data provided by management. The accounts conversion process does not Constitute an audit, hence our assessment is not based on audited financial statements.

In Appendix I, we present the company's Balance sheet as of 30th September 2009, converted to an international format. The Company had positive working capital of 478122 Tug (000), a substantial improvement over the previous year 2008. The current ratio is 1, 5:1. This business is not highly capital intensive and fixed assets total 62,641 Tug (000). The bank loan has increased by three times as compared to 2008.

In 2009, XYZ Flour Ltd. earned a net profit of 384,390 Tug (000). Once the price of wheat is dictated by market mechanisms, with Government taking a final decision on the level of subsidies, the profit level might decrease in the future. This is indeed a critical issue.

The company prepares annual budgets (seasonal and not monthly) but does not prepare projections for beyond one year in the future. Since long-term projections of earnings and cash flow are essential to our approach, a multi year forecast with certain revisions has been prepared.

Business Valuation Process

Introduction

The definition of fair market value, as stated at the outset of this report, provides that the objective of the business valuation is to determine the price that a buyer would pay for the business to be examined. There are widely accepted methods of valuing a business, viz. the discounted cash flow approach or the Earnings approach and the asset appraisal approach.

The basic steps to the discounted cash flow approach are as follows:

1. Analysis of future earnings, as well as a review of the necessary capital expenditures to maintain future earnings and other items that affect the total cash flow available to investors.
2. Determination of an appropriate discount rate, to adjust for the fact that the prospect of receiving a certain amount money in the future is less attractive than the prospect of receiving the same amount of money immediately.
3. Calculation of the present value of all future cash flows, through the application of the discount rate.

The total present value thus calculated is an estimate of the Fair Market value of the invested capital of the business. Since, the capital includes both long-term debt and equity, the long-term debt must be deducted to arrive at the estimated value of equity.

Cash Flow

An analysis of the company's estimate of future earnings before income tax is summarized in Appendix 2. The following adjustments have been made.

Depreciation: Depreciated is added back in the Cash Flow analysis since it does not represent a reduction of cash available to investors.

Income taxes: The tax rate is assumed at the same level for future.

Capital expenditure: Substantial capital expenditure would be required to replace the existing machinery. Hence, the investment for the residual year is taken at 10,000 (000) Tugrik.

Discount rate: The discount rate determines the way in which projected Cash flows are given a capital value. It is chosen according to the rate of return which investors would look for an investment in the business. The higher the required rate of return, the higher the discount rate and lower the capitalized value ascribed to projected cash flows. If the investor pays this capitalized value for the cash flows, his required return will then be achieved provided the cash flows occur as projected. The discount rate for this company was taken at 8 per cent, which is based on the cut-off rate, for similar enterprises in reforming socialist countries. This however needs adjustment to consider the risk profile of the business valued. The risks inherent in making investments in XYZ Flour Ltd. are of a nature and degree not normally encountered in relation to developed economies. These risks include:

- The economy has not been strong for several years, suffering from slow growth in GDP, increasing inflation, and sustainable convertible currency debt.
- There will inevitably be serious transition problems as the country moves toward a more market-oriented economy, compounded by years of under investment in the economic infrastructure of the country.
- The Tugric is not freely convertible into other currencies and is not internationally traded. If the Tugric becomes freely convertible into other currencies, its value may depreciate still further than it already has over the last few years against international currencies
- The Mongolian Stock exchange has only recently become operational and it may take considerable time before the exchange can provide the type of investment liquidity seen in some international stock exchanges.
- Accounting information is not prepared according to International Accounting Standards. Although, the accounts of some companies have been converted to an international format, there has been no history of auditing corporate accounts to an international standard, and therefore investors may be making investments on the basis of inadequate financial information.
- Politically, Mongolia is arguably at the crossroads between lessening its ties to the Commonwealth of Independent States (CIS) and other member countries of the defunct CMEA, while

attempting to strengthen its ties with other countries. This transition will no doubt have serious impacts on trading patterns.

Based on our consideration of these risk factors affecting investment in Mongolian companies, our discussions with individuals in the international investment. Community, and our experiences in advising clients in Eastern Europe, we estimate that a suitable range of risk premiums for investment in XYZ Flour Ltd. would be from 3 per cent to 8 per cent. Coupled with the discount rate for investments in the food industry of 8 per cent the range of discount rates to be applied to the present value of future cash flows of XYZ Flour Ltd. should be between 11 per cent and 16 per cent.

Results of discounted Cash Flow approach contained in Appendix 2 presents the discounted cash flow analysis, using the 11 to 16 per cent range of discount rates. The residual value included in the Appendix is calculated as the present value of a constant annuity, since no residual growth rate was assumed using the lower, less conservative discount rate of 11 per cent, we calculated a present value of 1775939 (000) tugrik. Using the higher, more conservative discount rate of 16 per cent yields a present value of 1181376 (000) Tugrik.

Conclusion

The previous sections of this report have described the valuation methods that we applied to XYZ Flour Ltd. In summary we used a discounted cash flow approach and an Asset appraisal method. The concluding stage of the analysis is to reconcile the two approaches. We also believe that it is prudent to continue to express valuation as a possible range of values.

Valuation method	*Range of indicated values in Tug (000)*	*Range of indicate values (USD)*
Discounted cash flow	1181376 to 1775939	2953440 to 4439847
Asset appraisal method		3367372
Average		USD 2953440 to 4439847

In conclusion, we have ascribed, on the basis of the assumptions in this report, a fair market valuation on the value of the equity of XYZ Ltd. which is in the range of USD 2953440 to 4439747.

Appendix-1

Figures in (000) Tugrik	*30/9/2009*	*31/12/2008*	*31/12/2007*
Tools			
Fixed Assets	54,154	54,154	46,231
Depreciation	(32,327)	(32,327)	(29,492)
Depreciation	(3,441)		
Cost of rep. FA	(763)	(763)	(221)
Cost of prep. FA	8,422		
Soc & ec fd	36,596	25,881	
		(9,606)	(2,104)
	62,641	37,339	14,414
CURRENT ASSETS			
Stocks	345,231	1,625,570	338,278
Goods in transit	5,091	21,211	4,839
Debtors	800,089	255,231	7,191
Cash	196,538	53,388	5,327
	1,346,949	1,955,400	355,635
CURRENT LIABILITIES			
Creditors	428,070	1,528,376	208,159
Taxation	83,520	84,257	8,827
Bank Loan	357,237	122,000	121,691
	868,827	1,734,633	338,677
NET CURRENT ASSETS	478,122	220,767	16,958
	540,763	258,106	31,372
Share Capital	49,400	49,400	49,400
Reserves b/f	314,626	(7,361)	(49,634)
Profit for year	176,673	216,076	31,606
Diff	63		
Diff cast	1	(9)	
	540,763	258,106	31,372

Appendix-2

Figures in (000) Tugrik	*Year 1*	*Year 2*	*Year 3*	*Residual*
Earnings before tax	55733	386174	384390	384390
Taxation	24127	165257	162750	170000
	316060	220917	221640	214390
Cash flow adjustment	1701	8333	3247	7000
Add: Depreciation				
	33307	229250	224887	221390
Less capital livestock	2692	8572	—	10000
	30605	220678	224887	211390
Discount factor 11%	.901	.812	.731	.731
	27575	179190	164392	1921727
			Terminal value 1404782	
			VALUE = 1775939 (000)	
Discount factor 16%	.862	.743	.641	.641
	26381	163963	144152	846880
			Terminal value 1321187	
			VALUE = 1181376 (000)	

Institutionalising the Process of Business Valuation

From the foregoing discussion it is clear that valuation is an important task to be carried out for restructuring purposes. It is not a question of whether to carry out valuation or not, but we should seek answers for the following:

1. When 2, How and by whom

When

Valuation should be carried out as part of the organizational diagnosis. Enerprises at the time of viability assessment should carry out valuation.

How

There are three perfected and time tested methods for valuation.

The Asset appraisal, the market comparison and the earnings capacity method.

The asset appraisal method needs to be used with a degree of caution. Rely on the asset appraisal for arriving at the range of values when the value is the least. Ignore the value when the method yields a higher value than the other two methods.

Whom

Valuation should be done by the local experts. Multinational accounting firms are expensive and do not understand the local conditions. The experience of Slovenia is worth mentioning here and as detailed in chapter 6. Also it is suggested that the standard valuation report should adhere to the format suggested.

Annexure-1

Outline for Standard Valuation Report

- Introduction
  - ➢ Description of the Rcport
  - ➢ Limitations of the Report
  - ➢ Descriptions of the Market Value
- Analysis of the Economic Conditions
  - ➢ The General Economy
  - ➢ The Specific Industry
- The Enterprise
  - ➢ Internal Enterprise Structure
  - ➢ Facilities
  - ➢ Employees
  - ➢ Customers
  - ➢ Competitions
  - ➢ Corporate Mission
  - ➢ Strengths, Weaknesses, Opportunities and Threats
  - ➢ Financial Performance
- Valuation of the Enterprise
  - ➢ Discounted Cash Flow Approach
  - ➢ Comparable Market Approach
  - ➢ Net Asset Value Approach
- Opinion of Fair Market Value

4
Change of Ownership Structure

A dominant theme in public policy commencing in the mid-eighties, throughout the world was privatization. Since then there has been a pronounced shift in the intellectual and political climate concerning the role of market and the state in economic and social life. Privatization refers to Change of ownership from Government to private hands and results in increased involvement of the private sector in an economy. Thus privatization of enterprises connotes transfer of property or control of productive economic entities from the public to the private sector.

Private and public firms pursue different objectives and serve different purposes. The observed under-performance or failure of public firms is generally the result of contradictory goals and inadequate incentives that public enterprises are facing (World Bank, 1995). The soft budget constraints that apply and the bailing out practices of governments towards public enterprises prevent these from achieving the same performance as private enterprises. Political interference (Shleifer and Vishny, 1994) distorts the objectives that management of public firms seek to maximize as well as the constraints they face, leading to lower efficiency. Ownership also matters because managers are subject to less adequate monitoring in public firms contrary to private firms. What do Britain and China have in common? How are India and Pakistan united? What do Mongolia and Germany share? The differences are quite obvious. Some are large, others are small. Some of these countries are rich and some are poor. Some lean right, some have left wing governments. The answer is privatization. Wayback between 1988 and 1993, almost 3000 state owned enterprises were privatized in over 95 counties raising over $ 350 billion. For so many diverse countries to adopt a common policy, there must be a compelling reason for it. The primary reason for privatization is to enhance efficiency with which the enterprises resources are used. There are other secondary reasons which are financial, social and political.

- To augment revenue for the government
- To decrease the burden of the government bureaucracy
- To create popular capitalism

A change in ownership from Government to private hands brings about fundamental efficiency related changes.

- Private enterprises are less subject to political influence
- Private enterprises are more capable of offering decent incentives
- Private enterprises are more subject to the discipline of commercial financial markets
- The interests of capital are better represented in private enterprises due to a stronger linkage between capital and management

Shehadi (2002) defines privatization as a policy with the general objective to enhance enterprise performance based on a number of hypotheses. He argues that regarding enterprise performance the following factors matter:

- Ownership
- Management
- Markets
- Competition
- Freedom to fail
- Regulation

Privatization comprises change in one or more of the above factors, thereby improving enterprise performance. Shehadi (2002) states that private management performs better economically and indeed competitive market demands should drive business decisions for better performance. He further underlines that a healthy market can only exists if unhealthy failing (public) firms are allowed to exit the market.

Table 4.1 summarises the basic organizational factors affecting the performances of both public and private enterprises.

Even though governments are well aware of the economic costs of keeping enterprises public they are often reluctant towards privatization. They often choose to spread the costs among unorganized taxpayers instead of facing well organized interest groups, like labour unions, who at first might stand to loose from a privatization track.

Table 4.1: Organizational factors affecting public- and private-enterprises' performance

	State-Owned Enterprises	*Private Enterprises*
General Characteristics	• Embedded in government • Goals influenced by national politics • Objectives diverse or not well articulated • Boundaries vague • Accountable to state	• Embedded in market • Owned by private investors • Clear profit maximization goals • Accountable to shareholders or private owners
Innovative Orientation	• Political and bureaucratic restrictions on innovation • Weak incentives to deviate from standard operating procedures • Civil service protected managerial positions • Organizational and technological changes driven by state budget resources • Able to survive as "loss makers" because of soft budget constraints • Fixed pay salary ranges • Limited interaction with external environment • Low levels of technological change	• Market opportunities provide freedom to innovate • Financial incentives for managerial risk-taking • Managers' employment depends on profitability • Salaries supplemented by opportunities for ownership stake • Extensive interaction with external environment • Potentially high levels of technological change
Human Resource Management	• Formalization and standardization in hiring • System-wide rules for promotion and removal • Limited ability to reward unique roles or performers • Limited incentives to use technology to increase labour productivity • Managerial behaviour driven by civil service rules • Difficult to remove or reassign employees	• Firm determines rules of recruitment Differentiated pay rates • Promotion and removal determined by performance • Strong ability to reward unique roles and performers • Strong incentives to enhance labour productivity with technology • Behaviour driven by incentives and firm strategy • Easy to remove or reassign employees
Productivity and Work Effort	• Difficult to provide feedback on performance • Limited freedom to design jobs • Limited control over group norms • Standardized pay and limited opportunities for extra rewards for effort	• Freedom to set goals and provide employee feedback • Flexibility to design jobs • Strong control over group norms • Strong work motivation driven by uncertain job security and opportunity for financial rewards

Source: United Nations (2005).

Rationale for Privatization

Ramamurti (1992) investigated the economic motives for privatization for developing countries. He divided the economic explanations for privatization into proximate and enduring causes, the proximate causes being fiscal pressure and international pressure on the government and the enduring causes being the excessive use of State Owned Enterprises (SOEs), the disillusionment with SOEs and the obsolescence of SOEs. The following conclusions were drawn from a detailed analysis of eighty-three developing countries.

1. Privatization seems to be associated with financial problems in developing countries.
2. Privatization seems less likely when budget deficits are financed with domestic borrowing, but the opposite applies if external borrowing is used.
3. The dependency of the developing country on the World Bank and the IMF increases the chance of privatization.

Proximate causes are thus much more likely to induce privatization than the enduring causes. It is important to realize that employment is a crucial determinant in privatization strategies. Governments lose their power to choose employment level when they privatize or they pay a high price i.e. through lower revenues from privatization, incentives and guarantees, when they demand private investors to maintain employment levels.

There is an increasing likelihood of privatization under pressure of the World Bank or the IMF. The World Bank whose prime cause is to reduce poverty, besides other objectives finds its efforts negatively impacted by SOEs, especially by their burden on developing countries government's budgets and their disproportionate share of credit. This explains why the World Bank within the framework of Structural Adjustment Lending and Sectoral Adjustment Lending often pressures developing countries to privatize their SOEs.

Privatization Methods/Strategies

The choice of method of privatization depends on the government's objectives and political, institutional and market-related constraints.

The following are the commonly used methods:

(a) Public offering of shares
(b) Private sale of shares
(c) Sale of Government assets
(d) New private investment in the enterprise
(e) Reorganization into component parts
(f) Management employee buyout
(g) Leasing and management contract
(h) A combination of the above methods.

The above methods/strategies facilitate transfer of State/Governmnet assets to private control. However, certain other actions are also referred to as privatization.

(a) Introduction of competitive features into an enterprise, to promote efficiency. eg providing incentives to efficient ports in a country,
(b) Economic policy reforms like liberalized industrial policies, easy entry exit barriers,
(c) Resorting to increased use of private sector financing of new activities, for example, Build, Operate and Transfer (BOT).
(d) Issue of revenue bonds/Revenue participation certificates by the Government.
(e) Mass privatization refers to a free distribution scheme involving bonds which are distributed evenly and free of charge among all citizens. In Poland, for example the bonds, were issued to citizens, which could then be used to pay for shares in privatized companies as a substitute for money. Free distribution of this kind was resorted to in Poland, Czekh and to some extent in Hungary.

Public Offering of Shares

Under this method, shares are offered to the public, through the stock exchange. Since such shares are issued for the first time, the transaction is handled as a primary issue. Hence, legal, financial and disclosure requirements need to be compiled with. A prospectus or a document in lieu of prospectus needs to be set out and registered with the relevant authorities. A decision has to be taken whether the shares would be offered domestically or globally. The process of business valuation needs to be carried out before such an issue, so that the shares are issued at the right price. Strategic and viable enterprises can be privatized by this method. Non-viable enterprises would require a prior restructuring, before issues are made to the public. After a period of efficient private management, the company's shares will likely appreciate in value. Once the shares have appreciated in value, they are sold to the public. One of the major justifications for retaining any percentage is ultimately to sell them at a better price to the public.

In a sale of shares to the public it is important to state, prior to the sale in the prospectus, how the shares will be allotted if the offer is oversubscribed. The three main issues are, whether there should be a maximum and/or minimum size of each holding, whether foreign investors will receive equal treatment, and whether employee participation can be encouraged.

It is a common policy to allocate shares to small investors first to achieve the goal of wider share ownership. The desire to encourage small shareholders should be weighed against the cost to the company of a large number of investors. The minimum share holding should be based on the targeted number of shareholders.

Limiting the share holdings to a few per cent of the shares prevents the concentration of ownership which enables shareholders to pressure management to improve its performance. To turn a company around, some core group may need to have and use a large stake in the enterprises. This is not an issue in a successful company with a strong technical partner, but is important when the business is under-performing or weak.

It will be useful to provide some global perspective regarding the size of holdings.

Jamaica—in the privatisation of the National Commercial Bank of Jamaica, there was a maximum holding of 7.5 per cent by any one individual or group of individuals.

Chile—law passed preventing an investor controlling more than 23 per cent for specific industries, more than 50 per cent should be held by shareholders who do not own, directly or indirectly, more than 10 per cent, and at least 15 per cent should be owned by more than 100 individual investors.

UK—in the case of British Telecom, a clause was inserted in the Articles requiring any investor who acquired more than 5 per cent to declare the interest. This was also the case in the privatisation of the Canada development Corporation.

In several African and Asian countries, Governments are faced with the need to take into account the distribution of ownership between various ethnic groups. In Malaysia, offer conditions ensured that the Bumiputra organisations owned at least 30 per cent of certain offers.

Limiting Foreign Participation

Most countries have allowed foreign participation in their privatisation programmes; some without limitation (New Zealand), others limiting foreign participation as a general policy set out in the privatisation Act (Brazil), and yet others have limited it in certain industries (Jamaica). Many have given priority to local investors.

Reasons for restricting foreign participation include political sensitivity of certain industries, national interest, or simple technological and financial requirements, such as retailing. Nigeria listed industries which required foreign expertise and stated the degree of foreign control permitted.

Most centrally planned economies (Mexico, Philippines) have required Ministerial approval for foreign control.

Restrictions can limit the inflow of foreign investment and excluding foreigners will usually result in a lower price being achieved. Key considerations are the needs of the enterprise for management, technology and new finance and their availability in the local market.

Malaysia permitted foreign control of industries if they involved higher technology, are export oriented and do not involve the processing of non-renewable resources.

Senegalese law specifies, for each enterprise, the proportion of shares available to local investors, in priority to foreigners and for what period the preference is maintained.

More common is a restriction in the Company Rules, giving the directors the right to refuse to register a transfer. These restrictions would then appear in the prospectus. Such a clause could be introduced into the Rules as part of the process of preparing the company for privatisation.

The method naturally presupposes the existence of a vibrant stock market. One of the prime purposes of stock exchanges is to provide a transparent market for the purchase and sale of shares. Selling shares to the public outside the exchange could result in accusations of lack of transparency-favoured allocation for example. However, in the absence of a well developed stock market, the Government should take sufficient steps to disseminate information about the proposed issue. The strategy thus ensures widespread ownership and is open and transparent. Thus the method is politically acceptable.

Private Sale of Shares

Thc Government sells all or part of its shareholdings to a preidentified single or group of purchasers. The sale of such shares can be a full competitive process with prequalification of bidders. The Government can also directly negotiate with the prospective investor. In many cases, the transactions have lacked transparency, because of discretionary procedures for identifying potential purchasers. Hence, in some countries, like Senegal, Philippines, Argentina the privatization law mandates a competitive process. and, minimum standards for bidding. The strategy is a preferred one for non-viable enterprises., as there is a scope for the enterprise to be made viable as a result of successful restructuring operation. Thus the strategy can be used as an initial step to or in conjunction with public offerings. This approach was extensively practiced in France. Private sale of shares is a feasible method in the absence of well developed stock market. The prospective owner can be evaluated for his capability to bring in a number of benefits such as management, market and technology, Resorting to this method for large number of transactions would result in inadequate spread of wealth in the country. Hence strict mandatory procedures need to be enforced in such situations.

General Aims of Tender Procedures

Tender procedures achieve the following objectives:

(a) to assist in the efficient operation of the privatisation programme from the viewpoints of the public, investors and Government;
(b) to ensure that potential investors receive fair treatment and that the bid, which is in the best interests of the enterprise and the country, is selected;
(c) to reinforce confidence in the aims of the programme among the public and investors;
(d) to ensure that potential investors are aware of the overall Government objectives of the programme and of the steps which they and the Government take to implement the privatisation.

Proper procedures bring an orderly and transparent process to the privatisation programme which safeguards the public interest and builds confidence in the process.

Sale of Government Assets

Unlike the first two methods described in the preceding paragraphs, this method involves sale of assets rather than shares. The Government may sell the assets directly, disposing of major assets. The assets may also be sold individually or sold together as a new corporate entity. The sale can be based on an open competitive bidding, carried out by auction or through a direct negotiation with a pre-identified party. The sale of assets can take many different forms. If the intention is to privatise only part of the enterprise, the respective assets may be sold, with the core enterprise remaining intact. The enterprise can be downsized this way. If the entire enterprise is to be sold, but is not saleable as a going concern, the same may be dissolved or liquidated and assets sold to a private party. In certain situations for financial, legal reasons, a sale of assets is considered, though the enterprise may be saleable as a going concern. In IRIs sale of Alfa Romeo to Fiat, all the assets and liabilities were transferred to a new company formed by Fiat Lancia. IRI wanted to keep Alfa Romeo as a shell company in order to write off its losses against other group profits.

The main problem in the usage of this method is the handling of existing liabilities. If the transaction involves full dissolution of the enterprise, all the restructuring issues will crop up. One way to overcome such problems is to have a hybrid approach. For example, the enterprise may be dissolved and sold, but under a contractual agreement the buyer may be obligated to rehire a substantial workforce of the seller company.

Reorganisation or fragmentation into component parts: This method involves the splitting/breaking up of a large enterprise into several separate entities. Reorganisation can take the following forms:

1. Break up into several legal entities. An electric utility being split up into generation, distribution, billing entities. A petroleum corporation split up into exploration, refining and distribution entities.
2. Transformation of a large Government enterprise into a holding company and number of subsidiary companies. The holding company has a majority shareholding of the subsidiary companies which have taken over the assets and liabilities of the original enterprise.

3. Hiving off certain activities (say productive, commercial) with the Government retaining the remaining activities (say non-commercial). For example, British Rail in the United Kingdom decided to privatize ferries, hovercraft, hotels, properties, consultancies, freight cars. A holding company, British Rail Investments Limited was set up to acquire some of the non-rail activities with the sole purpose of privatizing them.

The main advantage of this method is that it permits gradual/ piecemeal privatization. Also different methods of privatization may be applied to the different component parts which would maximize the efficacy of the whole privatization process.

New Private Investment in the Enterprise

New private investment in enterprises is a preferred method for alleviating the funding problems of under capitalized enterprises. The enterprise may be in need of substantial capital for capacity enhancement or for physical rehabilitation. The additional requirement of capital may be met by opening up equity ownership to the private sector. It should be appreciated that the Government is not disposing any of its existing equity in the enterprise, rather there is a dilution of the Governments equity position. This process of the Government encouraging private sector participation and gradually withdrawing from making any investment is known as a process of privatization by attrition. This process can be illustrated with the help of an example.

Government and Private Holding		*Initial capital (Government)*	*Private party*	*Total Capital*
Government	100%	$1billion	NIL	$1billion
Private	NIL			
Government	67%		$ 0.5 billion	$1.5 billion
Private	33%			
Government	50%		$0.5 billion +	$2 billion
Private	50%		$0.5 billion	

It can be inferred that the Government has caused a dilution of its equity to 50 per cent over a period of time, by encouraging the private party to provide additional capital.

Management Employee Buyout

From the foregoing discussion it is clear that the change of ownership from government to private hands is primarily for enhancing efficiency with which the enterprise's resources are used. This change of ownership can be either for those already working in the enterprise or outsiders to the company. Its but in the fitness of things that insiders are given the opportunity to own the assets and shares of the enterprise. This process of providing motivation to the insiders to own the assets and shares refers to the concept of buyout. Thus, a buyout operation can take the forms of—Management Buyout, (MBO), Management Employee buyout (MEBO), Workers Buyout (WBO). To operationalise the concept of buyout, there are two popular schemes Leveraged Buyout (LBO) and Employee Stock Ownership Plan (ESOP).

Leveraged Buyout (LBO)

Leveraged buyout is purchase of a private company through borrowed funds. LBO refers to the acquisition of all the stock or assets of a hitherto public company by a small group of investors financed largely by borrowing. Normally, debt financing represents 50 per cent or more of the purchase price. The tangible assets of the enterprise to be acquired are used as collateral for the loans. The cash requirements for servicing the debt would motivate managers to shed non-productive assets, improve operating efficiency and forego wasteful capital expenditure.

Employee Stock Ownership Plan (ESOP)

Employee stock ownership plan can be understood as an employee benefit plan like the pension plans. The pension plan is designed to provide for payments to participants after retirement. ESOP trust or fund is similar to a pension fund. Willing members join the ESOP scheme and make a nominal contribution as membership fee. Like pension funds, ESOPs may also provide for both employer and employee contributions. Governments mandate financial institutions to support the ESOP scheme. The financial institution is the source of borrowing by the ESOP. The financial institution lends cash to the ESOP trust. The sponsoring enterprise generally guarantees the loan. The ESOP trust purchases securities from the enterprise. The enterprise contributes cash to ESOP trust. ESOP trust ultimately makes payment towards principal and interest to the financial institution. The basic idea of ESOP is to link ownership with efficiency. Since, the members of ESOP realize that ultimately they would possess the shares, they would work with great zeal and enthusiasm. The amount standing to the credit of each employee will be converted into shares after a specified period of time or at the time of retirement, shares will be issued. The ESOP trust can frame appropriate rules and regulations concerning all relevant issues with respect to the operational details of the ESOP scheme.

In the Chinese economic system reform, management buyout was once regarded as one of the most efficient restructuring methods. However, a number of strict provisions were made to limit MBO by the Government at the end of 2003. This prohibited management from borrowing, and prevented the enterprises being used as security to finance MBO.

Leasing and Management Contract

Both leasing and management contract are intermediate methods which will ultimately facilitate the privatization process. The methods are purely temporary measures to bring up an enterprise upto an acceptable level of profitability. For example, most privatization transactions in France involved management contracts to turnaround the enterprises.

In a Management contract the contractor usually an individual or a firm manages the enterprise for an agreed compensation. The contract will define the rights, duties, obligations of the contractor. Usually details regarding a base remuneration and also an incentive for exceeding a fixed target form part of the contract.

Under leasing a private party leases assets owned by the Government. The lease deed sets forth the terms and conditions of the lease. Lessee has to make periodic payments to the lessor irrespective of the profitability of the operation. For both leasing and management contract the debt liabilities will be borne by the Government.

Regional Comparisons

In some countries, regions and industries, the state-owned activities still represent a significant share of GDP while in others this has diminished considerably. Trends show that transition economies and Latin American countries have been most active in privatization while other regions such as the Middle East and Northern Africa have not utilized privatization much as shown in Figure 4.1. In industrialized countries the share of

Table 4.2: Primary advantages and disadvantages of the most commonly used privatization methods

Method	Advantages	Disadvantages
Mass privatization	• Assures political acceptability • Supports development of local capital market	• Reduces governments proceeds • Imposes obstacles to foreign investment and the transmission of financial, technical and managerial expertise.
Public offering	• Transparency enhances political acceptability • Supports development of local capital market • Create broad ownership • Attract foreign investment	• Expensive process
Private sale of shares	• Offers flexibility to government • Technically less complicated • Cost-effective for smaller firms	• Does not support development of local capital market • Limits possibility of broad ownership
Mixed sale	• Transparency enhances political acceptability • Supports development of local capital market • Create broad ownership • Attract foreign investment	• Expensive process
Concessions	• Eliminates room for exploitation of monopolistic position	• Uncertainty of demand introduces constant risk of re-negotiation and re-nationalization
Employee/ Management buy-outs	• Leads to closer monitoring of performance • Aligns the employee and management incentives with those of the owners	• May seek objectives such as job security and job-based utility and forgo the increase of the value of the company. • Effective decision making can be hampered

SOEs in GDP has dropped to 5 per cent and on an average Latin American countries have almost reached the same levels. Consequently, the level of employment by SOEs has come down considerably.

Another trend is the declining public support for privatization. In Latin America for instance a survey from 1995 (Kikeri and Kolo, 2005) showed support levels of 75 per cent in favour of privatization while a

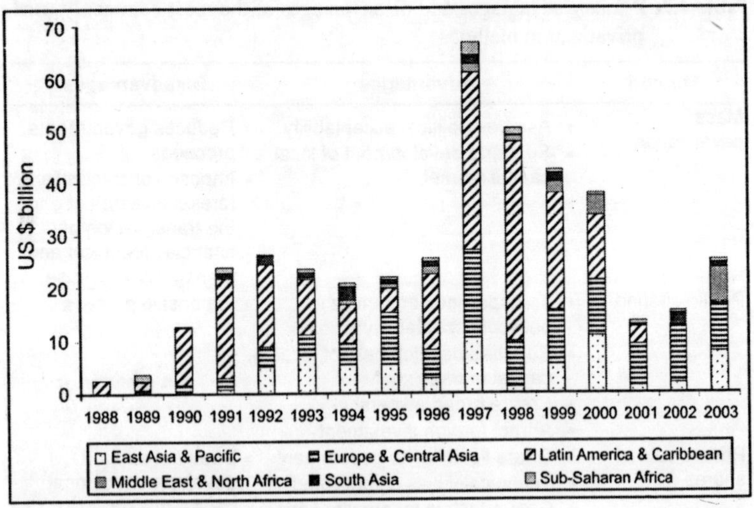

Source: World Bank Privatization Database

Fig. 4.1: Privatization proceeds worldwide

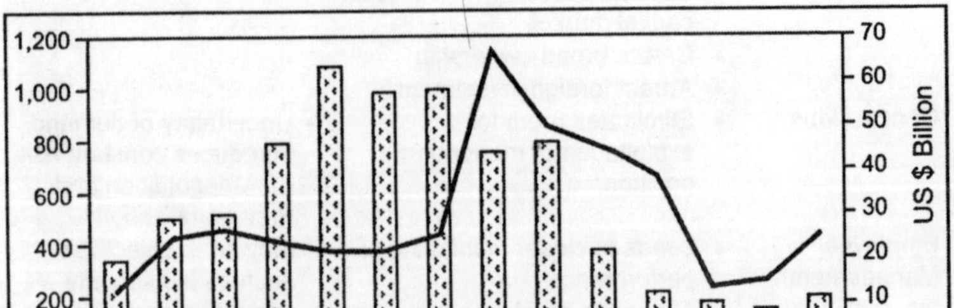

Source: Kikeri and Kolo (2005).

Fig. 4.2: Number of Transactions and Proceeds

more recent survey put the percentage in favour of private ownership at 35 per cent. At the same time only 28 per cent of respondents believed that privatization was beneficial for their country.

The Impact of Privatization

Numerous studies have been performed to research the effects of privatization. There have been case-studies, country-specific studies and cross country studies aimed to find changes caused by privatization. In general the impact of privatization and related empirical research can be categorized as follows (Kikeri and Nellis, 2001):

- Impact on financial and operational performance of the enterprise
- Fiscal impact and effect on economic growth
- Welfare effects
- Employment and broader labour market impact
- Impact on income levels and wealth distribution

The results of a number of authoritative studies on the impact of privatization in a wide range of countries and sectors revealed the following findings:

1. For non-transition economies profitability, efficiency, output and capital investment went up after privatization while the results on employment are ambiguous. The noted improvements are strongly related to the change in incentive and management structure and the improvement in corporate governance. The evidence further shows that the improvements are irrespective of the market structure, however competitive firms do perform better. In non-competitive markets deregulation is needed to speed up convergence of the firm to industry standards. Full private control is essential for achieving performance improvements. Results for transition economies are less impressive but still show improvements after privatization.
2. Regarding the macroeconomic and fiscal impact of privatization, sales proceeds, a decline in transfers (subsidies) to the firms and in due time- tax income from privatized firms benefit the treasury, causing budget deficits to decline. Important policy variables to achieve economic growth are fiscal discipline, price and trade liberalization, deregulation, privatization and clarification of property rights. Especially, the combined effect of these policies on economic growth is substantial. Privatization alone might not be the cause for economic growth but it serves as a proxy for structural reform. Also it is a strong signal of

reform credibility to investors. The use of proceeds from privatization is essential in realizing positive macroeconomic effects. The more proceeds are used to retire both domestic and foreign debt, the better the widespread economic benefits. When proceeds are substantial and used properly, interest rates and inflation drop and growth is stimulated.

3. Because of its complexity there are limited studies on the welfare effect of privatization. Even though these do point out positive contributions to the economic welfare, it remains an area that needs further research as the welfare effects of a privatization programme are critical to its acceptance and success.
4. The effects of privatization on employment are ambiguous. Drops in employment levels occur mainly when non-competitive firms are privatized. If the privatization involves a relatively efficient competitive firm the decline in employment levels is slight or non-existent. There is also evidence showing short-run decline but medium- and longterm improvements in employment levels. In addition the wage levels of the remaining work force increase. Overall privatization creates productive jobs and releases unproductive labour which had been employed at the expense of society, for more productive activities. The accompanying reforms and not privatization itself have to ensure that indeed the released labour is used in a productive way.
5. Little analysis has been performed regarding the distributive impact of privatization. However, it is obvious that the design of the privatization transaction strongly influences the welfare consequences. In the case of infrastructure firms the distributive impact has been shown to depend on the qualities of the regulatory system. In general the perception exists that the short-run distributive impact of privatization might be negative in the sense that upper income categories benefit far more than lower income categories. Still, further analysis is needed to arrive at conclusive findings.

Ramamurti's Multilevel Model of Privatization

Ramamurti proposes a multilevel dynamic model of privatization in emerging economies (EEs). This model offers an organizing framework to help understand the choice of SOE to be privatized, the choice of method applied and the performance implications of privatization in emerging economies. Figure 4.3 depicts the proposed multilevel model.

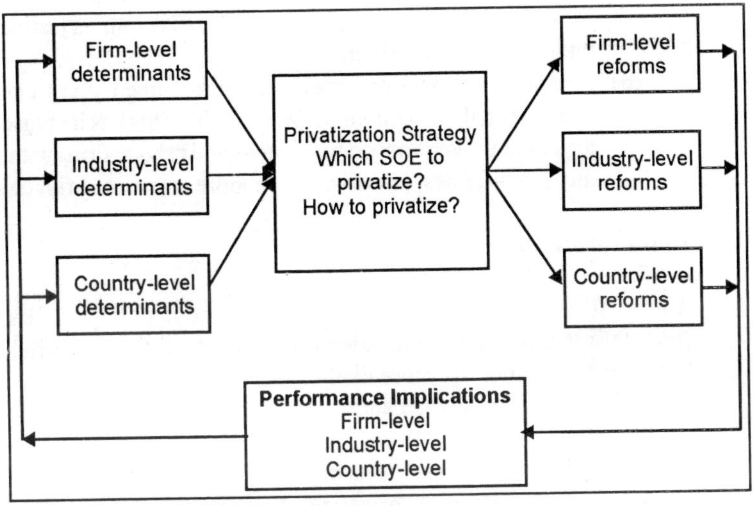

Source: Ramamurti (2000).

Fig. 4.3: Ramamurti's Multilevel Model of Privatization

Within his model Ramamurti uses privatization both in its narrow (the transfer of property or control of productive economic entities from the public to the private sector) and broad definition (increasing the involvement of the private sector in an economy through deregulation, liberalization, institution building etc.)

The model has the following distinctive characteristics:

1. It is multilevel because in order to understand the causes of privatization and the way it is implemented he believes that privatization should be looked at from firm, industry and country level.
2. It is dynamic because privatization is not a static one shot event but rather a staged process. Variables at all three levels determine which SOE is privatized, how it is privatized and therefore which reforms at each of the levels follow from these choices. In turn these reforms have performance implications at all three levels which then again influence the dynamics for the next round of privatization, either within the same firm, industry or country.

3. It is proposed for emerging economies because of two reasons:
   (a) Emerging economies (developing and transitional economies) are generally institutionally underdeveloped and the difference in this sense with developed countries justifies their separate treatment.
   (b) Emerging economies have in the past fifteen years been opening up their economies dramatically. This has increased the competitive strain on both public and private firms within these economies, providing even more reason to privatize.

Relevant Propositions

(a) Small SOEs are more likely to be privatized than large SOEs
(b) SOEs that resulted from nationalization or that are still partially privately owned are more likely to be privatized than SOEs that are wholly state owned and/or were greenfield investments by the state
(c) SOEs in competitive markets or potentially competitive markets are more likely to be privatized than SOEs in monopolistic markets
(d) Monopolistic SOEs in sectors that can benefit from regulatory innovations like vertical and horizontal breakup, yardstick competition, or price-cap regulation are more likely to be privatized
(e) SOEs in countries where the political leadership is ideologically committed to private ownership and market forces are more likely to be privatized than those where the political leadership is committed to state ownership and/or central planning.
(f) SOEs in countries facing a macroeconomic crisis are more likely to be privatized than SOEs in countries with stable economies
(g) SOEs in countries with weak market-supporting institutions (e.g., many transitional economies) are less likely to be privatized than those in countries with stronger institutions, especially if they are large, monopolistic firms:
   - Privatization is a policy with the general objective to enhance enterprise performance based on change in ownership, management, markets, competition and/or regulation. In addition privatization aims to strengthen the role of the private sector in the economy and to improve the government's financial health.

- The constraints faced when governments are privatizing are related to market structure, political scenario and institutional endowment. Three necessary political conditions for successful SOE reform and privatization are political desirability, political feasibility and credibility of promises central to SOE reform.
- Economic crises in developing countries increase the likeliness of privatization, however, less so when budget deficits are financed with domestic borrowing, but the opposite applies if external borrowing is used.
- Employment is a crucial determinant in privatization strategies. Governments lose their power to choose employment level when they privatize or they pay a high price in terms of revenue loss or incentives and guarantees when they require private investors to maintain employment levels.
- Pre-privatization restructuring is thought of as a means to improve the appeal of an enterprise to investors, to minimize layoffs or to increase the price. However, measures such as debt absorption have no effect on the net price while investment and efficiency programmes have a negative effect on the net price. Even labour redundancy programmes do not lead to the desired objectives. Restructuring should therefore be brief and limited to legal, accounting and organizational changes, leaving technology changes, capital investments and major purchases to the new owners.
- In general, profitability, efficiency, output and capital investment improve after privatization while the results on employment are ambiguous. Sale proceeds, a decline in transfers to the firms and tax income from privatized firms benefit the treasury and cause budget deficits to decline. There are limited studies on the welfare effect of privatization and little analysis has been performed regarding the distributive impact of privatization.
- Ramamurti's Multilevel Model of Privatization offers an organizing framework to analyze privatization from a multilevel and dynamic perspective. The model is multilevel because in order to understand the causes of privatization and the way it is implemented, privatization should be looked at from firm, industry and country levels. It is

> dynamic because variables at all three levels determine which SOE is privatized, how it is privatized and therefore which reforms at each of the levels follow. In turn these reforms have performance implications at all three levels which influence the dynamics for the next round of privatization, either within the same firm, industry or country.

Regulatory Reform Initiatives

Macro-economic reforms must be carried out along with enterprise reforms. It is important to strengthen, existing regulatory arrangements and set up sector specific regulatory authorities. Tariff revisions, consumer interest, social obligations, licensing procedures, intermediation and dispute settlements are the primary responsibilities of the regulatory authorities. As long as markets exist, there are bound to be risks of market failure. And there is a need for a regulatory mechanism to prevent this risk from exploding into a crisis.

A Comprehensive Illustration—Privatization in Suriname

Suriname, with a population of approx. 487000 and a land area of approx. 164000 sq. km, gained its independence in 1975 after three centuries of predominantly Dutch reign. In the past three decades, the country went through significant changes in political sense. Established as a constitutional democracy in 1975, Suriname experienced intermittent military rule between 1980 and 1991. The resultant steady deterioration of the economy, amplified after the Netherlands and the US withheld aid in 1982-1988, was the main factor leading to restoration of democracy in 1988.

Mining and manufacturing have been Suriname's largest sectors in 2004. Mining remains Suriname's leading foreign-exchange earner accounting for 8.3 per cent of GDP in 2003. Commerce and financial services accounted for about 11 per cent each and agriculture accounted for 5.3 per cent of GDP. The informal sector accounted for 14.5 per cent of GDP (EIU, 2005).

Also with regard to employment, mining is becoming more important as gold and other minerals ventures are being developed. Agriculture accounts for 15 per cent of total employment. The government remains the largest employer in Suriname, with 39,607 civil servants directly employed by the Central Government in 2001. Another 17,650 staff were employed by state-owned corporations.

The responsible government policies of 2000-2005, nurtured a stable economic environment with an average growth rate of 5.3 per cent in 2001-2004.

Politics and Privatization Policy

The Surinamese society is and has for centuries been segmented along ethnic lines. This caused the political system to develop based on ethnic identification rather than political ideology. Political parties lack ideological foundation and operate as organized interest groups. The segmented character of the Surinamese society, the nature of the political game and the weak economic basis in Suriname explain the absence of political ideology.

It is no surprise that in such a political environment, economic policy serves the aspirations and interests of the several ethnic groups. A long-term national development strategy to which successive governments commit themselves has been absent as a result of the diverse and fragmented (ethnical) interests. As a result the State is currently represented in nearly all sectors of the economy and has substantial stakes in key productive activities. The dominant role of the state in the economy has been costly. Poor performance of SOEs is more a rule than an exception.

In its multi-year development plan 2006-2011 the Government of Suriname considers privatization as a policy that leads to accelerated development, attraction of investment capital, and increase of revenues for the government. The plan announces a centralized approach towards privatization through the establishment of a Centre for Privatization of SOEs (CEPRIS) in 2007. The plan further indicates finalization of privatization of three current privatization undertakings by the end of 2006. These include the privatization of Surland from the Banana sector, the privatization of which had posed considerable obstacles in the past.

The World Banana Value Chain

Bananas are perennial crops that grow quickly and can be harvested all year round. Bananas are one of the most widely traded agricultural products in the world with annual exports valued at roughly 5 billion dollars. In terms of volume they are the number one exported fruit while they rank second after citrus fruit in terms of value. Bananas are grown throughout the tropical and sub-tropical regions of the world and are almost exclusively exported from developing countries to developed countries. In general there are two production systems, namely small scale plantations (0.1-10 ha) with average yields of 4-15 metric tonnes/ha, and large industrial-scale export-directed plantations (100-4,000 ha) with average yields of 25-60 metric tonnes/ha.

The banana industry is a complex playing field and involves a number of agents in several stages of its value chain. Figure 4.4 depicts the banana value chain together with the agents involved in the several stages. Only 7-13 per cent of value is controlled by producers. Labour accounts for 1-3 per cent.

World Banana Production and Trade

Total world production of bananas topped 70 million tonnes in 2003 increasing over 30 per cent within the last decade. World exports of banana make out roughly 20 per cent of production as most produce is consumed in local markets. About 80 per cent of the world exports are controlled by only four Trans National Banana Companies: Dole Food Company, Chiquita, Fresh Del Monte Fyffes, and National Banana Company: Noboa of Ecuador. This indicates the highly oligopolistic character of the export banana industry. The high level of vertical integration results from the special characteristics of bananas. Because of its high perishability careful control of growing, packaging, transport, handling, ripening and distribution is required.

Bananas are imported mainly by the European Union, the United States of America and Japan, which together accounted for more than 65 per cent of total world imports in 2010. The four leading banana exporting countries in 2010 (Ecuador, Costa Rica, Philippines and Colombia) accounted for more than 75 per cent of world exports. Ecuador alone provided more than 33 per cent of global banana exports.

Divergent patterns of trade regulation have defined two distinct trade systems for bananas: the Dollar Banana system based on the US market and the smaller ACP Banana trade between Europe and its former African, Caribbean and Pacific (ACP) colonies. Dollar Bananas have been regulated by free market conditions while ACP Bananas have been regulated by preferential market agreements between nations. The difference between these two regimes originates from a number of factors amongst which the historical relationship between producing and

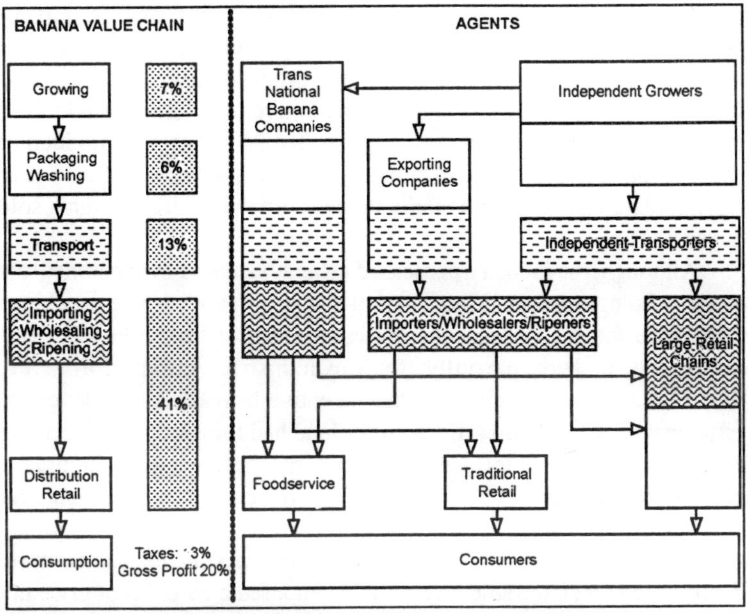

Source: Adapted from UNCTAD

Fig. 4.4: The Banana Value Chain

consuming countries, social and environmental factors, and the production systems used led to huge differences in cost structure.

The world market price is best represented by the dollar bananas because these are produced under free market conditions. The price differences among origins reflect the huge production cost differences between producer countries. Production costs vary between US$ 162- and US$ 740, per tonne.

Surland Overview

Banana plantations in Suriname were initially set up to replace the cocoa-plantations which had suffered from diseases in the beginning of the 20th century. However, these early initiatives did not bear the expected fruits. Diseases, the World Wars and economic crises prevented successful development of this industry and in 1957 the Government of Suriname decided to intervene. A division of the Ministry of Agriculture established large plantations and was responsible for central purchase of produce from individual farmers. In 1971 the Government of Suriname incorporated the banana plantations into the joint stock company "Surinaamse Landbouwbedrijven NV" or in short Surland of which it took full ownership and control. Surland produced from two locations: Jarikaba (approx. 1,353 ha) and Nickerie (approx. 1,012 ha) both located in the coastal area of Suriname. It controlled 95 per cent of production and 100 per cent of export. Until the temporary closure of Surland in April 2002 all produce was marketed and sold in the UK through a sole buyer, Fyffes.

Although, the industry possessed clear advantages over competitors in agro-ecological, logistic and market-sense, it was never able to achieve high performance. Perhaps the preferential treatment by the EU itself accounted, at least partially, for the industries low performance. Preferential treatment removed the incentive to reach higher levels of efficiency and production. Even so Surland had for a long time been the country's third largest foreign exchange earner before it was temporarily closed down in April 2002 after consecutive years of losses amounting up to US$ 33 million.

Preceding the closedown, Surland's financial situation had severely deteriorated when the sole buyer Fyffes imposed a 25 per cent price cut in 2000 and another 8 per cent price cut in 2001. Wind damages in the same year further increased pressure on the company's finances and early 2002 sales revenues covered only half of the company's production costs. Cash shortages forced the company to suspend production in April 2002 after it failed to pay up March 2002 salaries. At the time of its closure Surland employed around 2,600 people equaling 16 per cent of the total agricultural employment and 2.8 per cent of total employment while the banana production accounted for approx. 1.5 per cent of GDP.

Surland's export production varied between 23,000 and 40,000 tonnes per year, equaling .2-.35 per cent of worldwide banana exports, as shown in Table 4.3.

From 1994-1997 Suriname was subject to a quota of 38,000 tonnes which it however never was able to fulfil. Yields were as low as 17.7 tonnes/ha which is higher than world average but much lower in comparison to the dollar banana producers like Costa Rica with yields of 45-54 tonnes/ha. Besides, the low yield a high percentage of production, above 30 per cent, did not meet export standards and was rejected along the production line. It was the combination of high production costs, low yield, high waste rate, continually declining world market prices, erosion of the EU's preferential treatment, social unrest and the Governments inability to cope with these dynamics that eventually caused Surland to close down in April 2002.

Restructuring of Surland

By the end of the last century it became evident that reforming of the banana industries in ACP countries would be essential for their survival. In order to assist ACP countries to adjust to the market changes resulting from the diminishing preferential treatment, the EU allocated funds under Specific Frameworks for Assistance (SFA). In 1999 Suriname formulated a strategic plan for the restructuring and privatization of Surland, identifying the necessary actions aimed at improving competitiveness in a liberalizing environment.

After Surland closed in April 2002 the original strategic plan was revised. The revised plan was based on the creation of a new banana company to re-launch the banana production on a sound and sustainable basis while debts and social backlogs would remain the responsibility of Surland. In preparation thereof a new entity, the Foundation for Preservation of the Banana sector of Suriname (SBBS) was set up. In October 2002 the SBBS restarted the activities of Surland and was also endowed with the task of its restructuring and privatization.

An investment programme was devised by the French consulting firm SOFRECO (business plan 2002-2007) to achieve the targeted results. Over 2002-2007 capital investments of US$ 30 million were foreseen. The EU financed the largest part of this restructuring under the SFA-programme. In addition the Inter-American Development Bank (IADB) provided a loan of US$ 7.3 million for working capital. The SBBS started replanting in June 2003 and exports to Europe were resumed in March 2004 after a two-year break, with the marketing carried out by a French firm Agrisol. The targeted results of the revised strategic plan are displayed in Table 4.4.

To achieve the necessary improvements to gain and maintain competitiveness, the restructuring took place in four main areas, namely in finance, production, marketing and human resource management. The investment programme included investments in production systems like cableways, packing stations, drainage and irrigation systems and other infrastructural components. Surland's supply arrangements were now, as part of a forward integration strategy, based on spot market prices (FOT-basis) for its own brand of bananas (Switie), instead of fixed-term contracts at an annually negotiated minimum price which had been the

Table 4.3: Performance parameters of Surland 1995-2002

Year	1995	1996	1997	1998	1999	2000	2001	2002
Exports to EU (x 1000 tonnes)	27.98	25.96	29.25	21.22	39.02	34.23	28.72	6.55
EU market share (% of qty)	0.88	0.79	0.93	0.70	1.22	1.04	0.88	0.22
EU market share (% of value)	1.09	0.96	1.19	0.89	1.42	1.60	1.00	0.20
Quota realization (%)	70	75	59	n.a.	n.a.	n.a.	n.a.	n.a.
Yields (ton/ha)	23.1	22.6	21.0	17.7	25.5	22.3	19.8	19.7
FOB Value (x100 US$/tonne)	3.08	7.43	7.39	7.13	6.36	7.32	7.32	5.12
FOB Value (US$m)	11.3	17.6	24.4	17	21	24.9	21	3.4
Harvest Area (x1000 ha)	2.2	2.1	2.1	2.1	2.1	2.1	2.2	2.2

Sources: FAO, EUROSTAT, SOFRECO, NERA).

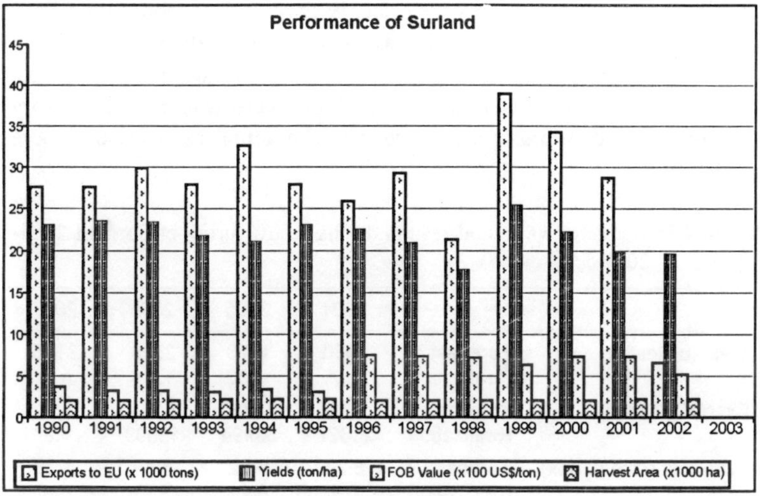

Sources: FAO, EUROSTAT, SOFRECO, NERA.

Fig. 4.5: Surland's performance 1990-2003

case under the agreement with Fyffes. To achieve higher yields and better output specific agro-technical measures were taken. The government settled approximately US$ 12 million of long-term debt while short-term debts of US$ 6 million remained. Several attempts to sell of unproductive assets (the company's rice plantation) turned out unsuccessful with bids

Table 4.4: Targets for restructuring of Surland

	Restructured company 2007	*Surland (2001)*
Foreign currency earnings (FOB)	>US$ 43 million	US$ 10.47 million
Direct rural employment	2600	2560
Rural income	US$ 8.5 million	US$6.6 million
Banana boxes sold and exported	5.4 million	1.56 million
Yield per hectare	2230 boxes (41.25 tonne)	858 boxes (15,9 tonne)
Cultivated area	2315 ha	1820 ha
Cost price (FOB)	US$ 5.70	US$11.32
Profit and loss account	US$ 5.035 million	-US$5.3 million
State revenues	>US$ 3 million	Losses US$ 32 million (1996-2001)
Indirect activities generated (plastic, pallets, port operations, transportation, in-vitro plants, banana boxes, trade)	>US$ 9 million	US$1.3 million

Source: SOFRECO/EC.

at less than 20 per cent of reserve price. With regards to labour the SBBS did not work with a union. Labour was attracted directly or indirectly on an individual basis. The former union active at Surland was not recognized.

The results which were projected along the restructuring trajectory are summarized in Table 4.5 along with the actual realizations where applicable.

Table 4.5: Budgeted vs Actual results during restructuring of Surland 2004-2007

		2004	*2005*	*2006*	*2007*
Yield (boxes/ha)	Forecast	1380	1978	2315	2195
	Realization	2259	1652	1316	n.a.
Exports (tonnes)	Forecast	38686	84282	100840	96586
	Realization	21327	39494	19099	n.a.
FOB-cost price ($/box)	Forecast	8.73	6.22	5.68	5.88
	Realization	8.8	8.11	7.15	n.a.
Reject rate (%)	Forecast	20	20	20	20
	Realization	37	35	35	n.a.
Cultivated (ha)	Forecast	1537	2322	2365	2365
	Realization	1424	1587	1589	n.a.
Labour force (qty)	Forecast	2124	2865	2985	2971
	Realization	1352	1750	1943	n.a.
EU licenses ($/box)	Forecast	1.1	1.1	0	0
	Realization	2.63	3.5	1.56*	n.a.

Source: SOFRECO/EC.

Notes: The realizations of 2006 are based on figures until the end of June 2006.

* not only license cost but includes tariff based on volume exported outside quota.

From Table 4.4 and Figure 4.6 it is clear that the restructuring of the banana industry did not meet its initial targets and the offset was quite substantial. In its monitoring report of June 2006 SOFRECO attributes these discrepancies to the huge unforeseen market access costs (EU license prices and duties). The financial difficulties resulting from these created operational problems which affected output. In addition the main estate Jarikaba performed much worse than expected due to weaknesses in field and packing operations leading to high waste rates and low yields.

It should be noted however, that the restructuring plan aimed at achieving competitive production in a liberalized environment. The question arises whether failure to meet this target should be attributed to the EU-market access costs. Surprisingly, the business plan which formed the basis for new investments of US$ 30 million did not include a sensitivity or a scenario analysis.

As a consequence of the underperformance, additional capital inflows were necessary to keep the company afloat. The partially state-owned Hakrinbank provided a total of US$ 4 million in 2004 and 2005 under State guarantees while the Ministry of Finance provided US$ 1.7 million in 2006.

In spite of the considerable investments in restructuring for the past 5 years amounting up to US$ 30 million and working capital loans for a total of US$ 13 million, Surland had remained unprofitable with long-term prospects threatened by the further erosion of its EU trade privileges.

Privatization of Surland

The objectives of privatization of the Surland were identified as follows:

1. Sustainability of banana sector restructuring. Within this context privatization should lead to—
   - Removal of burden on State budget
   - Prevention of political interference
   - Allowing market forces to work and as a consequence enhancing productivity and competitiveness
   - Capacity building of company (financial, managerial etc.)
2. Development of the banana sector or other tropical agricultural production
3. Revenue generation for the State
4. Exemplarity of privatization process

The constraints of privatization of the banana industry included:

1. Poor track record of the banana industry in terms of productivity and social stability
2. Confidence in outcome of the restructuring plan
3. Existing debt handling
4. Investment unfriendly environment
5. EU market development uncertainties

The government apparently decided to withdraw from the banana industry, however, with the intent to make the industry sustainable first. Two privatization strategy proposals were prepared and presented in 2004

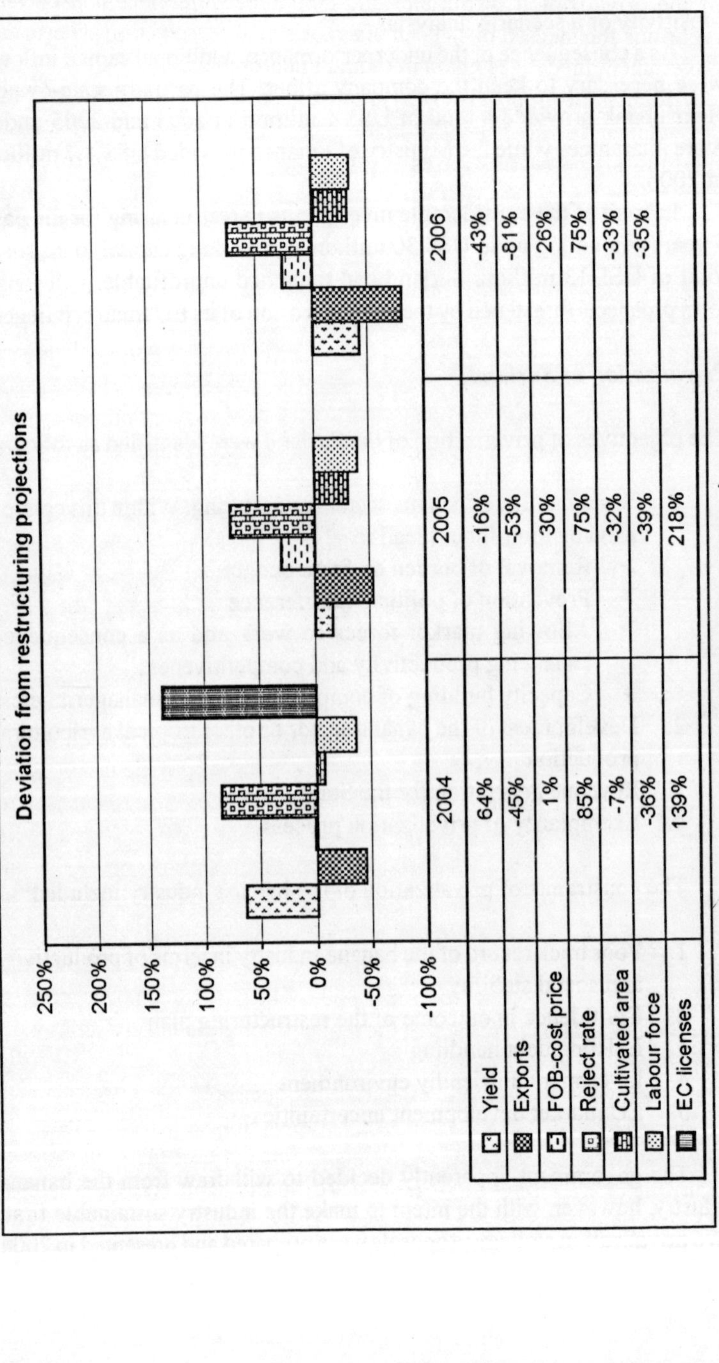

Fig. 4.6: Deviation from restructuring projections 2004-2006 in percentage points

and 2005. These proposals were based on the objectives and constraints of the privatization of Surland and contained guidelines and options regarding the method of sale, an investor's profile, selection criteria and government incentives guarantees and undertakings.

From these proposals a final privatization strategy was devised. Table 4.6 summarizes the privatization strategy. It was finally decided that a medium size strategic investor should be attracted with sufficient integration into the banana value chain and established presence in the EU banana market. Surinamese banana production would have to be indispensable within such an investor's strategy in order to preserve this industry, while the preferential treatment on the EU market would have to be utilized. The proposed method was to call for expression of interest followed by a formal tender restricted to a short list of investors established on the basis of the pre-selection criteria. The suggested method of privatization was a sale of shares of the new banana company. The proposed strategy also incorporates social and environmental safeguards required from strategic investors, and incentives and guarantees from the side of the government.

In 2003 the asset replacement value of the company was estimated at US$ 11.5 million, of which US$8.8 million for the Jarikaba and US$ 2.7 million for the Nickerie estate. In addition, a discounted cash flow value of around US$ 17 million was estimated in 2005. Based on lower output of the Jarikaba estate the revenue expectations from privatization were adjusted to US$ 12-15 million.

In July 2004 the government invited 29 operators on the EU market representing 90 per cent of trade to express interest in the privatization. Local investors were also called upon but none showed consistent interest while 6 of the 29 international operators did (Delmonte Fresh Food, Fyffes, Jamaica Producers, Grupo Caribana, Compagnie Fruitère, and GF Fruit). An open tender was issued in March 2005 restricted to the 6 short listed international operators. However, none of the operators entered in the bid process due to uncertainties which existed at that time regarding the EU banana regime after December 2005. The government was requested by these operators to re-launch the tender after these uncertainties would have been cleared.

Following the request of interested operators the government re-launched the privatization process in February 2006. Six operators (Fyffes, Agrisol/Katope, GF Fruit, Agro-Fair, Compagnie Fruitère and Mathias Durbeck) and one Surinamese company (American Suriname Development) expressed interest. Given the timeframe needed to implement the privatization (7 months) and the fact that SBBS ran into a substantial cash flow deficit, an intermediary solution was negotiated with Agrisol/Katope which already had a commercial agreement with SBBS to market its bananas in the EU.

Within the context of this solution Agrisol/Katope had provided the necessary finance and taken over management of the company for the period of one year ending in September 2007. The consultants of Sofreco responsible for development of and guidance throughout the restructuring and privatization process of Surland were recruited by Agrisol/Katope to execute this Management Contract.

The main objectives were to drastically improve the performance of the Jarikaba estate, to finalize the reinvestments as projected in the business plan 2003-2007 and to re-launch the privatization process in 2007.

Determinants of the Method of Privatization

Regarding the method of privatization of Surland, i.e. determining the targeted capital structure and investor in the sale of shares process, the following determinants can be distinguished.

At firm level the firm's performance and the firm's size are the most relevant. Surland had been underperforming for some years, with accumulated debts of US$ 33 million and a loss of US$ 5.4 million in 2001. The cost price stood at roughly double the world standard at US$ 11.32 per box FOB. In addition social unrest within the company deteriorated the firm's perspectives for improvements. The continuing underperformance supports government's withdrawal from this industry. The firm's size in this context also relates to its capitalization. Both asset valuation and a discounted cash flow valuation of Surland suggested a fair market value around US$ 12-17 million. Financially, capable investors would have to be sought.

At the industry level the extent of industry globalization primarily determines the method of privatization. The banana export industry comprises specific characteristics. About 80 per cent of world banana trade is controlled by only four Trans National Banana Companies: Dole Food Company, Chiquita, Fresh Del Monte, and Fyffes, and one National Banana Company: Noboa of Ecuador. This is indicative of the high oligopolistic character of this industry. Additionally only 7-13 per cent of value creation is controlled by producers. The high perishibility of the banana requires an integrated approach throughout the value chain,

Table 4.6: Summary of Privatization Strategy Surland

Factor	*Evaluated options*	*Choice of Option*
Method of Sale	Sale of Surland shares	
	Sale of Surland assets	
	New company with transfer of assets from Surland	X
Scope of Privatization	One single lot with unproductive assets	X
	One single lot without unproductive assets	
	Two separate lots: Nickerie/Jarikaba without unproductive assets	X
Management of existing creditors	Repayment by the state	
	State guarantee	
	Privatization law	
	Down payment by selected investor	X
Investor's profile	Financial investor	
	Strategic investor	X
Incentives, guarantees and undertakings	A priori definition of incentives and undertakings	X
	Incentives framework and undertakings proposed by potential investors	
Procedure of Sale	Direct negotiation with existing contract	
	Negotiated sales with selected investor after call for expression of interest	
	Open international tender	
	Open international tender restricted to a short list	X
Selection process	Award of bid to best financial offer	
	Award of bid to best aggregate technical and financial offer	
	Award of bid to best technical offer provided an acceptable financial offer is made	
	Award of bid to best technical offer if the investor accepts to match the best financial offer made by candidates reaching a given threshold in the technical evaluation	X

Source: SOFRECO/EC.

favouring Trans National Corporations in a privatization attempt within this industry.

At the country level, the determinants of the method of privatization relate to the macroeconomic crisis faced between 1997 and 2001 and the relatively weak institutional development in Suriname as well as the political power of the labour union at Surland. Since Suriname does not have a very well developed stock exchange, attracting capital through this channel can hardly be considered a possibility when privatizing. The choice for employee participation in a privatization capital structure depends on the worker's political power. The banana industry currently does not work with a labour union but with independent workers. The labour union which had been active at Surland prior to its closure in 2002 is not recognized.

Choice and Method of Privatization based on Determinants

Regarding the choice to privatize the banana industry in Suriname, the size of Surland in terms of employment and consequently political weight, does not favour privatization. This is further enhanced by the lack of political ideological commitment towards privatization. However, the firm's continuing underperformance due to agency/property rights failures and consequently its burden on state budget amidst an economic crisis (1997-2001) strongly favour the option for privatization despite the institutional underdevelopment at the country-level. Privatization seems almost inevitable due to the weak position of banana producers in the banana value chain and the oligopolistic character of the industry. In addition the choice to restructure and privatize the banana industry is driven by the availability of the SFA-programme.

Regarding the method of privatization i.e. determining the targeted capital structure and investor in the sale of shares process, the firm size in terms of value logically limits the choice of buyers to those financially capable. Local investors are less likely to be among those. The institutional underdevelopment also limits the options to attract local capital while the industry's structure favours TNCs -already integrated in the industry- as targeted investors. The workers current political power is low and the government is therefore not likely to target them as buyers.

Analysis of the Current Restructuring and Privatization Approach

The government's current approach regarding the restructuring and privatization of Surland is based on creating a new sustainable banana company through a pre-privatization restructuring programme, and to sell the company's shares to a TNC which is integrated in the industry and already present on the EU market.

Studies clearly show that while pre-privatization restructuring is supposed to appeal to investors and to increase the revenues from privatization the opposite occurs. Measures such as debt absorption have no effect on the net price while investment, efficiency programmes and labour redundancy programmes also do not lead to the desired objectives. These findings are quite understandable because enterprise performance is enhanced when changes in ownership, management, markets, competition and/or regulation occur. While privatization does cause one or more of the above changes, restructuring does not and therefore performance enhancements are not very likely. By entering into a Management Contract with Agrisol/Katope in September 2006, the government had caused a change in management of the company thereby increasing the likelihood of firm level performance enhancement.

Even though the restructuring programme considers substantial development of supporting industries, this will not be within the government's control when the industry is privatized. This is especially true because TNCs are targeted as investors. Integration within the banana value chain is essential for the viability of the banana industry and this is where TNCs are strong and producers are weak. The fact that privatization has been postponed already on request of potential buyers is a clear indication of the weak position of the government and the strong position of potential buyers.

Consequently, the likelihood of low privatization proceeds and costly incentives and guarantees forced upon by and to the benefit of investors is high. Investors could and probably will argue that sustainability of the industry is dependant on government's incentives and guarantees.

To summarise: (a) The choice to privatize the banana industry in Suriname is not favoured by:

- The size of Surland in terms of employment and consequently political weight
- The lack of political ideological commitment towards privatization.
- The institutional underdevelopment of Suriname

(b) The choice to privatize the banana industry in Suriname is favoured by:

- The firm's continuing underperformance due to agency/property rights failures and consequently its burden on state budget.
- The economic crisis of 1997-2001.
- The availability of the SFA-programme.

(c) The targeted capital structure and consequently the targeted investor in the sale of shares process is determined by:

- The firm's value of US$ 12-15 million
- The institutional underdevelopment, especially the lack of a well developed stock exchange.
- The industry's structure which favours TNCs as targeted investors.
- The workers current low political power which make them an unlikely target.

Current status: Surland filed for bankruptcy in 2002. The Belgium Company SBSS injected millions of Euro's from European Union funding. In 2014, Univeg Group from Belgium by acquiring 90 per cent stake,finalised the transition into private ownership, and operaion under the name of Food and Agriculture Industries.

5
Restructuring Strategies

Application of restructuring or turnaround strategies, assumes a basic understanding of the intricate operations of the enterprise and an insight into the functional areas of management *viz* finance, marketing, production, human resources, and potential applications involving e-business, supply chain, customer relationship management. It will be pertinent to mention at the outset, that there is no strict definition of what constitutes a restructuring or a turnaround situation. Enterprises or operating units, whose viability assessment signifies, a failure in the foreseeable future unless remedial actions are initiated, are ideal candidates for application of restructuring strategies. The suggested measures in this chapter are equally applicable for private enterprise, service undertakings, public utilities and are appropriate for both pre- and post-privatization restructuring of Government owned enterprises.

Formulating Restructuring Strategies

Appropriate set of Restructuring strategies should be identified and the same should be implemented in the shortest possible time, to revive an enterprise from decline. The following important factors determine the specific set(s) of measures to be used in a turnaround situation.

- The causes of decline.
- The intensity of the crisis.
- The attitudes of the stakeholders involved in the turnaround process.
- The enterprise's past strategy.
- The industry environment in which the firm operates.
- The cost price structure of the enterprise

The causes of decline described in Chapter 2, determines to a great extent the appropriate restructuring measures for a given situation. For example, if the cause for decline is poor management, the required measures are organizational change and decentralization and perhaps a new management to manage the affairs of the enterprise. It should be recognized that the causes of decline are usually multiple and thus for successfully restructuring an enterprise, one must deploy a number of strategies at the same time. The pragmatic actions initiated by the Restructuring/Turnaround Manager, during the initial stages would determine the efficacy of the restructuring programme. In a number of cases the task of implementing the restructuring strategies are normally entrusted to a Management Contractor.

Elements of a Successful Restructuring Strategy

The turnaround strategies employed in different situations might vary. However, the difference between restructuring situations that are successful and those that are not lies in the quality of implementation. Restructuring/Turnaround strategies, can be broadly categorized into the following types:

1. Asset Reduction strategy
2. Cost Reduction strategy
3. Revenue generation strategy
4. Debt restructuring
5. Financial restructuring
6. Labour redundancy
7. Strategic restructuring
8. Cultural restructuring
9. Legal restructuring
10. Physical restructuring
11. Organisational restructuring

The above measures are combined to formulate an appropriate recovery in a given situation.

Asset Reduction Strategy

Asset reduction is one of the most important measures and it is recommended that enterprises initiate this strategy to begin with. Most enterprises do have non productive assets, which do not in any way contribute to the revenue earning potentialities of the business. Hence, it makes sense to dispose off these non productive assets, realize cash and pay outstanding debts. This process is known as internal restructuring and has been successfully deployed in many enterprises

Asset reduction strategies encompass both fixed and short-term (current) assets reduction measures. These measures go a long way in making an enterprise 'lean and mean' and thus trimming down the organization. Asset reduction strategy can be accomplished by adopting the following measures:

Divesting Operating Units

Divestment of operating units would involve selling off all the assets of an operating unit in its totality. Divestment of an operating unit is a common recovery strategy for a highly diversified enterprise. There also is a scope for divesting subsidiary units in such enterprises. However, this measure may not be desirable for a small business. Divestment of operating units and subsidiary units may be extremely useful to generate cash inflow and minimize cash outflows resulting from severe operating losses. Enterprises do have a choice between divestment and liquidation of the operating units and subsidiaries. Liquidation no doubt would result in greater cash inflow, however a longer time would be required to wind up an unit than to divest it. Top management should endeavour to make a thorough analysis of the unit involved and identify the ideal potential purchaser. Also top management can seek the assistance of third parties to identify prospective buyers of the operating units. In many cases management lacks the time or might feel that they lack the selling skills. Management also would like to maintain confidentiality for a longer period of time, without divulging the name of the enterprise whose operating unit is offered for sale. For example, Levi Strauss divested twenty nine operating units in North America and Europe during the late ninetees when faced within a decline in market share.

Management Buy-Outs

The existing management of the operating unit or the subsidiary unit to be divested might perhaps be a potential purchaser of the unit being divested. Thus it will be useful, especially to inform the subsidiary units well in advance. However, the management might not possess the required cash for the buyout operation. Hence, to make the buyout operational.

schemes like the leveraged buyout and the employee stock ownership plan might be resorted to. Other useful options also might be explored. Management may identify a party with financial backing and together they could form a company to buy the operating unit being sold. The equity base is kept relatively small, to facilitate the management to subscribe for a substantial share of the equity. The bulk of the funds needed to buy the operating unit, is provided by the financial party either by way of term debt, preference shares or some form of convertible instrument.

Divesting Specific Assets

Divesting specific assets, relates to the sale of non-productive assets, which is not in any way contributing to the revenue earning potentialities of the business. Such assets should be clearly identified and earmarked for sale. The approach suggested earlier for divesting operating units, can be effectively employed for sale of assets. The specific approach would however depend on the type and value of the asset. More management effort and time would be required, depending on the value of the asset. In times of general economic recession, it may take a long time to find a buyer, for disposing the assets. Scrap value is normally low, depending on the type of machinery and generally the demand for second hand machinery is lukewarm.

Sale and Leaseback of Assets

In many enterprises undergoing a restructuring programme, large amounts of capital are locked up in fixed assets. Hence, management may decide to increase the cash inflow for some of the assets through a sale and subsequently having a leaseback arrangement. Implementation of such an arrangement is normally carried out for buildings, factories, plant and equipment. Management should work out the economics of a leaseback arrangement before embarking on such a proposal.

Reducing Working Capital

Large amounts of resources tend to be involved in working capital of enterprises undergoing restructuring and its mismanagement can lead to disastrous effects. Poor liquidity tends to be seen as evidence of an enterprise, in financial difficulties. The short-term assets or current assets of an enterprise, (inventory, debtors, and cash) tend not to be financed exclusively from long-term sources of finance. Most enterprises have access to two major short term sources of finance—(a) Trade credit (b) Bank overdraft. The relationship between these short term sources of finance and the current assets tend to be very close and hence it seems logical to deal with both of them, for reducing working capital.

Reducing Inventories

Inventories consist of stocks of raw materials, finished goods and semi finished goods. Broadly speaking, the level of investment in inventories by manufacturing enterprises tends to be relatively large compared with that of trading enterprises. The basic objective of inventory management is to secure maximum efficiency in production with the least investment in inventory. Enterprises should seek to balance the costs of holding stock with those of holding no or low levels of stock. Costs of holding inventory include, lost interest, storage costs, insurance costs and obsolescence costs. The costs of not holding inventory include, loss of customer goodwill, production dislocation, loss of flexibility and reorder costs. Models exist, to aid managers in their task of balancing costs, and optimum ordering quantities should be established for each item of inventory. These quantities should be periodically revised. Establishing levels for each item of inventory in terms of maximum level, minimum level, reorder level and danger level will be quite relevant. A common practice to alleviate inventory problems is fixing up the reorder level between the maximum and minimum levels, so that the level seldom reaches the danger level.

Perpetual inventory system, usage of ABC analysis are useful tools which merit attention. Implementation of Enterprise resource planning systems, in an effort to streamline the Supply chain Management functions would ensure smooth application of the suggested inventory management techniques.

Some practical measures for reducing inventory:

Budgeting and Planning: The importance of forward planning and budgeting should be recognized. Successful inventory management is concerned with an insight into the levels of demand for and costs associated with inventories.

Ratios: Financial ratios can be useful in managing inventory. The inventory holding period ratio (Average inventory × 365/annual stock usage) indicates the average period in days, for which inventory is held.

Cancel Outstanding Orders: Before the goods are sent by suppliers, efforts should be taken to cancel the orders. If, however, the goods are already in transit, the organization can always refuse to accept the delivery, barring legal implications.

Stop buying: If there is excess inventory, a stop order on purchasing is all that is required. If, however, there are supply contracts, management should renegotiate with the suppliers.

Return goods to suppliers: If the ordered goods have already been received and payment is yet to be made, the possibility of returning the goods should be examined

Sell Surplus Raw Materials to third parties: Obsolete inventory can be eliminated by selling to third parties. However the selling price is likely to be substantially lower than the cost price.

Just in time stock holding: Just In Time (JIT) approach implies that production and purchasing are linked closely to sales demand on a week to week basis, thus eliminating the necessity to hold buffer stocks to see the enterprise through unexpected demand peaks. However, effective implementation of JIT requires the acceptance of a particular philosophy and culture. A flexible attitude on the part of both suppliers and internal workforce to expand and contract output at a short notice is required. Also a focus on quality of outputs at each stage both by the suppliers and internal workforce is required. Thus a very close relationship between users and suppliers is a fundamental requirement for the success of JIT.

Accounts Receivable

An enterprise may sell goods/offer services both on cash as well as on credit. Credit is an important ingredient of sales promotion. The Quantum of sales can be increased by adopting a liberal credit policy. The outcome of a liberal credit policy may result in locking up substantial funds of an enterprise in the form of accounts receivable or trade debtors. Accounts receivable is a component of current or short term assets and are expected to be converted into cash within a short period of time. Sick enterprises in most cases suffer from liquidity problems and the ability of an enterprise to pay its short term obligations depends upon the quality of its accounts receivable.

A concern may sell goods on cash as well as on credit. Credit is one of the important elements of sales promotion. The volume of sales can be increased by following a liberal credit policy.

The effect of a liberal credit policy may result in tying up substantial funds of a firm in the form of trade debtors (or receivables). Trade debtors are expected to be converted into cash within a short period of time and are included in current assets. Hence, the liquidity position of concern to pay its short-term obligations in time depends upon the quality of its trade debtors.

Debtors Turnover Ratio

Debtors turnover ratio or accounts receivable turnover ratio indicates the velocity of debt collection of a firm. The ratio indicates the number of times average debtors (receivable) are turned over during a year. The two basic components of accounts receivable turnover ratio are the net credit annual sales and average trade debtors. The trade debtors also include the bills receivables. The average debtors is arrived at by adding the debtors in the beginning of the year and the debtors at the closing of the year and dividing the total by two. The provision for bad and doubtful debts should not be deducted from the debtors, as this may imply that some amount of receivables has been collected.

Example:

Credit sales $50000; Return inwards $2000: Debtors $6000; Bills receivables $2000

Debtors Turnover ratio = Net Credit sales/Average Trade debtors
= $48000/8000
= 6 times

Debtors turnover ratio indicates the number of times the debtors are turned over a year. Higher ratio signifies a better management of debtors and a better liquidity of the debtors. Low ratio implies inefficient management of debtors or less liquid debtors.

Effective management of trade debts, requires establishment and review of credit policy of the enterprise. In a restructuring situation, there are two aspects of debt management that need serious consideration: strict adherence to the established credit norms and policies and an actual reduction in the number of debtor days outstanding.

Establishing a Credit Policy

A credit policy is the blueprint used by a business in making its decision to extend credit to a customer. The primary goal of a credit policy is to avoid extending credit to customers who are unable to pay their accounts. The credit policy for some larger businesses can be quite formal., involving things such as: specific documented guidelines, customer credit applications and credit checks. The credit policy for most small businesses tends to be quite informal and lacks the items found in the formal credit policy of a larger business. Many small business owners rely on their instincts as their credit policy. The credit policy has a direct effect on the cash flow of the business. A credit policy that is too strict will turn away potential customers, slow sales and eventually lead to a decrease in the amount of cash flows into the business. On the other hand, a credit policy that is too liberal will attract slow paying (even non-paying) customers, increase the quantum of accounts receivable and eventually lead to cash inflow problems. A good credit policy attracts and retains customers without having a negative impact on the cash inflow. The extension of credit services is a deliberate marketing strategy designed to stimulate business and give an enterprise a competitive edge.

There are three basic types of trade credit:

1. Open Credit
2. Option terms credit
3. Revolving Charge

Open Credit

Open credit is a form of credit where short-term credit is extended to customers without requiring any down payment and without adding interest or carrying charges to the bill. It is usually extended for a thirty day period. This kind of credit is like the credit given out in the good old days during the great depression by mom and pop stores.

Option Terms Credit

This type of credit permits a customer to charge up to a limit and pay within thirty days of the billing date without penalty. An enterprise can assign a carrying charge for any amount not paid within that time period and release additional credit (upto a pre-set limit) as payments are made.

Thus the features of both open credit and revolving charge credit discussed below are combined in one plan.

Revolving Charge Credit

Revolving charge credit refers to the continuous releasing of credit ceiling as payments are made.

The enterprise should first of all consider whether it is appropriate to offer credit. There are costs associated with both granting of credit and restricting credit. In determining credit policy a balance must be struck between the costs of granting credit and the costs of denying or restricting credit. The costs of granting credit includes: Lost interest, loss of purchasing power, assessing potential customer's credit worthiness, administration and record keeping, bad debts and discounts. The costs of denying or restricting credit include: Loss of customer goodwill, inconvenience and loss of security of collecting cash. Once a decision is taken to extend credit, the credit policy should answer questions relating to:

(a) How much credit should be offered?
(b) What should be the credit period?
(c) Which are the customers to whom credit should be offered?
(d) What are the circumstances under which credit should be offered?

A decision to extend credit to any specific client or enterprise is generally based on what is called the FIVE C's of credit:

Character
Capacity
Capital
Collateral
Conditions

Character is usually referred to mean the applicant's willingness to pay bills when they are due. Hence, credit records must be studied to determine what kind of behaviour was evidenced by the applicant in the past with respect to debts. Relevant information may be obtained from the customer's bank, previous suppliers or from credit reporting agencies. An examination of the credit buyers financial statements and business plan may aid in making a correct judgement. As well, an analysis of their debt to asset and current ratios will also help in measuring their ability to pay. It is also important to look at any collateral which the credit buyer may offer as security. Finally the general economic as well as specific geographical and industry conditions which might speak positively or negatively about granting credit to any customer, should also be considered.

The next step is to ensure that the established credit policies are strictly adhered to. A common and effective practice is to evolve a system of debtor ageing analysis, which will reveal the debts outstanding by the number of days, since the date of invoice. Computer software packages for ageing analysis can produce a list of debtors with each category of debt analyzed by length of time for which the debt has been outstanding. A simple system like the one depicted in Table 5.1 can be established to ensure:

- No goods are dispatched until it has been confirmed that the current order will not take the customer above the predetermined credit limit,
- That invoices for goods supplied on credit are sent off to the customer as early as possible, thus encouraging the customer to initiate payment routines; and
- Existing players are systematically reviewed and slow players are sent reminders.

Table 5.1: Age-wise Classification of Accounts

	Amount outstanding ($)
0-30 Days	
30-60 Days	
60-90 Days	
Above 90 Days	
Total Debtors	100 per cent

In a restructuring situation, a reduction in outstanding debtor days may provide management with one of the easiest ways of improving the short-term cash flow. Fundamentally, it is a question of enforcing already established credit policies. Also a review of the enterprise's credit policy may in some cases indicate a need for immediate change. The following actions are suggested to for reducing the number of debtor days:

(a) Identify overdue accounts and place stop orders on them: No goods should be dispatched for overdue customers, until existing accounts have been settled. Customers need to be informed of such actions. An example of debt collection coversheet is given below:

Table 5.2: Debt collection cover sheet

Phone details			*Invoice records*		
Amount outstanding			Invoice Number	invoice Date	Invoice Amount
Terms and Conditions					
Date	*Contact Name*	*Days overdue*	*Action to be taken*		*Result*
		0 days	Account noted		
		7 days	Gentle reminder		
		14 days	Reminder notice pay within 7 days		
		21 days	Follow up reminder notice		
		25 days	Phone call to follow up reminder notice		
		28 days	Cease work on account Follow up phone call		
		35 days	Notice that debt collectors will be called		
		42 days	debt collectors called		

(b) *Contact customers*: This is a direct approach, which can be carried out through a personal/telephone call to the customers, urging them to pay up fast.

(c) *Tighten up on credit analysis*: In principle the enterprise may have decided that it is in the best interest to offer credit, however, unlimited credit sought by any potential customer should be avoided. The enterprise should establish a policy for investigating credit worthiness, and should not be prepared to grant credit indiscriminately. Once established, each customer credit limit should be vigorously observed until such time as there is some basic review by the management.

(d) *Establishing a policy on bad debts*: At some stage, it will become more expensive to pursue reluctant players than their debt is worth. The enterprise should decide about its policy on writing off bad debts.

(e) *Consider offering discounts for prompt payment*: The costs and benefits of allowing discounts should be assessed. If a decision is taken to offer discounts, care should be taken to ensure that customers are allowed to deduct discounts only when they have infact paid within the specified period.

(f) *Consider factoring debts*: Commercial banks and subsidiaries of banks provide a factoring service for debtors. The factoring firm will discount debtors, giving cash to the restructured enterprise as soon as the invoices are sent out. The factoring firm collects the debt on behalf of the enterprise. This arrangement relieves the restructured enterprise of the administrative and financial burden of granting trade credit, but at a cost.

(g) *Manage exchange risk*: When an enterprise is involved with credit sales in a foreign currency, an adverse shift in the exchange rate during the period from the credit sale to its settlement will reduce the value of the debt. Financial derivatives and instruments for minimizing foreign exchange risk should be taken recourse to.

(h) *Change settlement terms*: Reducing credit terms and cash discounts can greatly influence debtor behaviour. However, it should be ensured that the proposed changes in settlement terms are not out of line with those of its competitors.

(i) *Financial ratios*: As discussed earlier debtor collection period is an useful indicator in the management of debtors. The ratio conveys an overall impression of what is actually happening with debtors, which can then be compared with the enterprise's policy on debtor collection to provide a control device.

Practical Illustrations on Credit Policy and Operating Cash Cycle

Illustration 1

Inka Pharma Limited in Lima, Peru has recently undergone a Restructuring programme and seeks your advice regarding their credit policy for a newly introduced pharmaceutical product. The cost data for the product is as follows:

Sale price per unit	\$36
Variable cost per unit	\$18
Fixed cost per unit	\$8

At present Inka Pharma Ltd extends a credit period of 30 days to its customers and the credit sales amount to \$ 600000. The company is considering three options in terms of a credit policy. The proposed credit periods and the associated expected sales is given below:

40 days	50 days	60 days
\$ 630000	\$ 645000	\$ 650000

Inka Pharma Ltd has an estimated cost of capital of 15 per cent (The increase in debtors which results from each option will mean an additional cost to the company)

A cash benefit analysis needs to be carried out. For determining the right credit period, the cost of the increase in debtors from the current level should be compared with the benefits. The benefit is in the form of increased sales and the cost is the increased amount tied up in accounts receivable.

Illustration 2

Foodworld, a distributor of frozen foods, has initiated a restructuring programme, and seeks your advice about the measures to reduce the operating cash cycle. The profit and loss account for the year ended December 31, 2009 is set out below:

Profit and Loss Account for the year ended December 31, 2009

	$ 000	*$ 000*
Sales		820
Less: Cost of sales		
Opening stock	142	
Purchases	568	
	710	
Less: Closing Stock	166	
		544
Gross Profit		276
Administration expenses	120	
Selling and distribution expenses	95	
Financial expenses	32	247
Net Profit		29
Corporate Tax		7
Retained Profit for the year		22

Balance Sheet as on December 31, 2009

		$ 000
Fixed Assets at Written Down Value		
Freehold premises		180
Fixtures and fittings		82
Motor vans		102
		364
Current Assets	$000	
Stock	166	
Trade debtors	264	
Cash	24	
	454	
Less:		
Trade Creditors	159	
Tax	7	
	166	288
		652
Capital and Reserves		
Ordinary share capital		300
Preference share capital		200
Retained profit		152
		652

Foodworld Makes all Purchases and Sales on Credit

The operating cash cycle refers to the number of days between the outflow of cash for purchase of raw materials and finished goods and the ultimate receipt of cash from sale of finished goods. The following steps outline the determination of the operating cash cycle.

Average stockholding period

$$\frac{(\text{opening stock} + \text{closing stock})/2}{\text{Cost of sales}}$$

$$= \frac{(142+166)/2}{544} \times 365 \qquad \text{No. of days}$$

103

Plus: Average settlement period for debtors.

$$\frac{\text{Trade debtors}}{\text{Credit sales}} \times 365$$

$\frac{264}{820} \times 365$	118
	221

Less:

Average settlement period for creditors

$$\frac{\text{Trade creditors}}{\text{Credit purchases}} \times 365$$

$\frac{159}{568} \times 365$	(102)
Operating Cash Cycle	119

Foodworld's operating cash cycle is 119 days which is quite high This is primarily because of the inventory stockholding period which is quite long. The average inventory held represent more than three months sales. This may be reduced by reducing the level of inventory held.

The average settlement period for debtors is nearly equal to four months sales and there is scope for reducing the same. This would involve measures discussed earlier, like tighter credit control, offering discounts, charging interest on overdue accounts, etc. It may be noted that any policy decisions concerning inventory and accounts receivable must take account of current trading conditions. Foodworld can also reduce the operating cash cycle by extending the period of credit taken to pay suppliers.

Cost Reduction Strategy

Successfully restructured enterprises have zealously deployed cost reduction strategies. Enterprises in the past were forced to cut down costs, in order to simply survive and the response was primarily tactical. But enterprises these days are pursuing cost reduction as a strategic imperative. Cost is accorded the strategic focus primarily to fulfil two objectives:

1. Notable lead in the market, by widening the gap with the nearest competitors.
2. Redirect resources to invest in profitable growth.
   This paves the way for launching the company into an orbit of

global competitiveness and pursue a total cost management approach. Total cost management approach would ensure that an enterprise—(a) capitalises on continuous cost reduction to ensure better plans, (b) makes cost management an organization spanning issue to ensure total commitment, (c) Manages cost as a holistic entity. Total cost management covers all the functional areas of management, finance, marketing, production, human resources, information technology, etc. It encompasses the levels of strategic planning, management control and operational control. However, the aim is not mindless cost cutting, but intelligent optimization.

The evidence is best seen in the global aviation industry where both Boeing and Airbus are involved in a fierce fight for market supremacy. Boeing has been offering its updated version of the 737 aircraft at a substantial discount, based on a successful outcome of its four year long cost reduction strategies. Thus cost reduction strategies consist of measures pertaining to the real and permanent reduction in the unit cost of goods manufactured or services rendered without imparing their suitability for the use intended.

The unit cost of a product or rendering service in an enterprise can be classified as material costs, labour costs and overhead costs. Hence, It will be useful to broadly consider from a general management perspective different measures and finally consider approaches for managing resources in order to control costs.

As mentioned earlier, a total cost management approach is of utmost importance for implementing cost reduction programmes. Cost reduction is a continuous process embracing all the functions and divisions of a business. Thus cost reduction requires cooperation at all levels and the strategies should be so devised that a combined action is taken with the common aim of the benefit to the business. The organization for initiating cost reduction strategies would vary with the size and nature of the enterprise, and specific individual requirements. Normally a high powered committee/group is set up for the formulation of cost reduction plan and its operation. Services of experts from all the sectors of the business will have to be sought as cost reduction covers a range of areas and employs diverse techniques. The Committee/group should plan the programme, accord priorities and fix up responsibility for implementation of the programme. An individual manager should be made responsible for cost reduction and spheres under his control, just like the way he is made responsible for the costs incurred by him. Restructuring consultant's assistance may be sought to deal with specific problems.

Checklist for Cost Reduction

(a) *Product design:* The impact of cost reduction effected at the product design stage will be felt throughout the manufacturing life of the project. Scope for cost reduction should be investigated both when introducing new designs and when seeking improvements of the existing designs. Introduction of value analysis techniques at the designing stage would go a long way in achieving successful results. Efficient designing for a new product or enhancing the design for an existing product would result in cost reduction in the following manner:
   1. *Material cost*: Cheaper substitute, less quantity, less variety, higher yield—of materials—effecting reduction in storage cost and investment on inventory.
   2. *Labour cost*: Reduced overtime operation, increased productivity.
   3. Costs of jigs, tools and fixtures are minimized.
   4. Standardisation and simplification in variety enhances productivity and reduces cost.
   5. Designing reduces the loss on unsold products in case of seasonal demand.
   6. Reduction in after sales service costs

(b) Cost reduction from an improvement in the organization can be attained if the following considerations are looked into:
   1. Clear definition of function and responsibility
   2. Clearly defined channel of communication
   3. Motivating employees for cost reduction suggestions

(c) *Factory layout and equipment*

   The following aspects related to factory layout and equipment should be looked into:
   1. Elimination of wastage of materials and layout and optimum utilization of the available facilities.
   2. Need for replacement of plants, introduction of new techniques, or Expansion for facilities
   3. Economies of manual labour production *vis-à-vis* Machine Production Methods.
   4. Maximum utilization of plants and other facilities.

(d) Production plan, programme and methods An efficient cost reduction programme should examine the following aspects:
1. Minimum wastage of material and manpower
2. Scope for reducing idle capacity
3. Efficient procedures for control of materials (Purchases, storage and issues) and maintenance services
4. Reduction of labour wastage and increased productivity by eliminating faulty production methods, plant layout and design.
5. Existing methods of production, new improved methods
6. Production schedule versus delivery schedule
7. Improved tools and modernized equipments
8. Scope for reduction in indirect material and labour costs
9. Scope for reduction in overhead costs—whether budgetary system is in operation

(e) Selling and distribution methods
1. Efficiency of the channels of distribution
2. Promptness of the distribution and selling methods
3. Effectiveness of sales promotion
4. Adequacy of market research
5. Scope for reduction in selling and distribution expenses without impairing the efficiency of the sales division for both domestic and foreign markets.

(f) Human resources
1. Reduction in labour cost by work study and work simplification techniques
2. Improving machine loading and reduction in batch frequency
3. Labour cost reduction by improving labour relations and morale of workers through introduction of incentive payments, welfare measures and better working conditions
4. Introduction of training schemes and facilities

(g) Purchase and Materials control
1. Effective and economical purchase of materials
2. Adherance to Economic ordering quantities
3. Less investment in inventory
4. Control over material storage and issues
5. Economy in cost of material handling
6. Control and reduction of material utilization

(h) Financial management and Miscellaneous services

1. Scope for improvement in the system of control over utilization of finances, fixed capital investment, and working capital.
2. Minimising over investment and economic deployment of capital.
3. Economic supply and efficient utilization of power, fuel and water services.
4. Proper system of preventive and breakdown maintenance.

Tools and Techniques for Cost Reduction

A plethora of techniques are used for implementing cost reduction strategies.

1. Budgetary control and standard costing
2. Value analysis
3. Work simplification, work measurement, time and motion study
4. Standardisation
5. Economic batch quantity
6. Coding and classification
7. Improvement in design
8. Substitute material utilization
9. Automation
10. Operational research/Management science models
11. Quality control
12. Production planning and control
13. Inventory control
14. Job evaluation and merit rating
15. Training programmes
16. Business forecast
17. Market research

A set of specific strategies for managing resources in order to control costs follows:

Strategy 1: Convert Fixed Costs to Variable Costs

The key to this strategy is structuring costs so that they go up or down according to the extent to which a resource is needed and used, rather than having to pay a constant amount regardless of the usage.

For example, leasing rather than buying equipment that is used in varying volume levels is an example of this strategy. Leasing of copiers is a common example. Some copiers can be leased at a low monthly rate plus a per copy charge for copies made above a set threshold. This enables monthly costs to remain low when copier use is limited, with higher costs only paid in months where extra printing is needed, and can help produce a more sustainable cost structure. The same concept can work for other types of equipment.

Strategy 2: Change Policies for Expense Line Items

The typical way in which this strategy is employed is to simply add more restrictions- for example, more requirements or approval steps to make it harder to spend money. While this can help control costs, it can also introduce inefficiencies into operations that outweigh the benefits of the cost savings.

Strategy 3: Change Suppliers or Ordering Patterns

Public and non-governmental agencies alike have been successful in controlling costs by getting annual bids for phone service, office and general insurance, printing, accounting services and changing vendors when comparable services are found at a lower cost.

Strategy 4: Streamline Operations

Stremlining can be highly effective in producing lower costs that are sustainable year after year. The idea is to explore substitutions between a costly input and other inputs that could serve the same function. For example, offices have allowed staff to telecommute rather than work regularly in an office in order to reduce office costs.

Strategy 5: Obtain in-Kind Support

In kind contributions can provide much needed resources-supplies, staff time and other facilities. In kind contributions can come in the form of donated supplies from local stationary stores, donated time and expertise from community members and a variety of other ways. Not only will such in kind contributions decrease direct expenditures, but can be considered as matching funds for programmes and grants that require a local contribution.

Strategy 6: Collaborate for Cost Sharing

Opportunities to reduce costs by collaborating with other agencies are limited only by the imagination and willingness of local organizations.

For example, compare the cost of purchasing frequently used supplies and materials with partners and set up purchasing pools with low cost vendors that enable a consortium of agencies to obtain quantity discounts by agreeing to order from the same vendors.

Strategy 7: Outsource (or in source) Functions/Activities

Outsourcing is a strategy to manage costs by shifting specific functions, to an outside entity that is able to provide the function more cost effectively. It is most common to outsource payroll, accounting, programme evaluation and information technology support.

Strategy 8: Redesign the Organization or Components

Redesign involves more extensive restructuring of an organization in order to produce a more effective collection of programme and services at a cost structure that is sustainable. Another form of this strategy is to scale back or eliminate programmes with costs that exceed available revenue sources by a significant degree. In some cases, it is possible to transition programmes to or consolidate programmes with another agency better suited to provide those services in the most cost-effective manner.

Strategy 9: Defer or Eliminate Discretionary Costs

The strategy of "do without" should be a last line of defense to keep costs under control. The other strategies listed above, used consistently and effectively will eliminate the need to simply do without.

Examples of Cost Reduction

Zara-Spanish retail group Inditex reported a 28 per cent rise in nine month profits, helped by improved control over costs. The company's cost had risen in recent years alongside its fast paced global expansion. The initiative for cost reduction was taken by Chief executive Pablo Isla.

Revlon Inc., announced a broad organizational streamlining and consolidation that builds on the scope of the company's restructuring actions implemented earlier and meaningfully accelerates the company's efforts to reduce costs and improve profit margins.

Sierra Inc announced that it is undertaking a corporate cost reduction initiative which would reduce on-going annualized operating expenses by an estimated $25 million per year. The company's decision to initiate cost reduction activities is part of its on-going effort to improve its corporate operating performance and boost productivity across the organization.

Averion International Corporation, a clinical research organization specializing in oncology, medical devices, dermatology and nephrology, announced a cost reduction initiative to increase its operating efficiencies and improve its competitive position. Averion's new cost structure is expected to support its business growth strategy and assist the company in improving profitability. The cost reduction initiative is expected to reduce annual operating costs by approximately $2.5 million.

In a ground breaking global supply chain survey of 800 companies conducted in the US, results reveal a disconnect between business objectives and supply chain strategy. Despite the desire to improve service levels, almost half of the respondents cited reducing material, manufacturing and logistic costs as their top supply chain strategy. Thus it appears that manufacturing firms are still looking at a cost strategy in their supply chains, as opposed to speed, flexibility or service enabled supply chain strategies.

The Indian company Tata Motors initiated cost reduction measures through effective supply chain management. Setting the price and working backwards requied a fundamental shift in the way the car was designed, since many costs are fixed once the design is set. To accomplish this Tata Motors worked in collaboration with their suppliers very early in the process. They were able to provide functional goals for many parts rather than technical specifications. This approach tapped the ingenuity of the supply chain who delivered the parts that met the fuctional requirements at extremely low prices. To streamline its supply chain, Tata Motors reduced the number of parts suppliers by one third as it gears up to introduce new cars.

Revenue Generation Strategies

There are well recognized revenue generating strategies, commonly used in restructuring situations. The measures by and large are drawn from cardinal principles of marketing management.

A variety of specific measures can be implemented and it is

recommended that the measures follow the asset reduction and cost reduction strategies. It should be appreciated that the measures have a direct bearing on the customers.

(a) *Altering prices:* Raising prices is a common measure, if there are only a few sources of supply for the product on the market. Price rise may also be resorted to infrequently purchased consumer goods and products that have a high margin. Consumers are used to price increases during times of inflation. Substantial price increase however may result in, customer resistance and loss of goodwill. Volume (quantity) discounts and settlement (cash) discounts may lead to more customer reaction. Such discounts tend to be customer oriented, unlike price increase, which is product line oriented. Hence, cutting discounts should be used only as discretionary tactic.

(b) *Attaining Product-customer focus:* This action involves focusing on a small number of products and customers. Criteria for selecting products and customers include—sales volume, growth rate, gross margin, seasonality, and length of manufacturing cycle. Having chosen the customers and products, focus can be achieved by targeting selling and promotional efforts.

(c) *Enhanced selling effort:* Increasing sales volume is not a desirable strategy in a restructuring situation. Instead the sales force should refocus its efforts on the most profitable-customer segments. Endeavour should be to improve the cost effectiveness of the selling effort.

(d) *Product-line rationalization:* Many distressed enterprises have product line proliferation which is reflected in terms of a wide range of models, size or colours. Product line rationalization is carried out by a detailed analysis of sales and cost figures. It is better to cut out a product, if the sales are declining and the product is losing money, or the product is not covering the variable cost.

(e) *Implementing product-market change*: This measure involves developing and investing in selected business areas, while neglecting or selling off others. While there are number of tools for strategic analysis, it will be beneficial for an enterprise to go through the following fundamental steps: (i) Divide the enterprise into strategic business units or product market segments, (ii) Analyse the growth and profit potential of each strategic business unit, (iii) Determine which viable strategies are open to the enterprise in each product-market segment, and (iv) Determine the strategy the enterprise should adopt in each product–market segment considering the resources of the enterprise.

(f) *Generating revenue through acquisition*: Acquisitions involve acquiring enterprises in related or unrelated business. Acquisitions should be attempted only after the successful restructuring of the enterprise. Also the acquisition policies should ensure that a high purchase price is not paid and the post acquisition management is sound and good.

Examples of Revenue Generation

Novartis, one of the largest European drug makers devised a revenue generation strategy and the profits increased substantially as the company paid less than expected to withdraw its Zelnorm drug for irritable bowel syndrome while a bigger sales force gave a lift to its heart medicine Diovan. The CEO hired more Sales executives to introduce drugs like Tekuturna, the first new blood pressure treatment in over a decade, and Galvus for diabetes, which was delayed. With neither drug on the market, the new staff helped spur older medicines like Diovan instead.

Dutch Grocer Ahold NV, the Netherlands based super market operator, generates a majority of its sales and profits in the US. In recent years, Ahold has rebranded its US stores and lowered prices there under its "Value improvement programme" as part of its revenue generation strategy. The company generates 60 per cent of its revenue in the US.

Drug companies increasingly attempt to have a product–customer focus as part of their revenue generation strategies. Astra Zeneca introduced Iressa in 2002 for the most common form of lung cancer. The drug quickly fizzled when larger studies failed to demonstrate its effectiveness. But doctors began to notice that the drug still seemed to work in certain groups such as Asians and non smokers. Astra Zeneca is developing a new wave of genetically targeted drugs that could improve treatment of many types of cancer. Other drugs from Astra Zeneca that target specific genetic profiles include Herceptin for breast cancer and Erbitux for colon cancer.

Cadbury India, is the fastest growing in the Cadbury world and the strategic challenge according to the President Asia is to put more grams in more mouths. At a low per capita consumption of 54 grams as compared to the developed markets—the UK at 10.5 kilograms and the US at 5 kilograms—the market opportunity is huge according to the President. The revenue generating strategy is to have a low unit price strategy in place and a substantial increase in the volume consumption of chocolates.

Labour Redundancy

Today more than ever before, civil society as well as the market are demanding that enterprises exercise a socially sensitive approach for conducting business and treatment of workers, particularly during the process of restructuring. Also there is little social dialogue or consideration of affected employees interests during downsizing. Organisations must have a genuine work-related reason for a redundancy. Urgent action to reduce labour cost is an essential component of a restructuring programme. However, a forced redundancy programme—to reduce the size of the workforce may become a necessity. Enterprises may need to make changes in the workplace for a number of reasons such as:

- Improved technology
- More productive business processes
- Product changes
- Loss of markets
- A decision to contract out or divest some or all of the business.

Redundancy affects people in many different ways. They may feel despondent, but need to understand that it is the job that is made redundant and not the person. As redundancy is a life changing event, it can affect the health, finances, relationships, personal environment, self esteem of the employees. The decision to implement a redundancy programme is easy to make on analytical grounds, but the implementation process can be very complex and time consuming.

In most countries, the provisions of law would require employers to provide information to employees when they are considering changes that will affect their jobs. This would give them an opportunity to contribute to any decisions. The initial step is to refer to the employment agreement, since the same sets out the basis for the relationship and the procedures for changing its terms. If there are some significant changes the same cannot be imposed without the employee's agreement. Employees may be able to raise a personal grievance if they believe their employer has acted unreasonably in the event of a redundancy. For instance, the employer cannot use redundancy as a way of dismissing someone for reasons related to the employee personally. Employers may also have some specific legal obligations where a business is sold or transferred, or work is contracted out. Employers generally are required to take the steps as per the employment agreement to protect employees in such situations. Employers who employ staff doing certain catering, cleaning, caretaking etc have special obligations that provide continuity of employment protection to employees during restructuring. It should also be borne in mind that restructuring does not necessarily involve rendering labour redundant. Rehiring, retraining, voluntary retirement schemes, redeployment in alternative revenue generating projects and similar other options should be explored.

The following general framework is suggested which would assist the management in preparing a labour redundancy plan.

1. *Setting up of a core group/committee:* The first task in the implementation of a labour redundancy plan is to set up a small core group consisting of senior managers from each of the major functional departments. Other managers should be informed only on a need to know' basis.
2. *Redundancy and dismissal:* The legal position on redundancy and dismissal should be thoroughly examined by the core group. In the case of redundancy, no new employee is appointed in place of the redundant employee. When an employee is dismissed, a new employee is appointed on his behalf.
3. *Preparation of a short-term industrial relations strategy:* The objective of an industrial relations strategy in the process of implementing a redundancy programme is the minimization of disruption of work and utmost cooperation from both departing and remaining employees. One of the critical decisions to be taken at this juncture is the extent of discussion with the Trade Union. Most Managements prefer to get by with the minimum amount of consultation likely to be accepted to the unions under the law. The approach of the management should be to convince the union that the redundancy decision is an appropriate one, as compared to other alternatives.
4. *Evolving Contingency Plans:* Following the announcement of a redundancy programme, it is likely that there will be a disruption of work. Contingency plan for each of the following scenario should be instituted—

- Work to rule
- Go slow
- Short strike
- Long strike
- Sit in strike

  Management must have an assessment of the costs that will occur under each scenario and a detailed contingency plan for each scenario should be prepared.

5. *Work out redundancy details:* The details to be worked out include: the timing of announcement of the redundancy, the procedure for selecting the personnel to be made redundant, the quantum of redundancy payments, procedure for assisting redundant staff with new jobs.
6. *Preparation of a Master Statement and Communication Programme:* A master statement setting out clearly the rationale for the redundancy programme should be prepared. This statement will form the basis for the development of a communication programme. The communications programme will establish an understanding about the rationale for redundancy and the details to all the interest groups both inside and outside the organization.

Example:

Many industry observers feel that Italy's real reformer is Sergio Marchionne of Fiat. By breaking the mould of labour relations set through collective national bargaining, the chief executive of Italy's largest industrial group had taken on two powerful lobbies, confindustria, the main employer's association and the labour unions. He entered into more flexible contracts with major unions. Those who have jobs—a rare commodity in Italy's blighted south were happy with the deal accepting higher wages for shorter breaks, more night shifts, and tougher conditions on sick leave and the right to strike.

Financial Restructuring (including Debt Restructuring)

Businesses must grow in an environment of unpredictable terrain. An Organization's original business model can become obsolete, with constant changes in technology, the rise and fall of markets and a volatile consumer base. The mission and goal of a profitable business can be totally negated by increased debt burden and a matrix of suspicious creditors. Financial restructuring is a therapeutic amelioration for coping with a wide spectrum of these stressors.

Theoretically speaking financial restructuring encompasses: (a) Asset Reduction, (b) Cost reduction, and (c) Debt restructuring

The foregoing paragraphs described in detail, the asset and cost reduction measures. A detailed treatment of debt restructuring follows.

A well laid out strategy, which would include roping in qualified leadership/financial advisor/consultant, providing realistic forecsts, and encouraging administrative transparency are prerequisites for ensuring long-term financial viability. The financial advisor/consultant can assist in ensuring operational liquidity by projecting an honest forecast for creditors, shareholders and management. An important aspect of financial restructuring is to convince creditors and stockholders that the business is willing and able to carry out dramatic changes in order to satisfy outstanding debt by repositioning the business within its core market.

Financial restructuring is designed to increase the value of the firm. This would necessitate improving the capitalization, debt composition and change of ownership and control.

Financial restructuring involves restructuring the assets and liabilities of the business Including their debt equity structures.

Financial restructuring can create value by a judicious management of the assets and liabilities as depicted below:

Assets		*Liabilities*	
Fix the business	Operating	Debt	Fix the financing
	Cash Flows		
		Equity	

Fixing the business, would involve the following:

Assessing the worth of the business	Use Valuation Model-present value Of free cash flows
Divestitures	Value assets to be sold
Strategic partner or merger	Value the merged firm with synergies

Fixing the financing would include:

Improve the Debt Equity Structure	Revalue the enterprise under Different leverage assumptions least Weighted average cost of capital
Fix the kind of equity	Actions to be initiated to make the Equity more attractive
Fix the type of debt or Hybrid financing	Mix of debt best suited to the Business (short-term/long-term, Dollar/Euro/others, Bonds/asset Backed, convertibles/hybrids
Management or control	Value the changes new Management or control would result in

Thus, the actions with respect to debt and equity are as follows:

Debt

- *Restructuring of Secured Long-term Borrowings*: This action is resorted to, for reducing the cost of capital for healthy companies, for improving liquidity and increasing the cash flows for a sick company.
- *Restructuring of unsecured long-term borrowings*: The borrowings can be public deposits, private loans (unsecured) unsecured bonds or debuntures.
- *Restructuring of secured working capital borrowings*: Credit limits from commercial banks, demand loans, overdraft facilities, bill discounting and commercial paper fall under the working capital borrowings.
- Restructuring of other term borrowings like inter corporate deposits.

Equity

- Restructuring by consolidation of share capital or by subdivision of the shares.
- Restructuring by reducing or waiving off the dues from shareholders.
- Repurchasing the shares from the shareholders for cash, thereby reducing the liability of the company to its shareholders.

- Restructuring by writing down the share capital by certain appropriate accounting entries.

Thus, financial restructuring may mean refinancing at every level of capital structure and may involve the following actions:

(a) Securing asset based loans (accounts receivable, inventory and equipment),
(b) Securing mezzanine and subordinated debt financing,
(c) Securing institutional private placements of equity,
(d) Achieving strategic partnering, and
(e) Identifying potential merger candidates.

Debt Restructuring

An organisation's ability to bear debt reflects a choice about asset-liability structure. There is no standard yardstick for debt equity ratios, as the same would vary according to country conditions, stages of financial market development and financing and investment patterns. Nevertheless, there does exist in the corporate world, a naturally developed debt equity ratio, within which a certain amount of debt is considered normal. When the debt of an organization exceeds a certain limit, the same becomes abnormal liabilities. When an organization relies mainly on bank loans, these abnormal liabilities will become unhealthy claims reflected on the balance sheet of the bank. This situation is more pronounced in public/ state owned enterprises of emerging economies. As banks are saddled with non-performing loans (non-productive assets in some cases), it becomes imperative to analyse the debt rearrangement between the enterprises and the banks. It will be interesting to understand how a country like Peoples Republic of China is dealing with debts of State owned enterprises. Abnormal debts are divided into two categories: Fiscal liabilities and excessive liabilities.

Fiscal liabilities of enterprises include policy related losses due to price controls by the Government. These losses should have been actually made up by Public finance. Enterprises had to cope up with the losses with production capital, resulting in an increase in liabilities. Enterprises in the past were burdened by social welfare burdens, e.g. education, healthcare. Also losses have arisen due to improper management and errors in policy decision making and macro policy changes. The debts of the enterprises due to these causes are generally not repayable by them.

For the banks they are bad loans. Since this is a problem caused by economic system and history, the Government as the owner of enterprises should bear these debts.

In many countries, the notion that Governments should invest and operate the enterprises has not changed and the capital market is not sufficiently open. Thus, many enterprises still rely on bank loans without any loan repayment ability. The equipment and products are obsolete in these enterprises and no fiscal support is available to renew them which compel the enterprise to borrow from banks resulting in excessive liabilities. A realization has dawned on the Government, enterprises and banks that the organizations are solely responsible for such excessive debts and a restructuring mechanism should be in place for alleviating the same.

Thus, rehabilitation of the banking sector remains a key priority in most countries to facilitate subsequent corporate debt restructuring. Corporate debt restructuring is in the long-term interest of the banks. However, it is important that banks take adequate measures for loss absorption capacity and viability. Weaknesses in the banking sector could prolong the restructuring of corporate debt. At a broad level, Government intervention would be in the form of corrective macroeconomic policies, evolving legal and institutional framework aiding the process of corporate debt restructuring. Bank recapitalization, involving use of public funds has been a common feature to restore capital depleted by widespread corporate defaults. Government measures to facilitate bank restructuring and support the role of banks in corporate debt restructuring also include:

(a) Setting up specialized advisory and investment banking services to faciliatate negotiation between banks and enterprises and minimize coordination problems;
(b) Offering tax and other financial incentives to banks to facilitate out of court debt restructuring;
(c) Using supervisory powers to require banks to disclose claims to relevant negotiating parties;
(d) Ensuring strict enforcement of existing non-productive loans, classification and other regulatory guidelines to strengthen the banks incentives in debt restructuring; and
(e) Defining a clear and concise timetable for various stages of the debt restructuring process.

There is no single preferred course of action for restructuring debt.

However, the following are the commonly used methods for corporate debt restructuring.

1. *Complete Reorganization and Rescheduling*: Reorganization of debt may involve modification of the terms of a loan to provide relief to a debtor who could otherwise default on payments. The restructuring may involve extending the period of repayment, reducing the total amount owed, foregoing interest payment, reducing the size of interest payment, clubbing the interest with principal amount. The creditor thus expects to obtain more cash or other value from the debtor to increase the probability of receipt, by granting the concession than by not granting it. Some lenders may also accept modifications to non-cash terms such as covenants, waivers, recourse, provisions or collaterization. The debtor may negotiate with the creditor certain concessions referred to as modification of debt terms. The creditor may agree to reduce or delay interest payments. Sometimes the maturity amount is reduced or the maturity date is postponed to a later date. The more likely occurrence is that it will call for a combination of all these concessions.
2. *Repayment:* Debt can also be restructured through repayment. This can also be accompanied by sale of non-productive assets in the enterprise. This process is known as internal restructuring and needs to be encouraged.
3. *Asset Swap*: Under asset swap, the debt is settled through the use of an asset. The debtor must have an asset available for payment of the loan. The debtor may need to adjust the carrying amount of the asset to its fair value prior to recording its exchange for a debt. An asset swap will certainly bring a decrease in total assets and total liabilities. The total financial resources available for business operations will decline. Liquidity and long-term solvency will be affected because the decrease in total asset will have a bearing on the ability of the business to meet its future commitments.
4. *Conversion into equity*: Conversion into equity refers to the process of issuing shares to settle the debt, commonly referred to as the debt-equity swap. An equity swap has no effect on total assets because assets are not used to settle the debt. Liquidity and solvency position will remain the same. Total liabilities will decline as a result of the payment of debt while stockholders

equity will increase as a result of the issuance of the shares. Shareholders may favour an equity swap because there is not much effect on the financial position of the business. However, the equity interest of the stockholders may be affected with the infusion of additional issued shares. Ownership interest of the existing stockholders will be diluted with the conversion of the status of the creditors to that of stockholders.

Example: Dubai World, the Government owned conglomerate whose debt woes roiled markets in the year 2010, had a $ 23 billion of debt. They designed a debt restructuring scheme, lifting the cloud of uncertainty that hung over the emirate's economy. Under the deal, creditors will be repaid in full, but the payment period will be extended, while the Government of Dubai would convert debt into equity and help fund the restructuring. Emirates NBD and Abu Dhabi Commercial Bank, HSBC Holdings, Royal Bank of Scotland Group, Standard Chartered, Lloyds Banking Group, Bank of Tokyo Mitsubishi hold $ 14.4 billion and the Government holds the rest. The Government of Dubai converted $ 8.9 billion into equity in Nakheel, the real estate arm of Dubai World and committed to fund as much as $ 500 million of Nakheel's expenses and an interest facility of $ 1billion, while maintaining 100 per cent ownership of the company.

5. Arrangements for a third party to service the debt on behalf of the enterprise.

Asset Management Companies (AMCs)

Asset Management Companies (AMCs) have facilitated the restructuring of corporate debt, with the basic aim of maximizing asset recovery and rehabilitating viable enterprises over a period of time. Asset management companies also support the recovery of the banking sector, through transferring out bad debts, causing banks to recognize losses and focus on their core business. Thus the primary purpose of AMCs is to acquire non performing loans from financial institutions with the sole objective of recovering value from their resolution or disposal. AMCs together with a recapitalization agency can contribute significantly to the restructuring of banks.

Asset Management Companies (AMCs) have proved more effective in corporate debt restructuring, when there are a large number of distressed corporations having relatively homogenous loans. AMCs have also proved effective in situations when they bring in specific restructuring expertise unavailable in banks. As regards the institutional structure, AMCs could be Government sponsored, private or hybrid.

Government established AMC's performance leaves much to be desired. Mexico's Bank Savings Protection Fund (FOBAPROA), for example, witnessed massive disappearance of assets as well as failure to identify assets due to inadequate documentation. Turkey's AMCs were unable to quantify the stock of assets held by them. The AMC, Danaharta in Malaysia is the leading success and the Korea Asset Management Corporation (KAMCO) has been successful to a lesser extent.

During the late nineties, four largest Chinese Banks transferred $ 170 Billion in non-performing loans to four asset management companies. With headquarters in Beijing and thirty branch offices in various provinces, Huarong is the largest of the four asset mąnagement companies and a top performing AMC in the world. In order to implement the business plans of the AMCs, the Ministry of Finance injected each AMC with a paid in capital totaling $ 1.2 billion.

In India, The Corporate Debt Restructuring (CDR), mechanism was evolved in 2001. The CDR mechanism is a voluntary non-statutory system based on debtor-creditor agreement (DCA) and inter-creditor agreement. It is based on the principle of approval by super majority of 75 per cent creditors which makes it binding on the remaining 25 per cent to fall in line with the majority decision. The CDR mechanism covers only multiple banking accounts, syndication/consortium accounts where all banks and institutions have an outstanding exposure of INR 100 million and above.

Additional Government measures to facilitate bank restructuring and compliment the role of banks in corporate debt restructuring include the following:

(a) Support of the Government for setting up specialized advisory and investment banking services for a meaningful negotiation between banks and corporations.
(b) Tax and other financial incentives to banks, AMCs to expedite out of court debt restructuring.
(c) Supervisory powers mandating banks to disclose claims to relevant negotiating parties.
(d) Ensuring strict enforcement of non-performing loans classification and other regulatory guidelines to strengthen the bank's incentives to participate in debt restructuring.

Private Asset Management Companies (AMCs), tend to execute their functions more effectively. An innovative way of approaching AMC could be through hybrid public-private AMCs, leveraging both public and private resources and expertise. For example, Industrial Revitalization Corporation of Japan.

Certain broad inferences can be drawn from the experiences of the AMCs in different country situations.

(a) AMCs need transparent policies and procedures for the disposal of assets., which are designed within the framework of appropriate governance structures.
(b) Time is of the essence. Assets will deteriorate due to lack of maintenance, lack of commitment on the part of employees, supplier and customers.
(c) Assets should be acquired by AMC at a realistic price and disposed of at market price and not be focused on the historical cost.
(d) AMC should engage the private sector for disposing off the assets.
(e) Flexibility in the operation of AMC is essential as, a menu of financial instruments is necessary to deal with debt ridden enterprises.

Legal Restructuring

Many countries need to strengthen the legal framework for effective implementation of restructuring programmes. The legislations may need to be retailored as a result of changes to economic conditions resulting from a crisis.

For example, an effective insolvency framework is the prerequisite for efficient corporate restructuring. The objective of an insolvency framework should be to reduce legal and financial uncertainty, promote efficiency, and provide fair treatment to stakeholders in the insolvent firm. Weak creditor rights and slow enforcement limit recoveries and increases the risk of lending. Effective insolvency systems serve as a strong disciplinary force. In the debt restructuring phase, the effectiveness of an insolvency law may remain compromised due to market inefficiencies arising from the crisis. Reliance cannot be placed on the formal insolvency system alone. Thus a revision of other laws need to be considered to support out of court debt restructuring. These include corporate governance rules on the responsibilities of managers of the enterprise and the rights and liabilities of shareholders (including limitation of liability of shareholders and the subordination of equity to unsecured creditors). Also security and tax laws may need to be revised.

Legal restructuring may range from simple amendments to a document like the articles of association or to the winding up of the enterprise or transfer of the assets and liabilities to a new corporate entity. Again in the event of a Government owned enterprise being privatized, when the shares are to be offered to a private purchaser or to the general public, a number of specific legal steps may be required to convert the enterprise into a joint stock corporation or a public limited company. When the entity is a non stock enterprise, for example a statutory body established by an act of Parliament, the Government has to initiate steps to convert the entity into a stock corporation under the Existing Companies Act. Before the privatization of British Telecommunications, the entity was transformed from a public corporation into a public limited company.

In Peoples Republic of China, the Ministry of Finance and State Administration of Taxation, joinly released Corporate Restructuring rules entitled ' Several questions about Corporate Income tax treatments for Corporate Restructuring'. Restructuring rules which are retrospective from 1 January 2008, define types of corporate restructuring and lay down the prescribed conditions when the parties involved can opt for special tax treatments. The rules not only provide guidelines on the compliance requirements for corporate restructuring, but may also offer an opportunity for enterprises to achieve the above business objectives in a tax neutral manner. The rules provide detailed tax treatments for all of the different forms of corporate restructuring.

Strategic Restructuring

Strategic restructuring involves the preparation of a business plan. The preparation of a business plan would result in a redefined mission for the enterprise. As outlined in the earlier chapter, an assessment of the internal strengths and weaknesses and the external threats and opportunities would lend an insight into the profile of the enterprise. The profile would then enable a decision to be taken regarding the appropriate strategy(s) to be pursued viz cost leadership, market niche, product identity. A redefined mission followed by strategic plan and operative plans will comprise the business plan. It should be appreciated that most positive restructuring (non-surgical) efforts would involve strategic restructuring.

Physical Restructuring

Physical restructuring involves substantial capital investment for rehabilitating physical equipments and machinery. In many restructuring situations, there is always a persistent request for physical restructuring to be carried out at the earliest. This should be strictly avoided. As the asset reduction and other measures do not involve cash outflow, it is recommended that physical restructuring is carried out at the end of the restructuring process. The only exception, is in the case of severely undercapitalized enterprises, which just cannot be restructured without an initial investment for machinery and equipments.

Cultural Restructuring

There is a felt need in organizations that successful strategic implementation depends on having a positive corporate culture. This culture can help or hinder the success of an organization. Cultural restructuring facilitates a process to have an assessment of the desired culture to achieve the strategic objectives.

There should be a conscious effort for a multidimensional measurement of an organization's culture—the culture it currently has, the culture to which it aspires or both. The CEO and the Board should have an unvarnished view of their organisation's culture, allowing the organization to compare the culture it actually has with the culture that its branding messaging and strategic plan says that it has. This might shed light on appropriate cultural restructuring measures to be implemented.

Culture is based on past beliefs, experiences, expectations A set of beliefs, preferences would determine the culture prevailing in an organization. Multinational enterprises operating in foreign countries should adhere to the local culture. Similarly employees working in a foreign country should abide by the cultural practices of the host country.

British Petroleum (BP) had transformed itself from a typically old fashioned British company to an aggressive and dynamic corporate entity. BP's transformation into a successful energy company can be attributed to the radical changes in BP's organizational culture and their knowledge sharing initiative. Cultural restructuring in small steps contributed towards enhancing BP's ability to operate in teams. BP supports a liberal and supportive work culture. Informal means of communication are encouraged to enhance the team spirit of the employees in the organization.

The employees are encouraged to raise questions or issues with the management and team leaders. Employees can contact open talk confidentially through a 24 hour telephone helpline and voice their concerns without the fear of any adverse effect. BP's restructured work culture was exemplified in a meeting between the leaders of exploration and production of BP and Exxon Mobil in Texas at the beginning of 21st century. The BP team was dressed casually while all of Exxon's executives wore dark suits, blue shirts and red ties. The No. 2 in Exxon was the only one to speak on behalf of the company, while even junior members of the BP team put forth their ideas.

Carl Henric Svanberg was at the helm of Assa Abloy for almost a decade. He helped Assa Abloy turn into the World's biggest lock maker. Assa's growth has been underpinned by a large number of acquisitions. It bought more than 100 companies during the Svanberg years. Mr Svanberg helped identify potential purchases, winning the confidence of their owners—often families—at an early stage in the process. Carl Henric was very good at building relationships. He was able to convince people to sell to Assa at a reasonable price, feeling they were handing over their life's work to someone who would take care of it. He was very good at building team, and at the same time down to earth, no nonsense, straight talker. Mr Svanberg was famous for his attention to detail and figures. He operated a decentralized model with lean reporting lines and rigorous monitoring of cash flow and other financial targets. All operations were benchmarked once a month in terms of sales, cash flow and return on capital. It helped to push the underperformers. When Mr. Svanberg took over as CEO of Ericsson which had a typical bureaucratic culture, the challenges were more cultural than strategic. Mr Svanberg moved from a low tech business to a high tech business, from a company with twice as many employees as Assa. Ericsson is a technical company driven and dominated by engineers which for many years dealt with monopoly state telephone operators. Svanberg felt that cultural restructuring was the need at that juncture as the Ericsson group had not adopted to the developments at that time—deregulation, privatization, the mobile phone revolution, which had created hundreds of new operators. Inspite of his best efforts, the joint venture with Sony Ericsson resulted in a slight increase in market share, but did not make much money.

Looking out for cultural integration issues at the earliest stages of mergers and acquisition deal process, can help business leaders greatly improve the odds that the transaction will create, rather than destroy, shareholder value. Three years after the merger transaction between

Chrysler and Daimler, the market capitalization of the combined unit had not increased and the expected synergies were nowhere to be found. According to numerous observers, the happenings amounted to a textbook case of cultural misalignment. Chrysler had long been seen as bold innovator of vehicles for middle class Americans and a plucky survivor of four brushes with near bankruptcy. Daimler by contrast stood for uncompromising quality and disciplined German engineering. The two companies distrusted one another from the start. The cultural divide was reflected not only in the two groups products, but also in their management styles. Daimler Benz fostered a formal, highly structured work environment. Chrysler took pride in its more relaxed, freewheeling approach. Not surprisingly as Daimler asserted dominance over the combined companies, Chrysler began a steep downturn, with widespread departures among key executives and engineers, growing discontent among the rank and file, and mounting hostility between Detroit and Stuttgart. Hence, cultural restructuring should facilitate the development of an operational framework for a disciplined approach to cultural integration.

Organisational Restructuring

Organisational restructuring refers to the following actions carried out in the enterprise

1. Change of organizational structure
2. Divisionalisation
3. Change of ownership
4. Mergers and acquisitions

Change of Organizational Structure

Organizational structure primarily determines how the roles, power and responsibilities are assigned, controlled, coordinated and also how information flows between the different levels of management. The structure of an organization can be effectively organized through, (a) Military or line organization, (b) Line and staff organization, (c) Functional organization, (d) Line and functional organization, (e) Line, staff and functional organization. The appropriate structure would depend on the organization's strategic objectives. In a centralized structure, the decision making process is concentrated at the level of top management, which has an absolute control over the different departments and divisions. On the other hand, in a decentralized structure, the decision-making process is distributed and the various departments and divisions may have different degrees of independence. These days, with the proliferation of information technology, organizations are made to feel flat despite the presence of hierarchical structure. Also organizations appreciate the fact that information technology is organizationally natural. i.e. it can centralize a decentralized organization and decentralize a centralized organization.

For effective corporate governance, in times of restructuring organization can effect a change in its basic structure.

Organisational structure affects the culture of the enterprise and *vice versa.* The ability to identify the signs of oncoming organizational change is an important aspect during the restructuring process. This will facilitate implementation of policies that will keep the enterprise on a growth path. Besides, changes in the formal structure during restructuring, the following situations might also warrant a change in the organization structure.

Job duplication: Employees can be demotivated while trying to cater to more than one manager or employees may find ways to use opposing views by multiple managers to get what the employee needs. When employees encounter duplicate management positions, the structure of the organization needs to be altered to eliminate the excess positions and bring departments in line with the proper individual manager.

Marketplace changes: The structural needs of an organization changes according to the changes in the marketplace. For example, with increasing trend towards usage of e business, the marketing functions in organizations have undergone a dramatic change. The marketing department can draw the services of IT department as staff function.

Process changes: Structural changes can be caused by the way the enterprise does business. Suppose departments in an enterprise has been autonomous, a change to a centralized way of doing business will create change in the organization structure.

Acquisitions: Acquiring or merging with another company has a profound effect on organization structure. The deletion of duplicate departments will result in a saving in cost, however, the human resources from both enterprises can be utilized in the resulting corporate structure. Also job functions will be altered to fit the business model of the merged company and there may be elimination of management positions.

Divisionalisation: Divisionalisation is a common approach adopted during the restructuring of large organizations engaged in manufacturing/ undertaking multiple products and services. The large organization may be divisionalised through creation of responsibility centres. The individual managers have the authority over a given area of operation and freedom to make their own decisions. The process of delegating decision authority and responsibility in an organization is known as decentralization. The restructuring through divisionalisation may result in the creation of different types of responsibility centres—cost centre, revenue centre, profit centre, investment centre.

Change of Ownership

Privatization of State owned/public enterprises/parastatals is another form of organizational restructuring. Change of ownership from Government to private hands would call for alteration of the organizational structure. The senior leadership of the newly owned enterprise would have an assessment of all the functions and determine how they would like work activities to be organized and carried out. This process also identifies natural reporting relationships and chain of command. Reporting relationships can be both vertical as well as horizontal.

Mergers and Acquisitions

Both merger and acquisitions are essential aspects of organizational restructuring. As the subject has been dealt with extensively in the form of innumerable literature, a detailed treatment has not been included in this text.

It would be relevant to distinguish merger from acquisitions. Merger refers to a situation wherein two entities combine to form a new entity. In the case of acquisition, an existing company acquires another existing company and hence no new entity is created.

There have been several alternative forms of mergers. Horizontal merger refers to two enterprises operating in the same kind of business activity. A merger between two automobile manufacturing companies would represent a horizontal merger. Vertical mergers involve different stages of production operations. An oil exploration company combining with a refinery would refer to a vertical merger. Conglomerate mergers involve enterprises engaged in unrelated types of business activities, for broadening the product lines, wider geographical area for markets or merely as a diversification strategy.

In addition to mergers and acquisitions in the conventional sense, there has been an increased use of tender offers and joint ventures. In tender offer, a party normally a corporation seeks a controlling interest in another corporation—with a request to the stockholders of the firm it seeks to control to submit or tender their shares of stock in the firm. Joint ventures involve the intersection of only a small fraction of the activities of the enterprises involved and usually for a limited duration of say ten years or so. Two plus two makes five. This equation is very apt for a merger or acquisition. The logic behind a merger or acquisition is to create shareholder value over and above that of the sum of two enterprises. Two enterprises together are more valuable than two separate enterprises.

From the foregoing paragraphs detailing the restructuring strategies, it is amply clear that enterprise restructuring represents holistic changes which are realized in various spheres of the firm's activities. It is necessary to take into account that these changes do not affect separately but they are mutually connected and influenced. Thus successful restructuring process requires the realization of restructuring measures in all spheres of business activities—Finance, production, business, marketing, organization, information and human resources, ecology, social responsibility, business culture.

Conclusion—Being a Winner in Downturn

A survey carried out by Boston Consulting Group (BCG), some years back reveals that cost reduction strategy is the only measure enterprises have taken to guard against recession. Such complacency is highly risky. Enterprises should view any crisis/downturn as an opportunity. This calls for adopting an offensive approach to be a winner in downturn, and not be defensive. Besides the restructuring strategies, enterprises should gear up to face the downturn through some innovative actions:

Risk Assessment: The likely effect on sales, costs, and margins of the enterprise because of downturn should be studied in detail to have an insight into the vulnerability of the business. The following issues need a detailed probe.

- How cyclical is the business?
- Is the degree of cyclicality changing?
- Diversification plans for product lines, customer base, and target markets.
- Evaluation of competitors' ability to meet the downturn challenges.

Warning Signals for Downturn

On a regular basis, enterprises should monitor global, national, sectoral data. Periodically carry out the following analysis with respect to the enterprise.

- Mega
- Macro
- Meso
- Micro

The key is to identify the information that really matters for the enterprise and interpret the same correctly.

Get in Shape-Now

Restructuring implies making an organization lean and mean. Trim down the enterprise and get rid of the excess fat even in times of plenty. Such enterprises seek an answer for the following:

- Where can we trim operations, cut costs, release cash and add value?
- Can we outsource any process to low cost countries, in order to reduce costs and diversify country and currency risks?
- Can we delayer levels of management or staff to create a more leaner, agile organization?
- Can we develop collaborative partnerships, licensing agreements?

The above actions reduce risk, streamline the cost structure, affords flexibility, and opens up new opportunities.

Develop a Prioritized Action Plan

Action plan should be developed and prioritized, based on an understanding of the risk for the enterprise. Formulate the steps to be initiated to minimize the impact of the downturn and to achieve competitive wins. Make sure that management is aligned around the plan with a clear definition of the roles and responsibilities.

Think Counter Cyclically

The enterprise should keep competitors off guard by not doing the obvious. For example the common reaction in a downturn is to tighten customer payment terms. The enterprise can consider giving profitable customers more lenient payment terms. Terms can be made stricter for less attractive accounts. While others are cutting back on customer service to reduce costs, the enterprise can strengthen commitment to this critical area in order to make competitive inroads. The enterprise should plan to buy when others are selling. Still another approach is to identify and accelerate the projects that will deliver the biggest payback when the economy starts to recover.

Be Prepared for the Unexpected

The enterprise should stay flexible and not be rigid about the plans, as the unexpected is bound to occur. The enterprise should be ready to change course and initiate moves rapidly as conditions change. To enhance strategic flexibility, the enterprise can maintain a reserve of unallocated funds.

PART-II

6
Country Experiences

Europe—Slovenia*

Background

History

Slovenia is one of the smaller nations in Europe. Formerly part of Yugoslavia, it is squeezed between the upper reaches of the Adriatic Sea, the Alps and the Pannonian plains. Its population of 1.9 million live in a fertile territory of 20,251 sq km—the size of Wales or the state of New Jersey.

Historical ties of Slovenes with Austria to the north and Hungary to the east were established in the sixteenth century when most Slovene regions were under the control of Habsburgs. With the downfall of the Austro-Hungarian empire at the end of the First World War, a United Kingdom of Yugoslavia—Serbs, Croats and Slovenes—was proclaimed in 1918, with Belgrade as its capital. Political subordination and economic hardships within the Yugoslav federation then prompted Slovenia to begin building its own statehood. Attempted subjugation by its powerful neighbours during the Second World War further strengthened national feelings of the Slovenes. Yugoslavia became communist in 1945 but broke with Moscow in 1948, developing its own version of socialism.

---

* Reprinted with permission from Routledge U.K. "Revitalizing socialist enterprises: A Race against time (1993) Ed. by John Heath: Chapter 8 "Reforming Self Managed Enterprises in Slovenia"–R. Jayashankar, pp. 144-164.

The last two decades have seen Yugoslavia gradually slipping into political and economic crisis. Slovenes pressed for a looser confederation of states. This proposal was initially thwarted by the federal government. However, Slovenia's first free parliamentary elections in April 1990 pointed clearly towards the formation of a sovereign nation. The declaration by Slovenia of its independence on 25 June 1991 provoked military attack by the Serbian-led Yugoslav army. With the prompt diplomatic intervention of the European Community, the attack was subdued quickly and troops withdrawn. Eventually, on 15 January 1992, after centuries of Habsburg rule and decades of a communist regime, Slovenia was recognized as an independent nation by the international community.

Slovenia shares some common problems with eastern Europe in the transformation to a market economy and political pluralism, although its self-management system combined with (after 1948) an indicative form of central planning makes the adjustment relatively easy.

The communist system has given way to a more liberal democratic system, following which a comprehensive restructuring and stabilization programme is being implemented at both macro- and micro-levels. The shift towards a market-orientated economy implies tougher competitive situations, an impending fall in market share to imports and low profit margins for industrial enterprises. Thus a central element of the reform process is the restructuring of industrial enterprises.

The Industrial Base of Slovenia

The country's total annual GDP is approximately US$ 10 billion and its per capita GDP of US$ 6,200 is nearly double that of Yugoslavia as a whole.

The republic's average annual foreign trade turnover is US$ 12 billion and accounted for 29 per cent of Yugoslavia's exports in 1990 (with 15% of its population) and 18 per cent of GDP. Nearly 75 per cent of it is with developed industrial countries (60% with EC partners). However, trade with other republics in the former Yugoslavia has fallen away sharply, except to Croatia. Trade relations with Italy, Germany, Austria and Hungary are strong. Approximately 250 Austrian investments in Slovenia are envisaged, the primary interest being in banking, insurance and construction. However, Slovenia still needs markets, especially following the drop in sales to other republics of the former Yugoslavia.

The Slovene economy consists of roughly 12,000 enterprises, 90 per cent of which are small and medium scale (large-scale corporations have never dominated Slovenian economy as in other communist countries). Small enterprises (maximum 10 employees) employ 9 per cent of the 607,000 working population (a rising share), and there has been a rapid growth of self-employed persons, employees in the private sector and small private enterprises. However, large companies still employ 62 per cent of the total.

Manufacturing industry is the strongest economic sector of the Slovene economy, contributing 50 per cent of GNP. The main industries are electrical apparatus and machinery, metal processing, electronics, machine building, automobile production, textiles and garments, leather, wood processing and furniture, and pharmaceuticals. The raw material base of Slovenia is not very extensive. Half of the total land area is covered by forests. Other natural resources are coal, mineral and thermal springs and good agricultural land. For the country's energy requirements there is an adequate supply of power, particularly hydroelectric (with further potential). There is one nuclear power plant and a few thermoelectric power stations. Crude oil is imported mainly from the Commonwealth of Independent States.

The steel industry, machine building, manufacture of transport vehicles, textile and leather industries and base chemicals have experienced the greatest recession. Liquidity has deteriorated because of payment defaults, and there is no legal or personal security in business links with other parts of former Yugoslavia. Thus civil war, politics and economic conditions in Yugoslavia have changed the growth trends of industry and services.

Nevertheless, the Slovenian economy is further advanced than in many nearby eastern European countries. Its strong ties with the West have meant that it has been exposed to market economies—an advantage over other transforming economies. Its sophisticated labour force also distinguishes Slovenia from eastern and central European countries. The work ethic is strong.

The Workers' Self-Management System

The system of workers' self-management was unique to Yugoslavia in the socialist world. Its legal principles were codified between 1950 and 1953 and remained the basis of the system until 1974. Until that time enterprise self-management operated approximately as follows:

An enterprise comprised two legal entities—the *collective* (all permanent workers over 18 years of age, who produced, managed and distributed the income), and the *assets,* which were socially owned by 'all the people' (not by the state or the government).

The collective elected a *workers' council,* to which formal control for economic decision-making was passed if the enterprise membership exceeded 30. The collective had influence through electing the council, making personal proposals or choices in general meetings, or voting in the referenda that were called on most central issues. Large enterprises and multi-plant firms had more complex structures.

The workers' council determined overall policy and general direction. Its primary function was legislative, with the executive role played by a subcommittee it appointed—the board of management—and the director. The council therefore, set general aims and ensured that they were carried out by the executive, using a machinery of reports, rules (called 'statutes'), plans and accounts. It could have between 15 and 120 members elected for a two-year term, of whom 75 per cent had to be production workers (initially, the elections were *organized by the trade union but the role was later assumed* by the outgoing council). A rotation principle was introduced to ensure that there was a fast turnover, with members not sitting for longer than two terms consecutively on any self-management committee.

The board of management, the executive branch of the workers' council, had responsibility for the development and supervision of detailed plans to achieve the general policy goals framed by collective meetings, referenda and by the council. It included the director as *ex-officio* member and had 3-11 members, of whom 75 per cent had to be manual workers. It could appoint specialist committees. Membership of any self-management organs entailed no work exemption, nor higher earnings (except for expenses) but did guarantee freedom from dismissal, transfer or ordinary disciplinary procedures during the term of office.

The enterprise director, appointed by the workers' council, was the principal executive agent. He could only be dismissed during his years of office if he broke the law or if the enterprise was liquidated. The director's legal responsibility for business practices left the collective and the members of the various self-management committees free from legal liability. The director appointed a conventional enterprise hierarchy of managers who were responsible to him in the execution of policy, at the head of which was a 'collegium' of departmental heads.

Thus the system aimed at retaining decision-making at the enterprise level, with employees actively running the enterprises in which they work. They chose, worked closely with and supervised a management team. Workers possessed some of the property rights of ownership in that they had custody and *usufruct* of the assets they managed (the right to use and profit from certain property without damage to it). They could even, in special circumstances, alienate assets through sale. However, workers did not have unlimited rights with regard to the dissolution or change of form of the enterprise. The workers were not the owners in the strict, Western legal sense of the term. Three of the most important tasks for the self-management organs were the schedule of wage distribution, the distribution of net revenue and the adoption of internal statutes.

In principle the Yugoslav system of self-management was, and remains to this day, established by a fundamental distinction between decision-making, to be undertaken by the self-management committees, and execution, which is empowered to the managerial hierarchy. The imperfections of this distinction in practice, and in particular the fact that managerial staff appeared to dominate much of actual decision-making, has been a major theme in Yugoslav literature. It was a principal factor behind the 1974 reforms. These further devolved decision-making authority to the economic units later known as 'Basic Organizations of Associated Labour' (BOALs).

The constitutional system of 1974 sanctioned certain already accepted principles, with the goal of further promoting self-managements, and legally and materially guaranteed the organizations of associated labour. The Constitution of 1974 further stipulated that workers are entitled to receive the income of their BOAL, and a personal income for the satisfaction of personal, common and general social needs. The workers themselves establish the principles for the distribution of personal incomes and, in cooperation with other organizations of associated labour, jointly establish criteria for the distribution of income.

Slovenia has therefore never relied on the state as the most prominent form of economic ownership, as in conventional socialism. Self-managed enterprises were free to decide their market strategies and had great freedom in fixing prices and wages and in trading with foreign markets. Slovene enterprises were therefore much more used to markets and marketing, and were much better equipped, than their eastern European counterparts. The central planning system was more 'indicative' than controlling. Large multi-plant enterprises could be developed in most sectors of the economy, and market competition existed. The technical capabilities of many Slovenian enterprises were up to Western standards.

Some Problems with the Worker's Self-Management System

One of the prime considerations in its development was the efficient management of enterprises. A series of economic instruments was introduced for the purpose of placing enterprises in a position to make rational use of all the factors of production. These included a national system of inter-firm comparisons, using a variety of productivity ratios.

While the system provided good results in the beginning, it later became a barrier to development as it discouraged investment in new and more expensive technology. Workers' councils tended to take a short-term view, and employees took most of the proceeds. The basic way of financing investment therefore became credit approved by the banks on the basis of economic and technological proposals. Because of the great demand for investment resources, interest rates were high and loan periods short so that the annuities were also very high. The banks put a great burden on enterprises. This led to links between the administrative groups in the work organizations and the centre of financial power beyond them, and the influence and social position of the direct producers became weaker. There also appeared a tendency for individual managers to become rich, not on the basis of work but from their status, or because they disposed of social resources free of any control.

Privatization

Present Institutions and Policy

Two government institutions were established in Slovenia in December 1990 (one year before its independence) with the purpose of supervising, structuring and assisting privatization transactions in the Republic. These were:

1 *Agency of the Republic of Slovenia for Privatization* (which has a monitoring and control function), and
2. *Development Fund of the Republic of Slovenia* (which acts as the seller and recipient of the proceeds when shares of socially owned companies are sold, as well as the investor of privatization proceeds).

Both institutions are accountable to the Council of Ministers of the Republic of Slovenia. However, they enjoy a great degree of independence in their operations. The general principles followed by the Agency and the Fund in the implementation of privatization transactions are:

1 competitive and transparent procedures,
2 business and asset valuation on a standard and professional basis, and
3 assuring proportional voting and profit-sharing rights for socially owned companies in the case of joint-venture private (including foreign) investors.

In preparing for privatization, the company and (if appropriate) the foreign partner must follow certain procedures, required by the still-valid Federal Law on Social Capital, and the Company Law, supervised by the Agency for Privatization. These consist primarily of the mandatory business and asset valuation of the company and the rules for tender offers, auctions and public sale of shares through which the Agency tries to ensure the competitiveness and transparency of the privatization process. There are exceptions to the rule of competitiveness in the event that the potential investor has been a long-term contractual joint-venture partner with a domestic company. In that case the Agency adheres to the value assigned by a 'licensed business appraiser' and foreign investors should not expect to get major concessions on this value if there is no competition.

The licensed business appraisal system was set up by the Agency for Privatization. A core group of highly qualified accountants in Slovenia, recognized generally as being experts in the field of valuation and business appraisal, was appointed to form a Valuation Commission. They were granted licences on the basis of their valuation reports by international professional organizations. Their tasks were:

1 to prepare standards and principles for business valuation practice;
2 to prepare training courses and examinations for candidates applying for licences; and
3 to supervise the work of the business appraisers by reviewing their valuation reports.

If a candidate for a licence is not satisfied with the examination results he may appeal to the Agency for Privatization. The Agency will then forward the case to the Board of Examiners of the American Society of Appraisers for review and comment. At present there are 45 licensed business appraisers in Slovenia who have been trained and certified by the Agency.

The government cannot force a company into privatization because neither the government nor the state is owner. The initiative must come from the enterprise. But the Agency has to approve transactions and the creation of joint ventures where a socially owned enterprise contributes assets to the new company. In transactions involving the sale of shares of existing capital stock, the Development Fund (acting on behalf of the state) has the authority to sign the contract with the buyer.

The way to successful acquisitions and joint ventures in Slovenia therefore lies in achieving a consensus among various interests, ranging from the two government agencies, the firm's employees (workers' councils) and management, and sometimes even local communities. When this consensus is achieved, then practically any type of transaction is possible. So far, 20 privatization transactions involving trade sales and management buyouts have been executed by the Agency. The Privatization Agency and Development Fund would then ensure proper financial restructuring of these enterprises.

The workers' councils of some socially owned enterprises in Slovenia are to be transformed into social boards. They will comprise representatives of the state, creditors (typically the banks) and employees. Such boards will be vested with the power to hire and fire managers and to take other decisions typically made at the level of board of directors in a capitalist firm. The dilemma of whether to privatize first and restructure later, or *vice versa*, has been proven in practice to be no dilemma at all. The state is not able to restructure the economy on such a large scale. It is the future owners who will have to undertake the comprehensive restructuring, while the state will have to limit its actions to short-term financial reconstruction. If the state were able to restructure these companies and run them efficiently, it would have done this a long time ago and there would be little need for privatization.

A Case Study on the Work of the Agency and the Fund

The Tobacco Company of Ljubljana (TCL) was established 120 years ago as a state concern. This largest industrial facility in Slovenia has been run for the past four decades within the system of workers' self-management. Accordingly, the managing directors and heads of various organizational units were elected by the workers' council, which was chosen by the employees. The council did not interfere with management decisions and in most cases agreed to the proposed policies.

In addition to cigarette production, TCL was also a cigarette wholesaler and had retail outlets in Slovenia, Croatia and Serbia. TCL distributed 80 per cent of all cigarettes consumed in Slovenia. Its profits showed a progressive decline during the late 1980s and early 1990s. Both the national and international market share declined primarily due, it was thought, to the lack of attractive new brands to meet consumers' demands.

TCL's management felt that the company could be put on a sound footing only through a strategic alliance with a big international cigarette manufacturer. Other privatization techniques, such as management and employee buy-outs, sale of the company to financial institutions or individual investors, were not the desired options. Their aims were to produce a new brand of cigarettes, to have access to international markets and to introduce new technology and managerial skills.

The management of TCL identified two potential investors: Reemtsma/Seita from Germany and a large multinational company from the United States. Advice from both the Privatization Agency and the Development Fund was sought relating to the privatization plan, analysis of the offers and negotiating the deal with the winning bidder. The Privatization Agency was legally to approve the transaction, and the Development Fund had to sign the contract with the foreign partner.

Both bidders employed international accounting and auditing companies to appraise the value of the company. On the TCL's side the valuation report of the appraiser, licensed by the Agency for Privatization, was prepared according to Slovenian valuation standards and principles. After the completion of the analytical work, both prospective investors were invited to submit their offers, explaining the financial and commercial arrangements. A detailed plan of action was also sought about developing new products, modernizing technology, marketing strategies, changes in internal organization and developing human resources. During the first presentations it was felt that both proposals were satisfactory from the point of view of further development of the company. However, the offered purchase prices were too low in comparison with the appraised value. After two rounds of negotiations there was a significant improvement in the prices offered.

The selection committee decided in favour of Reemtsma/Seita, proposing a partnership that would preserve the tradition of one of the oldest Slovenian companies. A final draft of a sale contract was prepared and approved by the board of directors of Reemtsma/Seita, by the workers' council of TCL and the boards of the Agency and the Fund.

The structure of the deal consisted of purchase of a 76.5 per cent share of TCL from the Development Fund by Reemtsma/Seita. Firstly, the socially owned company was transformed into a limited liability company with the Development Fund as the only shareholder. During the bidding stage, both bidders were required to make an asset transaction. This involved the purchase of TCL assets by their newly established Slovenia subsidiaries. Following the awarding of the contract, these assets would be cashed in, the old company would be liquidated, and the residual money would go to the Fund. In order to allow the employees of TCL to take advantage of certain benefits expected to be guaranteed in the privatization law once passed, the remaining 23.5 per cent of the shares was reserved by the Fund for the future discount sale or even for free distribution to employees. Foreign purchasers were willing to accept employee-share participation only on the condition that employee shares stayed indivisible. The contract therefore established a new joint-stock company in which individual employees would be shareholders and for which the sole purpose would be to hold and manage the shares of TCL.

To ensure that there would be no redundancies, a modernization plan for TCL was prepared. A minimum of 20 per cent rise in real wages was promised and all fringe benefits were retained. This positioned TCL on the upper-wage-level range of companies. An extensive training programme was proposed to enhance productivity and to introduce new standards of quality for employees. A new seven-member board of directors was nominated. The chairman of the board was the chief executive of the buyer company. Three members of the board were nominated by the foreign shareholders; two of the other three were representatives of employees and one was a representative of the Fund. Specific provisions for corporate governance and minority shareholders' rights were contained in the shareholders' agreement. TCL took new orders after the acquisition and a new international brand of cigarettes was introduced in Slovenia. However, considerable discontent arose among employees as the work-load was substantially increased, though at present a strong sense of discipline prevails. The managing director retained his job and some new executives were nominated. The board of directors approved the business plans and introduced new incentive schemes. Due stress was also laid on training of managers and production foremen.

The Absence of a Privatization Law

Everyone in Slovenia agrees on the need to privatize socially owned enterprises, but the mode of doing so has evoked much controversy. Thus, although the Agency and the Development Fund have been in operation for two years, a law on privatization has not yet been passed by the Slovene assembly. There may be many reasons for this omission.

Firstly, the timing is wrong. In the extreme turbulence and terror of the civil war next door, and the severe adverse effect on Slovenia—dislocation and recession—a major privatization programme might be very risky. The government will want to keep a handle on the situation at this time since intervention in industry for over-riding national interest reasons may be necessary.

Secondly, there is no settlement yet of the restitution of property to former owners, and that must be cleared up first. Clauses to protect the interests of former owners have been accepted in principle. They entail separating parts of an enterprise, or a portion of the enterprise's capital, and putting them under government supervision pending resolution of the denationalization claim. This also protects future owners of privatized enterprises from later claims by former owners.

Thirdly, there are blocking actions by some former communist officials.

However, it is a sensible policy to position all of the legal structure and institutions of a private-sector market before the main privatization takes place, so the delay has a benefit. Also the Agency and the Fund are going through a learning process in preparation for the main thrust. The lessons can be fed back into the main policy initiative. It is a cautious approach so that Slovenia, when it decides on the main scheme, will get it right.

It is expected that the forthcoming comprehensive privatization law will mandate the initiation of the privatization process for each company and a definite time schedule will be implemented. It is envisaged that a certain portion of the equity of socially owned enterprises (perhaps up to 20%) will be given to employees free of charge or with substantial discounts. Along with this, the employees may have a first option for an additional 40 per cent of the equity that will otherwise be sold to domestic and foreign investors using traditional privatization techniques. The residual 40 per cent of the equity may be transferred to the Development Fund and a number of other financial institutions (investment companies, pension fund, compensation fund). These institutions would be free to keep or dispose of these shares. New boards of directors representing owners would replace the workers' councils in governing the companies. The full implications of such a law, which is expected to be passed in early 1993, on foreign direct investment are still somewhat unclear. However, there is little doubt that the current legal uncertainty in Slovenia will be greatly reduced when a law is passed.

Two Specific Privatization Options

Two detailed options are being considered by the government.

Firstly, there is a proposal by Dr Joze Mencinger, a prominent Slovene economist, that at least one-third of employees in a self-managed enterprise can purchase from the Development Fund a fixed 10 per cent of the company value in the form of preference shares, at a 50 per cent discount. The state would receive a 2 per cent fixed dividend, paid by the company, with no rights of management. The company itself also would have the right to purchase preference shares within the following 10 years, as would other institutions. At the end of the period any remaining preference shares would be converted to ordinary shares and given to the company.

Furthermore, employees would be able to buy up to a further 10 per cent of the preference shares, the purchase money being left in the company for its development.

If the workers' council of an enterprise decided not to accept either of these two tranches then the enterprise would have to be privatized by a direct method or public auction of all or part of its property, supervised by the Agency for Privatization. If none of these methods succeed, the state would itself attempt the sale.

The Slovene government has argued that the book value of companies will be lower than their actual worth. Leading Slovene economists argue that the 10 per cent 'threshold' for employee participation is too high and that if this proposal were to be adopted few companies would be privatized and would become a burden on the state.

The other proposal under serious consideration, called the 'Umek model', has been made by Dr Jeffrey Sachs, adviser to the Slovenian government. Share vouchers would be distributed free to all citizens rather than being sold to employees at a discount. Citizens would exchange them for shares in mutual funds (unit trusts), which would in turn hold shares in companies. The risk to citizens in holding individual company shares would therefore be reduced.

Four types of mutual funds are projected: an indemnity fund would receive 15 per cent of the value of enterprises being privatized, pension funds 20 per cent, various investment associations 35 per cent—and the remaining 30 per cent would be left in a national fund which would have to sell them within a few years or transfer them to other financial institutions.

Mutual funds would therefore take over all large enterprises and thus gain control over the present management. (Small organizations would be privatized according to Mencinger's model with some minor differences.) The Sachs approach is shock therapy, compared with the gradual approach of Mencinger. It prescribes a centralized blueprint to cover all enterprises, based on size. Its selling point is that it sorts out the tangled legal situation bequeathed by the social ownership system, under which property rights are frequently unclear.

The Banking System

Slovenian banking has inherited a peculiar feature of the Yugoslav federal system under which enterprises could establish their own banks. Enterprise managers could be represented on the board of their banks. A local bank manager could issue credit to the owned enterprise. There was, however, practically no accountability as the banking system was devoid of checks and balances.

The federal government initiated a process of restructuring the banking system in 1989. However, there were conflicting and vested interests at stake which prevented any effective reform. Enterprises accustomed to soft loans advanced by the banks and inter-enterprise banks were not in a position to survive without credits.

Successful banking reorganization was a necessary condition for a firm basis of the national currency. With independence in Slovenia and the establishment of the Bank of Slovenia as its Central Bank, measures have been initiated for effective credit and monetary policies for optimal liquidity management amongst the banks. The 'Agency for the Rehabilitation and Reorganization of Banks' was created in January 1992, comprising experts from the Bank of Slovenia. This agency has a large task ahead documenting the actual balance of accounts of the country's banks. Its first task is to ascertain the real value of the banks concerned.

The composition of the banking market in Slovenia is fairly unusual. Many have judged it to be monopolistic or oligarchical as the result of the privileged position enjoyed by the Ljubljanska Banka and its affiliated banks. According to a survey conducted by the Bank Association of Slovenia, the Ljubljanska Banka is the parent bank and the entire bank structure of the Ljubljanska Banka accounted for 60 per cent and 90 per cent respectively of the total balance sheet of all Slovenian Banks. The total number of commercial banks, including the ones set up after independence, is 30, and they have also begun diversifying the scope of their services. The restructuring of the Slovene economy and the enterprises to a great extent depends on the restructuring policies for the Slovene Banks.

Banking Problems

The problems facing the Slovenian banks are as follows:

1. *High provision for doubtful loans.* Ljubljanska Banka, which has a 90 per cent share of the Slovenian market, last year posted a provision charge of US$ 186 million against non-performing, bad loans and off-balance sheet exposure, which resulted in a net loss after tax of US$ 65 million.
2. *High unit costs of establishing and maintaining independent systems.* The number of employees in most banks is too high and this is linked to business costs.
3. *Temporarily unresolved relations with the National Bank of Yugoslavia.* In addition to the burden of non-performing loans of Slovene banks, the other problem is the claim against the National Bank of Yugoslavia (NBY), based in Belgrade. In the past, any foreign-exchange deposits made by Slovenes to the banks in Slovenia were transferred to NBY. Since independence the National Bank of Yugoslavia has not released these deposits to Slovenia (some economists in Slovenia believe that they have been spent). However, the rejection of the Slovene Banks' plea concerning their acute foreign-exchange shortage may be due to the intransigence of the NBY in impounding Slovenia's reserves. The problem is not simple and cannot be laid entirely at the door of the Yugoslav federal government. It also arises from Slovenia's flagging, uncompetitive exporting sector which brings in successively lower foreign-exchange inflows, while the level of domestic government spending remains unaltered.
4. *High investment in the retail network, new office space and information systems.* The Slovenian banks need an inter-banking

information system with stored data on their customers, accessible to all banks, which is the accepted banking practice.

Thus the greatest difficulty for the Slovenian banks is that their owners are to a large extent self-management enterprises which themselves have no owners (except the 'whole people') and are often debtors to their banks. The consequence is a large number of bad debts. It is unhealthy for the Ljubljanska Banka's lending to be controlled by its own client shareholders since this prevents healthy companies with no capital stake in it from obtaining investment funds, which much less deserving cases can access.

Banking Reforms

The Law of Central Bank was passed in June 1990 (a Law of Savings Banks is due to be passed early in 1993). The banking reforms were directed at minimizing the adverse effects just mentioned. They should also reduce the expenses of monetary trade, enable more favourable loans and a greater choice of services. Foreign banks do not contribute to this at present. They do not invest in the Slovene economy but only 'export' the foreign currency deposits of Slovenian customers. Only with the help of foreign capital will the Slovenian banks be able to extend their services and to modernize their technology.

The rehabilitation and privatization of banks will also offer the possibility that reformed banks could give loans to companies with a positive credit rating and to those who wish to become the banks' shareholders, thereby changing the bank's loan into their share investment in the bank.

There is a debate on the level of statutory reserves deposited with the Central Bank. The banks' claim is that the interest paid by the Bank of Slovenia does not keep pace with inflation, which under the conditions of restrictive monetary policy negatively reflects on their liquidity.

When Slovene banks and the Bank of Slovenia were cut off from Yugoslavia's foreign-exchange reserves, amounting to some US$ 2.6 billion, savers were left without their own cash. However, the sale of socially owned apartments to their existing tenants increased Slovenia's external liquidity and foreign-exchange reserves because many savers had their deposits put in safe places abroad, and when the sale, at favourable prices, of 230,000 apartments began, a large amount of these deposits was drawn back to domestic banks. In allowing the privatization of state-owned apartments the government combined its privatization and monetary goals into one.

Monetary sovereignty was established with the introduction of new Slovene currency, the 'tolar' (shortened to 'SIT') on 8 October 1991. The tolar (a Slavic version for the old German 'thaler') was initially fixed at one to one against the (Yugoslav) dinar, but within a few days a dinar was worth only 0.75 SIT.

Development of a Capital Market and Stock Exchange

The absence of the capital market over the past 50 years, and the common ignorance of, and mistrust in, long-term forms of the mobilization of capital, have given way to a range of laws designed to provide for the financial and economic restructuring of the economy. A turning point in the introduction of a capital market into Slovenia came on 12 December 1989, when 33 banks and financial institutions founded the Ljubljana Stock Exchange. At present 25 securities, with a total capitalization of nearly DM 500 million in value, are traded on the Exchange.

The funding statutes of the Exchange restrict its ownership to banks—only they are permitted to buy its shares although other institutions may become members. Discussions are under way to allow other financial intermediaries, such as insurance companies and pension funds, to become shareholders.

Membership of the stock market is open to both public- and private-sector companies, provided they are from Slovenia. There are still limitations on the participation of foreign brokers in stock-market trade. A foreign broker can only become a member of the domestic stock market through the foundation of his own firm in Slovenia. Similarly, securities issued by foreigners are not admitted to the market except those issued by joint-venture firms. However, these limitations may be changed with the anticipated privatization legislation.

Most of the trading (88%) is accounted for by bonds, primarily the bonds of the Republic of Slovenia. In certain periods it was possible to buy the bonds of the republic at a price ensuring a 14 per cent or higher return on maturity. Shares account for an insignificant part of stock-market trade for the time being.

Securities traded on the market can be bought by domestic and foreign investors alike. Investments by foreign persons are not subject to special legal limitations, barring investments in the purchase of immovables. Reinvestment of profits from direct investments are not liable to tax. The repatriation of profits, interest and invested capital is guaranteed by law. Minor limitations do exist still in the repatriation of foreign and domestic securities, where a special permit is required from the Bank of Slovenia. Domestic and, foreign investors are both exempt from payment of capital gains tax until the end of 1993.

The present situation on the capital market still leaves much to be desired. The consequences of deficient legislation, and the lack of firms capable of providing good quality services to those interested in participating in the capital market, are sharply felt.

Foreign Investment

The most popular and widely used format of foreign investment in Slovenia is an equity joint venture with a socially owned enterprise. This type of deal is closed directly with the company. However, for the inscription of the new legal entity into the court register, approval by the Agency for Privatization is necessary. Where shares representing social capital are sold, close cooperation with the Agency and the Fund (acting as the seller) is even more important.

Foreign investors are required to contact the Agency or the Fund in the early stages of the process to avoid potential problems in the final stages of negotiation, particularly when the proposed transaction includes complexities such as organizational and financial restructuring prior to the transaction, restitution issues and deferred payment schemes.

The Slovenian attitude is positive and realistic towards foreign investments which are designed to integrate the republic into international economic process and qualitative restructuring of the economy in general. According to the current foreign investment law, foreign capital can be engaged in business in Slovenia in various legal forms:

1. wholly or partially foreign-owned company;
2. contractual joint venture;
3. concession; and
4. a build-operate-transfer agreement.

A company owned by a foreigner may take the form of a joint-stock company, limited liability company or partnership. A special form of partially foreign-owned company can be created under the current Company Law by partial sale of a socially owned enterprise or by raising additional equity capital. In this event, foreign private equity coexists with social capital stock that has no clearly defined owner.

Foreigners can invest in any company on a contractual basis. The foreign investment itself does not change the legal status or ownership structure of the enterprise in which it has been made. Investment capital on a contractual basis in a domestic enterprise does not entitle the foreign partner to ownership rights in the enterprise. He acquires the right to participate in its management and to share in the profits in proportion to his invested capital.

Concessions may also be granted to a foreign investor operating from abroad or through a wholly owned Slovenian enterprise. Although private ownership of natural resources is not allowed, the investment rules permit the granting of a concession to a foreign investor for the exploitation of a given renewable or non-renewable natural resource or public good.

A foreign person may also be allowed to build, manage and exploit for a fixed period of time a certain facility, installation or plant under conditions specified in the permit. Once the contract expires, the facility becomes a public property and is constituted as a public-sector enterprise. The foreign investment law specifies the form which domestic and foreign capital contribution may take. These include cash, tangibles and rights. The law does not specify a minimum or maximum percentage for foreign investment and hence ho ratio of domestic to foreign investment is prescribed and all combinations are possible.

Thus the Foreign Investment Law has been strategically drafted to define the different ways in which foreign capital can be invested in Slovenia and the attitude towards these investments. This was not clearly spelt out in the former Yugoslavia and hence investments were haphazard. Establishing a clear policy in relation to a foreign investment is the essence of the strategy. When the Slovenian market economy is entirely open and the risk is transferred to individual companies, such a legislation will be redundant.

So far, most investments are from Italy, Austria, Germany and France. Slovenia is a country where some risk exists and the new legislation will help to safeguard the interests of foreign investors. The priority tasks that Slovenia wishes to carry out with the aid of foreign investments are projects concerning the rehabilitation of Slovene waterways, air and waste management.

Slovenian Taxes

The first reform in the economic field, implemented by the new Slovenian government after the first multi-party elections, was tax reform. In December 1990 Slovenia changed the previous system of 48 direct taxes and social contributions to a system of personal income tax, corporate income tax and three social contributions towards the pension fund, social security and unemployment. The most important Slovenian indirect tax-the sales tax-remained as it was until a new sales tax was adopted in January 1992, in preparation for the introduction of a value added tax.

The tax reform from December 1990 has, through the introduction of the above mentioned taxes, also introduced other changes. Prior to the personal income tax, a complete decentralization of tax policy existed in Slovenia. Within the state only certain taxes and contributions were fixed and the communes had a large degree of autonomy in fixing rates, tax exemptions and many income-tax reliefs. The same was true also for all social contributions (except for the contribution to the pension fund). Such decentralization of the tax policy caused much confusion in Slovenia, especially in Ljubljana, which consisted of five city communes, divided by particular streets.

The second important consequence of the reform was the introduction of an integral budget at the level of state and communes. Prior to this many independent budgets existed in the state and in the communes, with the help of independent taxes. Thus public consumption was indeterminable and the savings measures were inefficient. Public money dispersed through particular accounts was not enough for the special tasks of the state.

The third important consequence of the tax reform is the tax equality of citizens. Prior to the reforms, the citizens of Slovenia were divided according to their profession in special tax groups, with the tax on income ranging between zero and 35 per cent. With the tax reforms introduced in December 1990, Slovenia now has a law on financing public consumption which represents the main law of all public finances.

Management Education

Development of managerial skill is an integral part of enterprise restructuring. The interaction of central planning, 'self-management' and the market, previously provided an overall conceptual system. Changes in the weighing of different parts of the system will lead to a new balance of forces.

The market dimension will be greatly enhanced. 'Macro-economic management by government' will replace central planning, and more independent trade unions might be a substitute for 'self-management'. Managers will have to interact with both government and trade unions.

Hence management training, to be effective, should be focused on managers performing their role in the new circumstances.

At present in Slovenia long-duration management programmes at the postgraduate level are offered by the University of Ljubljana and the University of Maribor. The International Centre for Public Enterprises launched an international MBA programme in 1989 by collaborating with the University of Ljubljana. There are also other training centres offering short-term executive development programmes.

Because of the large number of managers in need of development, there should be short-term executive development programmes in basic areas such as accounting, finance and marketing for middle management and supervisory staff. Strategically orientated programmes should be the focus for top-level management. It is also essential to have relevant cases prepared over a period of time to introduce trainees to situations prevailing in the transition economies. The most effective way to transfer knowledge is through training of capable local management teachers. Most of the existing training institutions rely primarily on foreign faculty. Thus there is a need to train Slovene trainers, as in the end only local faculty will be relevant and most effective.

As the perceived need to address uncertainty in the strategic planning process is assuming importance, a few firms have begun to use 'scenarios' as tools of management. Enterprises should devise contingency plans as part of the strategic planning process, to test strategies against major sources of uncertainty. In the restructuring process of the Slovene enterprises, 'scenarios' can be a powerful device for taking account of uncertainty in making strategic choices. Also, decision support systems, which deal with unstructured decisions through the facility to provide answers to 'what if and 'goal seek' questions, can be extremely useful in such situations. In the transformation process of Slovene enterprises, such approaches can be of special relevance.

Concluding Remarks

Slovenia, unlike its neighbouring republics from the former Yugoslavia, has not allowed nationalism to prevail over pragmatism. Efforts are being directed towards establishing an export-orientated industry structure, to be achieved through privatization, liberalization, economic transformation and restructuring. Where the practice of self-management has been abandoned it has resulted in a better work ethic and improvements in productivity.

Restructuring and privatization of socially owned enterprises, coupled with the growth of private business units, will accelerate the growth of the economy. Speedy restructuring and internalization of Slovene enterprises will be faster once the privatization law is passed. Private property is gaining recognition and the existing social enterprises are being transformed into companies with share capital. The process of privatization has commenced. The introduction of a securities market has facilitated the transition from loans to venture capital investments.

The Slovene economy has already gained a considerable foothold in the European economic arena. The relations with western Europe are very important for Slovenia's further development. In the longer term, Slovenia hopes to become a member of the European Community. The aim of becoming closer to Europe in the monetary field has been achieved through introduction of the Slovene national currency and liberalization of the exchange rate. The range of economic measures, such as the liberalization of imports, the restrictive monetary policy and the changed role of the Bank of Slovenia, will support the development of a competitive and export-orientated market economy. The work carried out by institutions, enterprises and the Central Bank serves to reassure the international community and foreign investors that Slovenia is stable. Given the desired accessibility to exports, finance and markets, confidence and stability can be a permanent feature in this part of Europe.

Latin America—Peru

Around the year 1930, the majority of Latin American governments started to take a protagonist role in their respective economies to dim the negative effects caused by the Great Depression. During those years, several institutions had been built in order to regulate some productive areas for goods and services. During the 1950's under the guidelines of The Economic Commission for Latin America (ECLA) and other multilateral agencies such as the World Bank and International Monetary Fund (IMF) countries were stimulated to intervene as an active agent in economic issues.

With this mixed system of public and private enterprises, Latin America experienced a high economic growth rate through the 1950's and 1960's as public sectors developed at a rapid pace. However, the ups and downs in global economies and the oil crisis during the 1970's called for a paradigm shift and there was a felt need for market liberalisation, deregularization, privatization, and State liberalisation in economic matters. Particularly in Latin America the situation was aggravated by severe stagflation and deficits in the balance of payments.

Latin America strongly started privatization processes during the 1990's. It can be said that presidents from the region acted in favour of market liberalisation and that the region was a pioneer in privatization transactions.

Between the 1960's and the end of the 1980's Peru has had a strong State prominence in its economy. During the first governance of President Belaunde (1963-1968) the state launched the Imports Substitution Programme, which indeed promoted public enterprises. Furthermore, between 1968 and 1975, during Velasco Alvarado governance, the number of public enterprises increased extensively and were assigned with a strategic role in order to control the access to the basic public services, create a national intensive economy based on capital, control the financial sector as well as to export the natural resources. Indeed, between 1970 and 1990, public enterprises experienced a robust growth in the Peruvian economy totaling 186. By the late eighties, these enterprises controlled between 15 per cent and 20 per cent of the GDP, 28 per cent of the exports and more than 26 per cent of the imports. Peruvian State was the major economic agent and the most dynamic one during this period. It also had the monopoly of the basic services such as electricity, hydrocarbons and telecommunications.

The first privatization efforts in Peru were initiated in 1975 in the fisheries sector. Again, during the second governance of Belaunde between 1980 and 1985 the adverse international economic situation frustrated the intentions of privatization. Peru was overwhelmed with its external debt crisis and balance of payments. During Alan Garcia's first governance (1985-1990) privatizations were not handled in a coherent manner and the few privatizations deal did not have much economic impact.

Finally, the ninetees came to symbolise the most important restructuring period for Peru. President Fujimori had imbibed a hyperinflation economy left by Alan Garcia. Hyperinflation, external debt crisis, excessive bureaucracy, lack of productivity and efficiency were the predominant problems. The privatization process took a proper shape in 1991 with the promulgation of the Law of Promotion of Private Investment in Public Enterprises. This law established the creation of the Commission for Promotion of Private Investment in Public Enterprises (COPRI in Spanish) and defined the following modalities for private investment:

- Transfer to the private sector all or part of the shares or assets.
- Capital increase through contributions made by individuals or legal entities of private law established in the country or abroad.
- Celebrating partnership contracts in participation, services leasing, management, and entities of public or private law established abroad.
- Disposal or sale of assets upon its dissolution or liquidation.

During the periods 1991-1999 cement industries, electricity, telecommunications, banks, mines, fishery plants, construction companies, steel mills, airlines, and many others were privatized. By the year 2001 more than 200 public enterprises had been transferred to the private sector mostly through auctions and through the stock market. Concession arrangements were also resorted to. These privatizations generated an income of US$ 9,249 million for the Peruvian government and investment of US$ 11,428 million. Peru initiated innovative strategies and in the words of Armeane Choksi of the World Bank—

> "If I compare what Peru has done, by ways of reform, the way it has maintained with them against the existing difficulties; I believe there is no other country that has been able to do so. Peruvian reforms are superior than the Chilean ones, that at some point were considered as outstanding and as a role model for other countries, as same as the Mexicans; the Peruvian reforms had reach much more deeper levels and are being executed much more quickly."

Stages of Privatization Process in Peru

In late 1991 the number of state-owned enterprises amounted to 223. Of these, about 150 were operational while the rest were non-operational, in liquidation process or in bankruptcy.

Restructuring of Public Enterprises: 1990-1991

Since 1990 a set of instruments designed to reverse the prevailing crisis in state enterprises, were evolved. Basically restructuring contemplated legal aspects, reorganization, administrative as well as the rationalization of expenditure and staff. Non-viable enterprises were also liquidated.

Exhaustive Step: 1992-1996: During this period more than a hundred state enterprises were privatized. These first privatizations generated revenues totalling US$ 7,200 million which corresponded to 76 per cent of the total revenue generated throughout the process. During this period major privatizations were carried out in the telecommunications, electricity, hydrocarbons and the financial sectors

Stagnation: 1997-2000

This period was characterized by a dramatic decrease in the rate of transfer operations of public enterprises to the private sector.

Resurgence: 2001 Onwards

The Peruvian government that took office in 2001 announced a policy of open doors to foreign investment. The privatization of public enterprises, especially in the electricity sector and the concession to the private sector of the national infrastructure, assumes significance. Numerous concessions in the operation of ports, airports, telecommunications, roads, irrigation, water and sewage services were also resorted to.

Role of Multinational Agencies

The Multinational agencies that played an important role in one way or another in the restructuring processes carried out in Peru were the International Monetary Fund (IMF) and the World Bank (WB).

During the 1950's both World Bank and IMF, recommended and disseminated the idea of State intervention as an active entity in economic affairs. Most of the Latin American countries including Peru adhered to the prescribed policies. However, with changed orientation of the policies of the World Bank and IMF, all the Latin American countries, started to liberalize their economies.

Critical Sectors

Public companies in Peru by the late eighties recorded alarming imbalances in their operations. The sector with the highest negative results was the energy sector led by Petroperu and Electroperú (Table 6.1).

The critical sectors in Peru by the year 1990 can be identified not only by the ways of their economic losses but by measuring the impact on specific sector generated in terms of transactions (which represents income to the Peruvian Government) as well as the projected amount of money it needed to invest in order to be successful and competitive (committed investment).

Almost 85 per cent of the transactions since 1991 carried out in Peru through privatizations were concentrated in telecommunications, electricity, mining and hydrocarbons. The telecommunication sector represented 39 per cent of the total transactions, followed by the electricity sector with 23 per cent and by mining and hydrocarbons sectors with 13 per cent and 10 per cent respectively as shown in Fig. 6.1.

Furthermore, the projected committed investments were led by the mining sector with a participation of 40.4 per cent followed by hydrocarbons and telecommunications with 25.3 and 13.7 per cent respectively.

Thus it can be inferred that the most critical Peruvian sectors for restructuring were mining, telecommunications and hydrocarbons due to its high transactional levels and its high committed investment requirements.

Mining

Peru has a long mining tradition due to the presence of leading worldwide companies and its enormous geological potential: The Andes range, is considered as the main source of mineral deposits in the world, along its entire territory. According to official figures, in 2011 the mining activity reached US$ 27,361 billion, approximately 59 per cent of the US$ 47,200 billion of Peruvian total exports. Globally, Peru is among the top producers of numerous metals (gold, silver, copper, lead, zinc, iron, tin, molybdenum, tellurium, etc.) which reflects the abundance of resources and the production capacity of Peruvian mining (Fig. 6.2).

From Figure 6.3 it can be seen how gold production had an impressive growth around the year 1992, just one year after mining privatizations had taken place. So it can be inferred that indeed the privatization of mining sector was very important and critical for Peruvian sustainable economic growth objectives.

Telecommunications

The telecommunication sector prior to its privatization was characterized by technological backwardness, poor coverage, high costs for users, high degree of bureaucracy and long waiting periods for telephone lines. There were two public enterprises in charge of providing the service: Compañía

Table 6.1: Profit of Major State Enterprises.

	1986	*1989*	*1990*	*1991*	*1992*	*1993*	*1994*	*1995*	*1996*	*1997*	*1998*
Energy	**–197**	**–766**	**–1223**	**–213**	**121**	**111**	**–89**	**94**	**130**	**207**	**97**
Petroperu	–155	–515	–827	–230	6	84	–238	65	37	62	19
Electroperu	–33	–176	–301	11	97	25	148	29	93	145	78
Electroliza	–9	–74	–95	6	18	3	–	–	–	–	–
Mining	**–87**	**–129**	**–1353**	**–636**	**–261**	**–29**	**41**	**50**	**10**	**9**	**4**
Centromin	–69	21	–556	–333	–157	–45	40	68	10	9	4
Hierro Perú	–10	–36	–85	–85	–77	–	–	–	–	–	–
Minero Perú	–7	–114	–715	–218	–27	16	1	–17	–	–	–
Comunication and Transportation	**–27**	**–120**	**–250**	**–44**	**–10**	**–20**	**–26**	**–24**	**–54**	**–35**	**–34**
Entel	0	–39	–10	2	7	6	–	–	–	–	–
Aero Perú	2	–59	–92	–	–	–	–	–	–	–	–
Enafer	–17	0	–71	–47	–49	–43	–26	–25	–59	–34	–44
Enapu	–12	–23	–77	1	32	16	1	1	5	1	10
Industry	**–22**	**–47**	**–116**	**–96**	**–73**	**–123**	**–213**	**–20**	–	–	–
Sider perú	–24	–43	–113	–52	–35	–89	–180	8	–	–	–
Paramonga	2	–4	–6	–45	–38	–35	–33	–27	–	–	–
Other Sectors	**23**	**–75**	**–102**	**–41**	**–14**	**27**	**33**	**39**	**40**	**58**	**49**
Sedapal	–5	–59	–103	–23	–15	20	28	32	32	40	24
Rest	28	–16	1	–18	1	7	5	7	8	18	15

Source: Banco Central de Reserva del Perú.

Table 6.2: Privatization Results per Economic Activity Peru

(In million dollars)

Sector	*Transactions*	*Proyected Investment*
Telecommunications	3,611	1,565
Electricity	2,101	698
Mining	1,199	4,618
Hydrocarbons	915	2,889
Industry	604	51
Financial	422	30
Fishing	166	0.1
Transport	100	1,424
Tourism	48	23
Agriculture	44	50
Others	39	80
Total	**9,249**	**11,428**

Source: Osiptel.

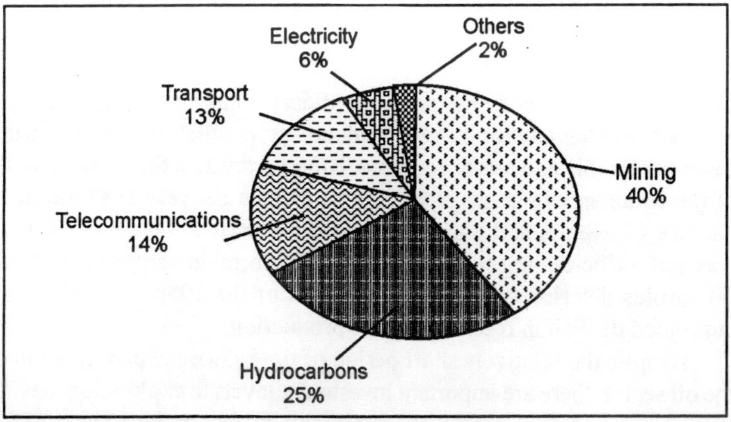

Fig. 6.1: Committed Investment by Economic Sector

de Teléfonos del Perú (CPT) that offered the local telephone service in Lima and ENTEL Perú which operates the local telephone service in the rest of the country as well as the national and international long distance calls. By the year 1993, the telephone coverage in Peru was 2.9 phone lines per hundred inhabitants, there were 660 thousand telephone lines, average waiting periods to get a telephone line was 118 months and the cost of acquisition was US$ 1,500.

The critical situation of the telecommunication sector in Peru by the year 1993, dramatically improved in just 6 years because of restructuring and privatization.

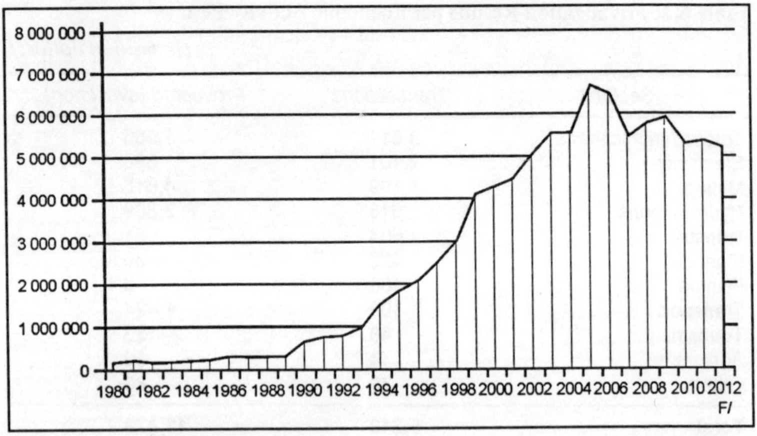

Fig. 6.2: Peruvian Gold Production
Source: INEI.

Hydrocarbons

The hydrocarbons sector has an extraordinary importance in the Peruvian economy and society for its high productivity, profitability and for being a non-renewable and scarce resource. Noteworthy, that the oil is the basis of the commercial energy production and since the year 1987 the trade balance of exports and imports of crude oil tends to be deficient. Peru was self-sufficient in oil until 1986 with exportable surpluses. But this oil surplus deteriorated in the second half of the 1980´s resulting in a continued decline in reserves and oil production.

Despite the relatively short period of time since the privatization of the oil sector, there are important investment levels in exploration, having been signed several contracts with many oil companies since 1993. Unfortunately, none of the boreholes has been successful so far,

Role of Restructuring/Privatizations

As previously stated, restructuring in Peru generated an income of US$ 9.249 million and committed investments for US$ 11,428. According to the Economic and Financial Crime Investigating Commission (Comisión Investigadora de Delitos Económicos y Financieros), US$ 6.445 million of those incomes entered the Peruvian Treasury. Almost 35 per cent of the money going to the Treasury was directed to Public Savings and

Pension Reserves while 19.19 per cent was destined to Public Debt. Other 15.35 per cent was spent in Weapons Acquisition.

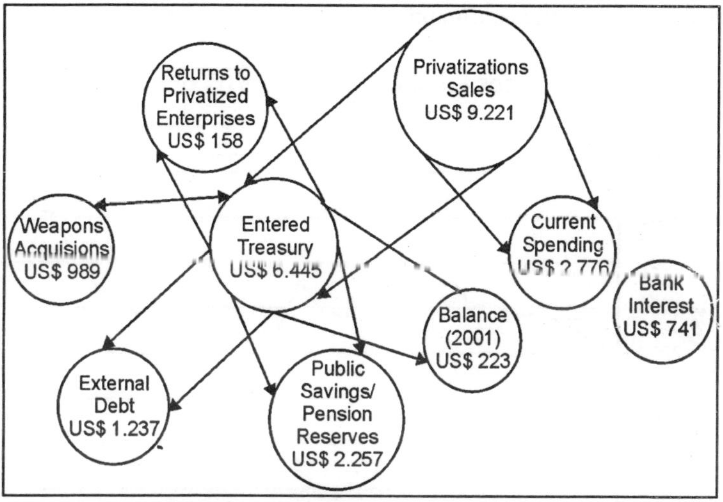

Fig. 6.3: Use of Privatization Incomes.
Source: Comisión Investigadora de Delitos Económicos y Financieros.)

Thus, it is apparent that an amount of US$ 840 million has not been accounted for. In addition, it can be concluded that the Peruvian Government did not invest these incomes strategically in the most relevant sectors of the country in order to increase wealth and employment.

On the other hand, it is believed that at least some of the valuations of public enterprises that were afterwards privatized had been sub-valuated and that many of the new operators did not accomplish the investment plans agreed to. For example in 1996, 75 per cent of the shares of the oil refinery La Pampilla were sold of at US$ 180 million to Repsol, while in the year 1994 the enterprise had generated incomes for US$ 657 million and operating profits of US$ 85 million. This meant that in less than three years the investment was retrieved. Additionally, it is known that Repsol has nowadays an outdated refinery due to the breach of the investment programme. Finally, one of the main objectives of privatization was to increase and improve the quality of employment. However, by 1999 Repsol had dismissed substantial number of employees.

Nevertheless, the Peruvian GDP per Capita has been in an upward trend since the year 1993. This can be attributed to: (a) the political stability gained after almost 25 years of terrorism, (b) the economic model driven comprising and promoted by the Government, (c) the very high international metal prices, (d) the efficient performance of private sector, (e) the explosive development of internal and external tourism, and (f) the growth of domestic consumption.

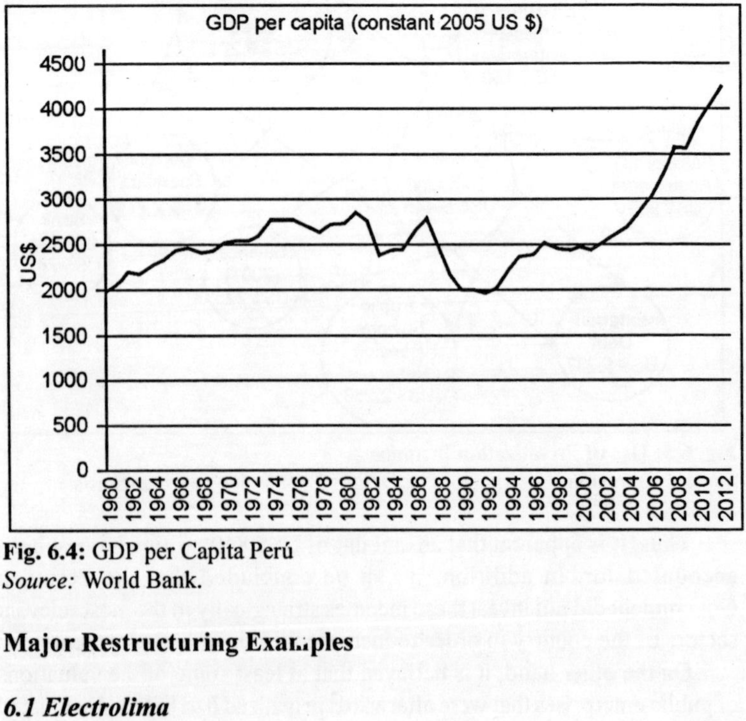

Fig. 6.4: GDP per Capita Perú
Source: World Bank.

Major Restructuring Examples

6.1 Electrolima

Electrolima was fragmented into five companies for privatization purposes: EDGEL (power generator), Luz Del Sur, Edelnor, Ede-Chancay and Ede-Cañete (all of them distributors). Overall, the sale of the shares was for US$ 1.213 million and generated investments projects for US$ 312 million.

The privatization of EDGEL was for 70 per cent of the shares worth US$ 600 million. The first sale was made in October 1995 for 60 per cent of the company. This acquisition was made by Generandes consortium comprising of Energy Corp. (USA), Endesa (Chile), Granay Montero and Banco Wiese (Peru). Generandes provided US$ 524 million (including $ 100 million in debt papers) and committed investment of US$ 42 million.

Luz Del Sur is the enterprise that has the concession to supply

Metropolitan Lima. Its total shares were sold for a value of US$ 407 million of which 60 per cent was acquired in July 1994 by the consortium Ontario Quinta, formed by Ontario Hydro (Canada) and Chilquinta (Chile); workers subsequently acquired 10 per cent in December 1996 and sold the remaining 30 per cent through the sale of shares in domestic and international market. The international sale was made through the New York Stock Exchange (US$ 24 million) and local sale through institutional investors (US$ 42 million) and the Citizen Participation Programme (US$ 96 million) in which were involved over 150 thousand investors. By 1997 it supplied 49 per cent of the total demand for electricity of the country with more than 640 thousand customers.

EDELNOR holds the concession for the north area of Lima. Its privatization included the sale of 64 per cent shares for a total value of US$ 187 million. 60 per cent of these was purchased in July 1994, by Distrilima Holdings, consortium consisting of Endesa (Spain), Chilectra (Chile), Enersis (Chile) and Cosapi (Peru). Later the workers acquired 4 per cent. The remaining 35 per cent still remains in state hands.

Petroperú

The main units privatized were Refinería La Pampilla (RLP), oil fields 8/8x Lot and Block X, the supply terminals, the service stations and Petrolube, obtaining a combined US$ 705 million investment and a commitment of US$ 119 million.

The privatization of RLP was made in June 1996 with the auction of 60 per cent of the shares for a total value of US$ 181 million including US$ 38 million in debt papers. The auction was won by Refinadores del Perú, a consortium comprised of Repsol (Spain), YPF (Argentina), Mobil Oil of Peru SA, Inversiones Grana y Montero and The Privatization Fund of Peru. In November 1997, workers acquired 8 per cent of the shares for a total of US$ 23 million. Currently, 32 per cent of the shares of the refinery is held by the Peruvian state. The refining capacity of the company is 100 thousand barrels of oil and supplies 65 per cent of fuel consumption Metropolitan Lima (45% nationally).

The privatization of the oil field 8/8x in 1996 by the consortium Pluspetrol Peru Corp., was formed by Pluspetrol Peru Corp (Argentina), Pedco (South Korea) and Daewoo Corp. (South Korea). It was paid $ 142 million including $ 25 million in debt papers. This lot is located in the north eastern jungle of Peru and has an output of 26.8 thousand oil barrels per day.

As to Lot X, this was auctioned in the same year and was acquired by Perez Companc (Argentina) which paid US$ 202 million with an investment commitment of US$ 50 million. The output of this lot is of 13.1 million oil barrels per day.

Finally, in December 1997, Petroperú conducted the auction for the contract operation of fuel storage terminal for 15 years, being acquired by GMP consortium, led by the company Granay Montero, for the operation of the north and south terminals and Serlipsa for the operation of the central terminals. The total value of this privatization was for US$ 99 million, of which $ 9 million was paid by subscription rights contracts and $ 90 million to be paid from fees in the period of the contracts besides the implementing investment commitment of US$ 18.8 million over a period of 4-5 years. These plants have systems for receipt, storage and delivery of fuel, being the sources of supply for the whole country, as well as access to fuel imports.

Tintaya

Tintaya is located in Cusco and is the second copper producer nationwide. Its auction took place in October 1994 and was acquired by the American company Magma Copper Corp. to provide US$ 277 million including US$ 55 million in debt papers at face value and an investment commitment of US$ 104 million. Workers bought shares of the company worth $ 2 million. Since January 1996, the new owner of Tintaya is the Australian The Broken Hill Proprietary Co. In 1994 Tintaya sold 164,000 metric tonnes of copper concentrates. Before privatization the company processed daily 8 thousand MT of copper and by 1998 it significantly increased its production capacity to 12.5 MT. By 1998 the company had invested over US$ 117 million (more than the US$ 104 million that was committed in the agreement).

Pitfalls in the Process

The results of the privatization process in Peru are ambivalent. The expansion of the coverage of public services, technological modernization and high levels of investment particularly in the mining sector are some of the most positive features. The Peruvian privatizations were especially notable in comparison with other Latin American countries due to accelerated pace of execution. However, privatizations were marked by irregularities that in many cases generated price increases, and poor control mechanisms.

It can be said that in the electricity sector, the different strata of the urban population of Peru significantly reduced their consumption due to the increased rates, while the increase in coverage can be mainly explained by the Rural Electrification Plan implemented by the Ministry of Energy and Mines.

As for the telephone sector, the increase in the price of local calls and the constant increase in the fixed monthly fee had reduced the consumer's surplus in homes since 1997. Moreover, most of the service coverage is still concentrated in Lima, were more than two-thirds of fixed lines and 75 per cent of mobiles are established.

In the hydrocarbon sector, the objectives that the privatization of Petroperu pursued were not accomplished. It has been seen that oil production, oil reserves and the number of oil exploration wells have declined significantly. Peru has registered in recent years a growing deficit in its trade balance of hydrocarbon. Clearly, the country has lost competitiveness in this sector compared to other Latin American countries.

Privatization generated a high social cost due to loss of shareholder rights or due to dismissal suffered by workers to clean up companies before sales process. It is estimated that during the nine years of privatization over 120 thousand jobs were lost of which only one third was absorbed by the new entrants.

Another aspect that can be inferred is the fragmentation of the operations in the process of privatization. This fragmentation can in fact reflect the buyers' selective interest in the most profitable units of a determined enterprise, leaving to the state those which are less profitable.

Finally, we have seen that the resources generated from privatization were not adequately invested and that almost 70 per cent of it were destined to the acquisition of weapons, external debt and to different public funds, wasting a clear opportunity to invest and develop other interesting and potential sectors.

In conclusion, the Peruvian experience shows to some extent that privatization has not generated solutions to the system of public financing in the long-term but instead a short-term palliative that ends as soon as the sale ends.

The Road Ahead

Restructuring and privatization must continue in order to have a sustainable economic growth. Obviously adjustments in the restructuring processes must be properly executed. The government must review aspects such as increasing the participation of Peruvian capital in these processes, as its participation has been insignificant compared to the foreign ones. And last but not the least, the government must increase the control and monitoring mechanisms in order to assure the correct execution of the committed investments agreed.

AFRICA—GHANA AND TANZANIA

Ghana

Historical Background of Restructuring in Ghana

As part of the Economic Recovery Programme (ERP) of Ghana, the State-owned Enterprise Reform Programme was launched in 1988 as measures to improve the performance of public enterprises and to rationalize the sector through a programme of divestiture. Around this period the state controlled about 350 enterprises across all sectors of the economy. Majority of these State Owned Enterprises (SOEs) were not performing satisfactorily due to the lack of technical expertise, over-staffing, lack of urgency towards state business and excessive bureaucracy. The reform programme was therefore, seen as a tool to make SOEs more efficient and to operate profitably like any private limited liability company. In addition, the programme was aimed at boosting Foreign Direct Investment (FDI) into the country and conforming to the recommendations of donor agencies like the IMF and the World Bank.

The State Enterprise Commission (SEC) oversees the corporate governance of SOEs and it encourages the running of state enterprises to be operated like limited liability companies in order to maximise profit through government support to loss making enterprises.

The Divestiture Implementation Committee (DIC) was set-up in 1993 by the Government of Ghana to implement and execute all government policies regarding programmes of divestiture. The legal framework under which the DIC operates is set in the Divestiture of State Interests (Implementation) Law, 1993, (PNDC, Law 326). The law states the following as the functions of the DIC:

- to plan, monitor, coordinate and evaluate all divestitures;
- to arrange for the effective communication of Government policies and objectives for any divestiture;
- to develop criteria for the selection of enterprises to be divested

and assume responsibility for preparing such enterprises for divestiture;
- to make appropriate consultations for successful processing of all divestiture programmes, and
- to ensure consistency in procedures for divestiture, in particular with regard to valuation, invitation for bids, negotiation of sales and settlement of account [Divestiture Implementation Committee (DIC)- Ghana, 1999].

The DIC uses a bidding process and interested bidders are evaluated using laid down criteria including the assessment of business plans, financial resources and management skills. The private owners are expected to convert the enterprises into productive ventures that are profitable and pay taxes as well as provide employment for Ghanians.

The Role of the Multinational Institutions (IMF, World Bank and DFID etc.)

The reform programme was a condition for the IMF and World Bank overall Structural Adjustment Programmes (SAB). For the Government of Ghana to continue to be supported by these institutions and other donors, it was required to fulfil their recommendations to reduce the size of the overblown public sector and take the state from operating enterprises that are inefficient. The donor agencies have major influence on the economic policies of Ghana, because the economy depends on them for financial assistance and external loans to finance its development projects and budget deficits. Total debt/GDP ratio was 129.4 per cent as at the end of 2000 whereas Gross Domestic Investment (GDP) as at the same period was 23.7 per cent, with total external debt standing at US$ 6.7 billion. The ERP was therefore used as conditions for loan agreements and financial supports. For instance, in 2004 the World Bank supported the privatisation of the water sector with an amount of US$ 103 million for an "Urban Water Project" (The World Bank, 2004) while the Nordic Development Fund supported the same project with US$ 5 million.

The DIC was provided advice and financial support by the World Bank to carry-out its activities. In addition, the Department for International Development (DFID) of the United Kingdom formerly the Overseas Development Administration also provided technical assistance to DIC in the form of legal, financial support and other aspects of divestiture.

Critical Sectors

Prior to the period of restructuring/privatisation, SOEs dominated the entire sectors of the economy. The government after independence in1957 pursued an industrialisation policy based on socialist ideals, leading to the establishment of and the involvement by the state in running corporations. Several strategic corporations were established across all sectors of the economy making the state a forerunner in the productivity of the country. The energy, utilities, mining, food, business and financial services sectors were dominated by SOEs. In addition, the communications, transportations, construction and wholesale and retail trade sectors were predominantly state-owned enterprises. A major step in the privatisation process was in 1994 when the government floated 30 per cent of its 55 per cent shareholding in Ashanti Goldfields Corporation (AGC) on the London and Ghana stock exchanges. In the financial sector, the government privatised Standard Chartered Bank, Social Security Bank, Ghana Commercial Bank and recently, the National Investment Bank and the Merchant Bank as well as the State Insurance Corporation. In the telecom sector, the Ghana Telecom was divested and in the transport sector the State Transport Corporation (STC) has also been divested.

In general, most of the SOEs in the manufacturing and consumer goods sectors have been divested. Government still has minority stake in the banking, airport and harbour management sectors. In addition, government still has partial ownership in the extractive sector. Currently, only a small number of SOEs remain, affected by poor financial conditions. The leading state-owned enterprises are Tema Oil Refinery, the Ghana Airport Company and the Ghana Ports and Harbour Authority.

How Much Divestiture has Taken Place

After over a decade of implementation of the privatization programme, about 335 companies have so far been transferred to the private sector.

The privatisation process begun with a total of 350 SOEs, and between 1988 and 1993, 55 SOEs were divested. The process continued steadily after the establishment of the Divestiture Implementation Committee (DIC) in 1993 and by December 31, 1997 a total of 201 SOEs (full or partial) were authorised for divestiture by the Office of the President. The number increased to 212 by December 1998. According to the Bank of Ghana (2005), about 335 SOEs have been privatised after over a decade of the reform programme implementation. In 2013, the newly reconstituted

DIC was tasked to divest the remaining government assets in addition to other residual assets before 2016. In all six (6) enterprises were identified including EREDEC Hotel in Koforidua, GNTC House in Tamale, Catering Rest House and the Bolga Meat Factory both in Bolgatanga, Abosso Glass Factory and Bonsa Tyre Factory. Most of these enterprises are in poor financial conditions. The programme has brought considerable amount of foreign direct investment to the country. Most of the companies have been modernised and their productivity has improved. The mode of divestiture included sale of assets, sale of shares, joint ventures, leasing and liquidation. The Bank of Ghana (2005) explains the mode of divestiture as follows:

- Trade sales to a private sector investor or consortium of the enterprise's assets (either as a whole or in parts if the enterprise comprises a number of distinct businesses or divisions).
- Total acquisition of shares by private investors while the government absorbs the existing liabilities of the company.
- The creation of a joint venture companies between the state and the private investor with the state as minority shareholder while management control remains with the private investor.
- Leasing of plant and equipments, where the investor undertakes the necessary investment to upgrade the asset and manage them for an agreed period with an option to acquire them within the lease period.

Figure 6.5 shows the total number of firms privatised between 1990-2002, according to the mode of divestiture.

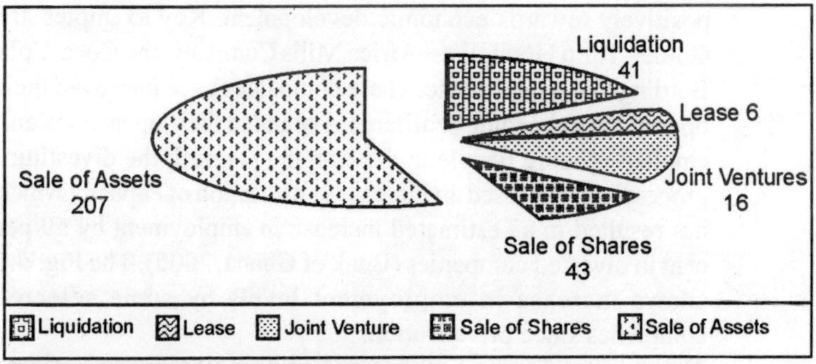

Fig. 6.5: Mode of Divestiture (1990-2002)
Source: World Diplomatic Guide, 2014.

Some Examples of Restructuring

Major restructuring and privatization exercises include the following:

(i) Ghana Water and Sewerage Corporation (Ghana Water Company): Management contract given to Aqua Vitens Rand Ltd (AVRL) for the period 2006-2011
(ii) Ashanti Gold Fields (now AngloGold Ashanti): Sale of government stake
(iii) Ghana Commercial Bank: Sale of part of government shares
(iv) Ghana Telecom: Sale of government stake
(v) Golden Tulip Hotel: Sale of government stake

Role of Restructuring/Privatisation or other Appropriate Agencies

The Enterprise REstructuring Programme (ERP) was comprehensively developed to achieve certain objectives that would promote the productivity of the public sector. Since inception in 1983, the restructuring/privatisation has played major roles in the development of the economy. In accordance with the objective of the programme, the following are some of the major roles of privatisation in Ghana.

- The key objectives of the programme was to implement policy reforms that would ensure that SOES operate in a commercial manner, through increased competition, new policies and procedures for financial support by government to public enterprises. Many of the divested enterprises have become more productive and competitive and are currently contributing positively towards economic development. Key examples are Golden Tulip Hotel, West Africa Mills Company, the Coca-Cola Bottling Co. (GH) Ltd etc. These companies have improved their operations to become profitable, expanded their operations and employing more people in the country. Overall, the divestiture process has witnessed an increase in utilisation of capacity which has resulted in an estimated increase in employment by 59 per cent in divested companies (Bank of Ghana, 2005). The Fig. 6.6 shows increase in employment levels by some selected companies since privatisation:
- The programme also aimed at instituting major institutional and legal reforms to give autonomy to managers of SOEs that are

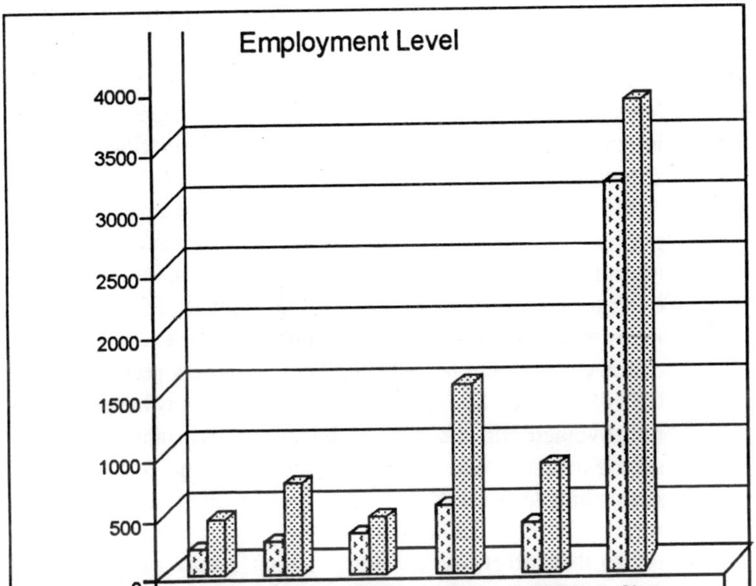

	Golden Tulip Hotel	Tema Steel Company	West African Mills Co.	Ghan Agro-Food	Coca Cola Company Ltd.	Ghana Rubber Estates
Pre Divestiture	116	130	170	494	340	3085
Post Divestiture	346	584	345	1570	700	3833

Fig. 6.6: Employment Levels
Source: World Diplomatic Guide, 2014.

critical and financially viable. The Tema Oil Refinery and the Ghana Ports and Harbours Authority are examples of SOEs being given institutional and legal autonomy. Through this, the Tema Oil Refinery invested greatly towards the current discoveries of oil in Ghana.

- The privatisation also played a major role in reducing the managerial and financial burden on the government. The key problems of SOEs prior to the restructuring programme were overstaffing, lack of technical expertise and operational inefficiencies. The rationalisation of the public sector has improved the deficit position of the government and allowing government to focus on more relevant development activities. The state no longer funds SOEs in their acquisitions of plant and equipments and it has stopped to guarantee loans and other facilities to divested companies. The improved companies operate profitably and pay taxes to government and those under joint venture arrangements pay higher dividends to the state.

- The programme also played a major role in efficiency and management of SOEs through trainings of managers, reduction in staffing, installation of management information systems, corporate plans preparations and financial audits.
- Apart from above, the programme also boosted private sector participation in the economy through deregulations. Private investments increased tremendously, opening the country to other parts of the world for trade. The amount of foreign direct investments increased, bringing more foreign exchange to the country. For example, in 1996, the government received about US$ 454 million from privatisation. The economy has registered improvements in the general business environment through serene investor perception though more still needs to be done. According to a Bank of Ghana (2005), domestic as well as foreign investors hold positive perception about fundamental issues that affect investment decisions. Factors such as good governance, costs and efficiency of infrastructure, political issues, the internal and external investment policies of government among others, improves the country's international competitiveness in attracting private capital inflows.
- In addition, there has been major technology transfer through the privatization programme as many companies under new ownership are investing in new modern plants and equipments to replace existing and non-functional ones. The skills of the workforce are upgraded to assist in building the much needed technological capabilities to effectively and efficiently utilize the productive resources.

Pitfalls of Privatisation

Lack of Transparency

Lack of transparency of the privatisation process has been a major issue. Many intellectuals and the public have raised eyebrows against the process because they think some of the transactions especially through sale to a strategic investor or sale of assets were not transparent. The disposal of assets of some major enterprises were done in secrecy aggravating the fear of corruption in the system. Many believed that some enterprises were sold to power brokers or party affiliates at considerably low prices, proceeds of which should have yielded more than US$ 873 million to state by end of 1997. The DIC has come under serious criticism from the general public due to the following reasons:

- Lack of transparency in its operations.
- Lack of involvement of operators in the private sector in its membership.
- The divestiture activities perceived to be increasing the unemployment rates in the country.
- The secretariat is perceived to have some inefficiencies in its operations.
- The supremacy of the Social Security and National Insurance Trust (a government organization) resulting in the crowding out of the local private sector.

Social Cost of Privatization

The restructuring process was characterised by staff lay-offs, redundancy and other problems related to labour, making it rather unpopular. This was deemed to be creating unemployment problems, raising labour agitations and the Trade Union Congress (TUC) contested vigorously the privatisation of some enterprises. The situation has since affected the effective operations of enterprises under new owners due to labour unrests. For example, there have been frequent closures of Sabbat Motors (formerly ATS) due to labour unrests. Besides, workers can decide to run down an enterprise upon information that it is listed for privatisation. The social effects of unemployment caused by restructuring has major impacts on society which is further compounded by low average incomes to pay for goods and services at higher prices resulting from removal of government subsidies.

6.3 Politicization

The privatisation programme has been politicized with opposition parties using it a tool for campaigning against the current government. The opposition really do not see anything good about the programme and every aspect of it has been condemned. Like many developing countries, economic reforms are usually faced with such factors as varied interests through class, ethnic, professional groups or geographical factors. In

Ghana there have been public protests against privatisation of certain enterprises deemed strategic and essential, for example, the electricity and water companies. The attempted sale of government shares in the Agricultural Development Bank has been opposed by both workers and farmers association making it difficult to implement the programme to the fullest. Besides, the politicisation of the opposition, incumbent governments also tend to portray only the good aspects of the programme in a bid to push their way through without considering its effects on other aspects of the economy. To achieve good results, a better strategy is to adopt a balanced approach that would capture the interests of various stakeholders.

Tanzania

History of Restructuring

In 1967, the government of Tanzania nationalized all the commercial activities which led to several parastatal enterprises in all sectors. However, the nationalization policy proved to be a failure since all the enterprises depended on the government for their finance and managerial requirements. Due to this, gradual reforms were initiated in the 1980s by price reduction and later on the elimination of price controls. In 1992 the state pulled out of the commercial sector and retained its role in law and order maintenance and provision of economic and social infrastructure.

In May 1992, the government commenced a privatization programme in which more than 400 loss-making public enterprises were to be sold. There were 339 commercial enterprises and 56 non-commercial enterprises as well as several holding companies. The parastatal sector contributed to 24 per cent non-agricultural employment with whole ownership in utilities and major ownership in agriculture, banking, mining and manufacturing. The key monopolies such as the container terminal of the Tanzania Harbour Authority and Tanzania Telecommunication Corporations Ltd (TTCL) were still initiating reform measures.

The restructuring process of the public enterprises involved three types of reforms namely:

(a) Ending of government subsidies to the parastatals.
(b) Partial or complete privatization of public sectors holdings, and
(c) Liquidation of non-profit making entities.

Role of Multinational Agencies

World Bank and International Monetary Fund (IMF) contributed to the post structural reform policies in the liberalized and privatized economies. The World Bank supported the privatization through its project known as World Bank Privatization and Private Sector Development Project. The project contributed to the following requirements:

- To finance technical assistance and advisory service to the divestiture procedures.
- Formation of new regulatory institutions.

The state was supposed to phase out price controls, production, marketing, transportation and the allocation of foreign exchange. Furthermore, state owned enterprises such as banks, cooperative societies, marketing agencies which were running unprofitably were sold to private sector.

Among the structural change brought about by World Bank and IMF was the inflow of foreign exchange when the Tanzanian currency, shilling was devalued, subsidies on maize meal and fertilizers were lowered, trade barriers to international markets were abolished and prices of rice, maize and other crops for export were raised.

Critical Sectors

The critical sectors which needed restructuring in Tanzania were all the commercial sectors owned by the state. These include—

- Banking
- Industries
- Agricultural cooperatives
- Infrastructure
- Telecommunications

Privatization Agencies

- In 1991 Loans and Advances Realization Trust (LART) Act was enacted with the aim of recovering of non-performing debts in which the public enterprises with huge debts were supposed to transfer their debts to LART for collection.

- Later on in 1992, the Government of Tanzania under the Public Corporations Act of 1992 established Presidential Parastatal Sector Reform Commission (PSRC) which was then amended in 1993 and 1999. The aim of PSRC was to coordinate the economic reforms in the implementation of privatization.
- PSRC assessed which parastatals were strategic that is they contribute to GDP, provide employment or use local inputs. Those which were viable and commercial were to be sold and those which were unprofitable were to be liquidated.
- In 2007, Consolidated Holding Corporation (CHC) formerly known as NBC Holding Corporation which was enacted in 1997, was vested with the remaining activities of LART and PSRC.

Major Restructuring Examples

More than 400 public enterprises were privatized in Tanzania; however, some major restructuring/privatization include the following:

National Bank of Commerce (NBC)

NBC was deregulated in 1997 where it was divided in three entities which are NBC Holding Corporation, National Microfinance Bank (NMB) and National Bank of Commerce (1997) Limited. The bank was later privatized by selling of shares to ABSA Group Limited now known as Barclays Africa Group Limited. To date the shareholding in the bank is as follows:

- ABSA Group Limited (Barclays Africa Group Limited) 55 per cent.
- Government of Republic of Tanzania 30 per cent.
- International Finance Corporation 15 per cent.

Water Sector

A ten year contract was signed to supply water in urban areas between the state and two foreign companies namely Biwater from Britain and Gauff Ingenieure from Germany are involved.

Tanzania Railways Corporation

A 25 year contract was signed between Reli Assets Holding Company (RAHCO) on behalf of the Government of Tanzania and Tanzania

Railways Limited (TRL) a subsidiary of RITES Limited of India to run the Tanzania Railways Corporation. The Government of Tanzania will own 49 per cent of the shares and TRL will own 51 per cent shares. TRL will invest US Dollar 40 million which will be used to buy locomotive, coaches and wagons.

Pitfalls in the Process

The privatization of agricultural sector seemed to be progressing faster compared to the industrial sector, however, lack of enough capital in agricultural sector needed for transportation and storage of the produce have made it difficult for the investors.

Some of the foreign companies opted to open branches or subsidiaries in the country rather than buying the existing parastatals. This would eventually lead to the liquidation of the assets of those companies which cannot be sold.

In the banking sector, most of the banks needed capital injection after the restructuring process; so as to allow the natives to invest in the private sector. To tackle this challenge, there must be some partnership with other companies so as to raise the capital.

In the utilities sector, privatization resulted in the rise of the prices in the water sector with poor supply of water and in the long run termination of the contract with the investor Biwater from UK. Although the adjustment policy on water infrastructure was established, only 40 per cent of the rural population and 70 per cent of the urban population have piped water and the rest of population get water from unsafe sources.

ASIA—BHUTAN AND SRI LANKA

Bhutan

Overview

Bhutan is a strategically located country bordering India, Nepal and China. India being a former British colony is an influential neighbour historically. India is also the major economic and development partner, accounting for 100 per cent of its expenditures during the first 5 year plan (1961-1966) down to about 28 per cent in the 8th 5 year development plan (1997-2002). Bhutan's guiding philosophy is "Gross National Happiness"—by avoiding destruction of the environment, with

Government taking all efforts to preserve the country's culture, identity and environment and good governance. Democratic form of Government was initiated in the country in March 2008, with its first democratic election for the Prime Minster. It was under monarchic rule in all of its existence prior to that.

Role of Multinational Agencies

The development of Bhutanese economy can be mainly attributed to the Government of India, which has been rendering assistance towards its planned activities right from the initiation of First Five Year Plan in 1961. The Government of India had been a major development partner from 1910 when British ruled India and this cordeal relationship has continued since then. Besides India, multinational agencies have provided financial grants to enable the government of Bhutan plan and implement the plans smoothly as per the emerging needs. Government plays a vital role in every aspect of the area in tackling the constraints the country faces and strengthening its economy at the same time. A huge chunk of the responsibilities fall on the shoulders of the government as most of the businesses are still state owned. Asian Development Bank (ADB) started to support Bhutan from 1982 and was committed to the private sector growth. It plays the role of a broker, expedites the discussions whenever necessary between the policy-makers and the stakeholders and helps realize the viable plans into real projects. ADB provided assistance in 1997 for reforming the financial sector under the following broad guidelines:

- Loan grant of $ 4 million for policy-based reforms to Government of Bhutan for aiding the financial as well as private sector, help in the privatization of Bhutan National Bank.
- Credit facility and development loan of $ 4 billion financed but administered by the Ministry of Finance.
- Investment in equity through common shares of Bhutan National Bank.
- Provide assistance to all financial institutions in technical areas to enhance the capabilities through grant of $ 500,000.

The diagnosis of inviting banks and having foreign partnership was discussed and elaborated with the consultants of ADB. The Government of Bhutan had consensus on this issue as there would be capital injection and human resource expertise in related fields along with support in technology.

Bhutan got a grant of over 37 per cent of Bhutan's aggregate revenues during the Country Partnership Strategy period of 2011-2014. The World Bank Group identified the need for laying the base for the medium and long-term commitment in ICT, private sector development and employment for youth.

India was the major revenue assistant partner to Bhutan. The country has received grant and aid since 1960s through the Colombo plan from several countries not only in monetary terms but also in the form of kind like farm machinery, motor vehicles, school and library books and laboratory equipments. Also livestock, agricultural help through distribution of seeds, dairy kit, medication and help in irrigation systems were provided.

Below is the list of Multinational agencies offering grants for restructuring/privatization in Bhutan (Table 6.3). These agencies help to explore opportunities along with the Government of Bhutan to help private

Table 6.3: Multinational agencies offering grants for restructuring/privatization

Development Partner	*Area(s) of Engagement*
Asian Development Bank	roads, urban, rural infrastructure, financial sector, private sector
United Nations Development Programme	rural development, urban development, health, education, governance, disaster risk reduction, labour and employment, private sector development, gender, institutional capacity building, human resource development, social protection
UNICEF	education, health, water and sanitation, gender, institutional capacity building, human resource development
UNFPA	education, health, water and sanitation, gender, institutional capacity building, human resource development
World Health Organization	health, institutional capacity building, human resource development
World Food Programme	rural, education, health, social protection
Food and Agriculture Organization	agriculture, rural development
IFAD	agriculture
Helvetas/Swiss Development Cooperation	education, culture, rural infrastructure, renewable natural resources, civil society, state sectors
Austrian Coordination Office	electrification, hydropower. efficient ovens, tourism
Japan International Cooperation Agency	agriculture, power, roads, telecommunications, health, education, good governance
SNV (Netherlands)	water, sanitation and hygiene, smallholder cash crops, forest products, pro-poor sustainable tourism
Liaison Office of Denmark	education, health, urban development, environment, governance, decentralization, media
Save the Children (US)	early childhood care and education, basic education adolescent and youth development. child protection

sector development. Their role is to take charge for the investment and programmes for advisory activities. They also discuss issues related to strengthening the financial sector, tourism, education and telecommunication and challenges of the private sector.

Bhutan has a few bilateral country partners from various countries like, Japan, Denmark, Switzerland, Austria, Netherlands and Canada. The other development partners include ADB, the European Union, Norway and Australia. India has always been Bhutan's largest development partner.

Critical Sectors

The critical sectors contributing to Bhutan's economy in both manufacturing and non-manufacturing are Tourism, Hydropower, Finance, Agro products, paper, handicraft, minerals and chemicals, Bio medical, ICT and hydro related parts. The potential for market and revenue generation capacity is shown in Figure 6.7.

Hydro-power

In 1986 Chukha Hydropower Project was established. It was the first project and it contributed to 7 per cent share to the GDP in that year. Hydro-power capacity of 1488 MW was established in the country. The hydro power share to the GDP recorded a growth of about 20 per cent since 2007. With this contribution, hydropower is seen as the single largest contributor to the economy of Bhutan. Bhutan exports around 80 per cent of the power generated yearly to India and the balance 20 per cent is consumed locally. Presently, there are 28 hydropower plants operating in Bhutan. According to their capacity, 5 of them are large whereas the rest 23 of them fall under small, mini and micro power plants.

There are several other additional projects in the pipeline which would provide more contribution to the country's economy as well as earnings by exporting the energy. The plan of Bhutan is to electrify all of the country using conventional grid extension and use of renewable energy. The Austrian Development Cooperation supports Bhutan in this objective through the promotion of rural electrification.

Tourism

One of the main drivers of growth in Bhutan is the Tourism sector. It has a considerable growth potential. 64,028 high end tourists visited Bhutan

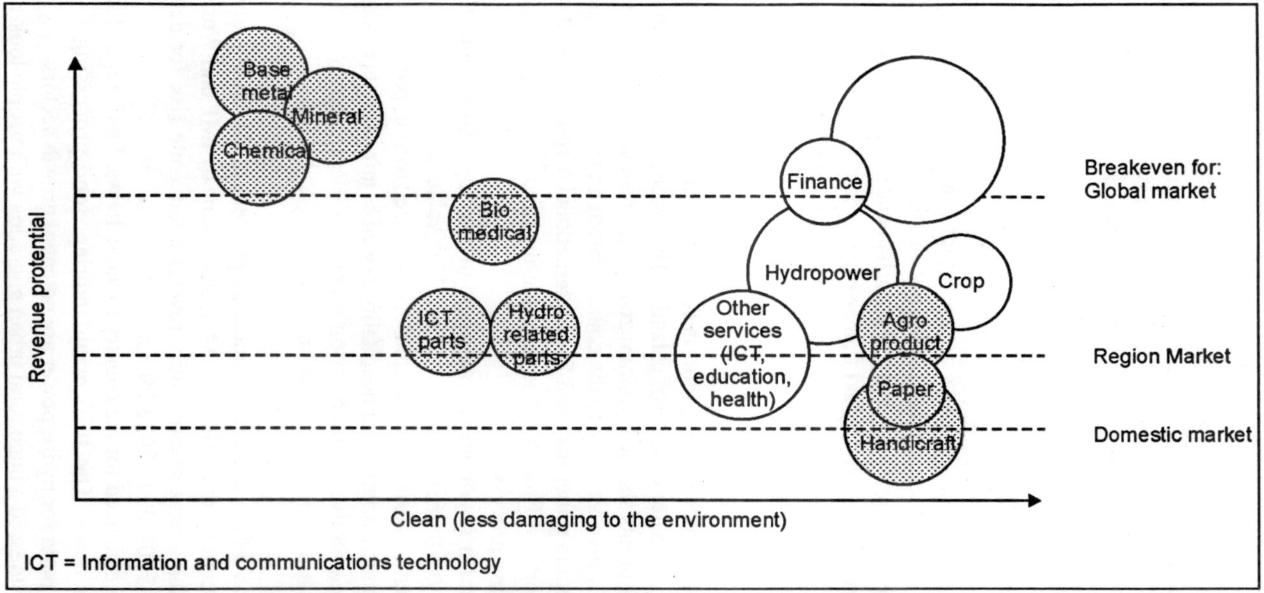

Note: Size of the bubble shows the potential for job creation. Manufacturing is shown in dotted bubbles and non-manufacturing in white bubbles.

Source: Bhutan Critical Development constraints, 2013.

Fig. 6.7: Critical sectors

in 2010 contributing to 6.8 per cent of the GDP. It is a service sector which employs a huge number of educated labour force.

More than 25,000 tourists visited the country with more than 400 Tour operators in business till year 2010. The total number of all tourist arrivals in 2012 was 105,402 which generated total revenue of US$ 227 million. More than 6 per cent of GDP was contributed through Tourism and it also provided employment to 25,987 people.

The Restructuring Process

The Government of Bhutan plays an important role in restructuring/ privatizing the enterprises or even framing policies that eventually govern the activities of enterprises. Firstly, the parliament is responsible for enacting required laws: institutional framework for identification of firms to restructure, evaluation, tendering, negotiation and restructuring. Regulatory framework like Royal Monetary Authority, Druk Holding Investment is necessary for post restructuring controls.

(i) Without proper air transport in the country, it could prove to be a huge disaster in times of calamity. The process of immigration check points should be minimized and the restructuring process should involve entry to the country through the east and south of Bhutan rather than just Paro International Airport situated in the north of Bhutan. Thus restructuring of tourism sector is an ongoing process.

(ii) The most important characteristic of the Royal Government's policy in tourism is the concept of high value, low with volume element. Tourism services must be enhanced with improvement in human resources for hospitality as well as infrastructure. Also the ineffective harmonization amongst different government regulations affects the tourism sector.

Bhutan has a debt burden of almost 60 per cent of the GDP and it rose to 75 per cent by the year 2013-14. A study done by IMF and World Bank on Bhutan's debt sustainability reveals a moderate risk for debt over the years 2008-09 to 2028-29.

There is a dire need for the country to move forward and expand its private sector more. The ICT, manufacturing, food processing and production of parts for hydro power are potential growth sectors.

Bhutan witnessed a huge rural urban migration with people looking for better opportunities. This brought down the GDP contribution of Agriculture from 58 to 14 per cent from 1981 to 2011. In the meantime Industry contributed to the GDP at 11.7 per cent in 1981 and increased to 44 per cent in 2011. 60 per cent of the population depends upon agriculture for employment. The GDP of Bhutan for 2012 was US$ 1.780 billion.

A brief history of various restructuring process that took place in Bhutan since the first 5 year plan in 1961 is mentioned in Table 6.4.

Major Restructuring Examples

The following are some examples of major organizations and the sectors restructured:

- *Creation of National Pensions and Provident Fund*: In March 2000, through the technical assistance of ADB, the restructuring of Government Employee Provident Fund (GEPF), resulted in introduction of National Pension Scheme in Bhutan. The GEPF functioning as one of the Departments under the Royal Insurance Corporation of Bhutan, was restructured as an individual enterprise.
- *Government and State Owned Corporation*: In mid-1999 during the 77th National Assembly, the Royal Government of Bhutan was restructured into 10 Ministries implementable by 2002. Bhutan Telecom was converted to state owned public corporation from the Telecommunication Department and Bhutan Post was also segregated as autonomous public sector corporation. In mid-2001 the government adopted restructuring process in replacement of skilled expatriates with Bhutanese national for various jobs and it was aimed that the expatriates will be reduced from 50000 to 12,500 by end of 2002.
- *DHI Companies Restructuring:* Druk Holding and Investment is an investment wing of the government and looks after all the corporation which has some state ownership and was established in 2007. With its establishment, it has carried out organization restructuring on companies like Bank of Bhutan Limited, Bhutan Telecom Limited, Druk Air Corporation and Bhutan Power Corporation limited to make these sectors more efficient.
- *Financial Sector Reforms*: With the technical assistance of IMF, World Bank and ADB, the Royal Monetary authority, the central

Table 6.4: History of Restructuring Process

5 Year Plan	*Years*	*Sectors Restructured*
1st Five Year Plan 2nd Five Year Plan 3rd Five Year Plan 4th Five Year Plan	1961-1966 1966-1971 1971-1976 1976-1981	✓ Road network ✓ Education and health infrastructure ✓ Agricultural production ✓ Education ✓ Forestry ✓ Roads ✓ Water supply
5th Five Year Plan	1981-1987	✓ Hydropower development ✓ Forests ✓ Tourism ✓ Power
7th Five Year Plan	1992-1996	✓ Human resource development ✓ Social services ✓ Communications ✓ Agriculture ✓ Privatized resource mobilization and service industries ✓ Corporatized agencies involved in airlines, post, financial institutions and municipalities ✓ Established technical assistance programmes for the private sector ✓ Simplified the rules and regulations for imports and export ✓ Liberalized the licensing system to encourage and promote enterprises.
8th Five Year Plan	1997-2002	✓ Human resource development ✓ Application of technology ✓ Gross national happiness implemented ✓ Power ✓ Social services ✓ Roads
9th Five Year Plan	2002-2007	✓ Promote and enhance participation of private sector ✓ Uphold culture and environmental preservation ✓ Fiscal decentralization ✓ Decline in certain public services ✓ Handed over powers of decision-making at the local level
10th Five Year Plan	2008-2013	✓ Hydropower ✓ Tourism ✓ Manufacturing industries ✓ Technology in Information and communications ✓ Human capital ✓ Good governance ✓ Rural connectivity projects ✓ Agricultural production

bank of the country has initiated series of restructuring measures known as Financial Sector Intermediation Facility.

- *Bhutan Carbide and Chemical Limited*: The Privatization history in Bhutan can be traced back to the year 1990-91 when the joint state and Tashi Group of Companies owned company was privatized after the government disinvested its shares to public. Tashi Group now owns 51 per cent shares and 49 per cent owned by the public. The BCCL was established in 1985 through grants provided by World Bank for a sum of US$ 9 m loan interest free for 50 years and the grant from Kuwait Fund for Arab Economic Development (KFAED), to harness the carbide deposit in Bhutan and also to meet the rising needs of Hydropower sector.
- *Bhutan National Bank*: The government disinvested 40 per cent of its equity to Asian Development Bank and Citibank making it the first Institution in country with foreign Investment and established Bhutan National Bank in 1997. On November 1, 2006 ADB offered 25 per cent of 109.603 shares to the employees of Bhutan National Bank as employee buyout option and only 9560 shares were lifted by the employees. The second phase began on 8th December 2009 offering the remaining shares of ADB to general public, which met with over subscription and ended the ownership of ADB and Citibank.
- *Tourism Sector*: The tourism sector was privatized in Bhutan in 1991 due to increased tourists visiting Bhutan. However, till 1998 the licensing process of tourist agency was restricted to 33 licenses. From 1999 after the silver jubilee coronation of the 4th King Jigme Singye Wangchuk, tourism industry was liberalized with around 400 tour operators bringing in approximately 25,000 tourists per year.

Table 6.5 provides details of organizations, the respective sector and the type of restructuring carried over a period of time.

The Road Ahead

Bhutan stands out as one of the fastest growing economies in the region of South Asia. Its reliance on the hydropower exports alone could prove to be harmful. There is a dire need for the country to move forward and expand its private sector more. The ICT, manufacturing, food processing

Table 6.5: Organizations, Sectors and Type of Action

Sl. No.	*Name of Organizations*	*Year*	*Sector*	*Type of Action*
1.	National Pension and Provident Fund	2000	Financial sector	Legal restructuring
2.	Bhutan Telecom Limited	1999	Telecom sector	Management Restructuring
3.	Bhutan Telecom Limited	2012	Telecom sector	Strategic Restructuring
4.	Bhutan Post Limited	1999	Communication	Asset reduction restructuring
5.	Royal Insurance Corporation of Bhutan Limited	2006	Financial sector	Labour redundancy measures
6.	Royal Insurance Corporation of Bhutan Limited	2009	Financial Sector	Strategic restructuring
7.	Ministry of Labour & Human Resources	1999	Government	Labour redundancy measures
8.	Drukair Corporation Limited	2011	Airline	Strategic restructuring
9.	Bank of Bhutan Limited	2011	Financial sector	Strategic restructuring
10	Bhutan Power Limited	2011	Power	Strategic restructuring
11.	Bhutan Carbide and Chemicals Limited	1990	Private	Sale of government shares
12.	Bhutan National Bank	2006 2009	Financial sector	ESOP Public offering of share
13.	Tourism	1991	Tourism	Leasing
14.	Unit Trust of Bhutan	1992	Financial Sector	Legal Restructuring

and production of parts for hydro power are potential growth sectors. These areas need to be restructured and privatized.

It is vital to establish a powerful and effective agency to be responsible for the overall restructuring process.

Sri Lanka

Socio-economic Profile of Sri Lanka

Democratic socialist republic of Sri Lanka is a tropical island located just below the southern tip of India. By the year 2012 its population exceeded 20 million with an annual growth rate of 1 per cent. The country became independent in the year 1948 after 500 years of western colonization. In economic perspective Sri Lanka is considered as a lower middle income country with an annual GDP of $ 59 billion in 2012 and

7 per cent GDP growth rate in year 2013. Although, Sri Lanka is considered as an agricultural country where 31 per cent of labour force is engaged in agriculture, sector contribution to GDP is only 11.1 per cent in 2012 whereas service sector contributes 58.5 per cent and industry sector contributes 30.4 per cent. Sri Lanka has a huge negative trade balance of $ 409 million because its imports are almost double the exports in 2012.

Sri Lanka is better in social indicators compared to its neighbouring countries. Its literacy rate is 93 per cent, life expectancy 74.9 years at birth while human development index is 0.715 in year 2012. Infant mortality rate is 14 per 1000 live births and maternal mortality rate is 35 per 100,000 live births in year 2010 being the best among SAACC countries.

History of Restructuring and Privatization Process

Sri Lanka adopted the welfare state concept and the Government increasingly was involved in both social and economic activities from its independence in 1948. The government spent a significant part of its resources for three major social development programmes namely the food subsidy programme, education programme and health services within last five decades and made a significant progress in those sectors.

State intervention was not limited to social development. Public sector dominated in agriculture, manufacturing and service sectors. In this period, government created a state monopoly in several sectors by setting up new public enterprises and nationalizing number of private entities. Setting-up of corporations in the trade of cement, steel, ceramic, paper, fertilizer, salt, petroleum, tyre, etc. and nationalizing private bus companies are worth mentioning.

The government could get the support of general public for these policies by convincing them with attractive goals like more employment opportunities, controlled prices for essential goods and services, balanced regional development. Public sector was the owner of one-third of investments with 40 per cent of formal employments in the country.

A new Government in 1977, opened up the economy under market liberalization with more market oriented policies. But still the government was the implementer of huge donor-funded infrastructure projects like Mahaweli irrigation and hydropower project. The popular concept of building one million public houses and building new parliament complex also were some of the popular government economic activities.

Most of these SOEs were unproductive, and inefficient due to overstaffing, politically appointed poor management and a myriad of other reasons. The government had to pump in huge amount of public funds into these SOEs in the name of subsidy for their survival.

This is the underlying reason for the restructuring and reforms wave in the eighties and ninetees. Major aims of these reforms were to reduce excessive state intervention in economic activities and strengthen market mechanism. As most of state interventions were done by SOEs it was necessary to privatize them. Although the government realized the necessity of restructuring SOEs they were reluctant to do it, because by that period these SOEs had become a vehicle to provide thousands of employments to their political supporters.

A "pro-western oriented" capitalist regime came to power in 1977 and ruled the country for seventeen years and made some radical changes in the economy. The regime created an executive presidency through constitutional amendments in order to make radical centralized decisions without consulting the legislature. This government made significant policy reforms in the economy, which brought a lot of FDIs and donor aids into the country. World Bank, IMF, ADB or any other fund came in packages with conditions including restructuring and privatization of SOEs. Therefore, the real restructuring process started in mid 1980s in Sri Lanka under united national party's government.

First Era of Privatization

Until mid-eighties, the government was not able to initiate privatization primarily due to resistance from employee unions of SOEs. Also government had no expertise or competent institution to implement privatization. However, pressure from funding agencies, compelled the Government to take up ownership transfer. Ownership transfers were carried out mostly to family members or relatives of political leaders. Privatization was not done on a large scale during this period and only primary methods such as liquidation of easy pick-ups, franchising, management contract and partial divestiture were taken recourse to.

Second Era of Privatization

This second era of privatization commencing in the late eighties was more systematic compared to first era. In this period a presidential committee for reforms was appointed and two legislations also were enacted. These legislations enabled to convert corporations and government owned business units into public companies which was the first step towards privatization. Since, the Government was still facing the trade unionists and social resistance against privatization, the Governmnet preferred the term "peoplization" instead of privatization.

Third Era of Privatization

The people's Alliance party came to power in 1994 and established the Public Enterprises Reform Commission (PERC) in 1996 to carry out public sector reforms in a more systematic and structured way. PERC used the methods of selling SOE's golden share to corporate investors through open tenders, competitive bidding, and management contract or management buyouts. The Government earned Rs. 46.2 billion in this period by restructuring number of public enterprises including utilities like telecom and gas also. PERC and central bank report that 86 SOEs had been privatized during 1989 to 2002 in various sectors including financial, utility, service, manufacturing, agriculture, trade, plantation and petroleum. But the remaining 70 odd loss making SOEs still make an annual loss close to 2 per cent of GDP. By end of 2005 the government had privatized 98 SOEs and liquidated 17 entities. However, the present regime has stopped privatizing public utilities due to increasing social unrest regarding privatization.

Role of Multi-National Agencies

The World Bank, IMF and ADB were the major actors in providing financial aids to Sri Lanka. From time to time US Aids, JAICA. COICA, UNICEF, WFO, AUS Aids and some other international donors also contributed to technical and financial assistance.

The agreement of the Government with the IMF in 1977 reform package related to the following aspects:

- Macro-economic stabilization
- Market reforms and price liberalization
- Restructuring and privatization
- Legal and institutional reforms

Although Government agreed with above terms the privatization part was not given priority till mid-1980s.

In 2004 IMF initiated the Poverty Reduction Growth Fund (PRGF) for four main areas of action as given below:

(i) *Fiscal measures*: This involves further rationalization/streamlining of the tax system including the continued shift to indirect taxation, reducing import taxes and setting up and implementation of the Revenue Authority to enforce fiscal discipline.

(ii) *Financial sector reform*: This essentially involves restructuring of the two state banks and easing of capital account restrictions.

(iii) *Public enterprise reform*: Continuation of the privatization process and reform of the Samurdhi programme to enhance targeting.

(iv) *Labour market reform*: To increase flexibility of the labour market through retrenchments schemes

World Bank

In 1985 World Bank highlighted the need to reduce the massive burden of budgetary provisions on loss making SOEs. In 1987 the government announced privatization as a state policy with the objective of achieving following goals.

- Reduce debt burden through proceedings
- Reduce fiscal burden to government by improving efficiency of SOEs with private sector practices
- Develop an entrepreneurial middle class
- Active capital market and broad-based share ownership

In this effort the government carefully used the word "peoplization" instead of privatization and stressed that no worker will lose their job due to privatization.

Due to some adverse external shocks, internal political violence and entrenched structural rigidities in year 2001, Sri Lankan economy recorded a negative real growth rate of 1.4 per cent for the first time after independence. Public debt was equal to 103.6 per cent of GDP.

Both IMF and WB encouraged and forced Government of Sri Lanka to take following steps in exchange of their financial packages.

- Trade liberalization.
- Devaluation of exchange rate.

- To take policy measures for attracting FDI.
- Encouraging private sector.
- Dismantling price controls and a massive public investment programmes.

Restructuring Critical Sectors

Restructuring unimportant easy pick-ups will not bring expected results to an economy. As well restructuring critical sectors like education, health, finance, utilities also should be done carefully because the positive or negative result will have a critical impact on the general welfare of the citizens.

Sri Lanka started privatization, selecting some easy pick-ups which were not critical and utilities like telecom were taken up only at a later stage. Two state banks are in the agenda for a long period. No regime has attempted to privatize health and education sectors as those are very sensitive to the day to day life of general public.

Role of Internal Agencies and Strategies for Restructuring and Privatization

The Act No. 22 and 23 of 1987 which were enacted with the intention of converting GOBUs into public companies and the act that established PERC can be considered as some of legal frameworks in the vicinity. Public enterprise rehabilitation act also was enacted in 1996 to re-vest seven privatized unsuccessful institutions and abolished within six months due to it's anti-privatising nature.

Presidential commission on privatization or presidential committee on peoplization, public investment management board, and Commercialization of Public Enterprises Division (COPED), the new plantation restructuring unit and special unit in ministry of industries were the institutions that implemented privatization in 1987-1995 period.

The Public Enterprises Restructuring Commission (PERC) was established in 1996 under an act of Parliament to take the overall responsibility in the privatization programme in Sri Lanka fulfilling the need to take the whole process under one umbrella. This brought the privatization programme to some structured and transparent environment.

A strong and an effective regulatory framework is a must to ensure expected distributional and allocative efficiency from privatization programme. When essential utilities are privatized, it needs strong anti-competition laws to protect customers from monopolistic behaviour of mergers and opportunistic entities.

The department of internal trade, fair trade commission, consumer affairs authority are some of regulatory institutions which played the consumer protection role in the country with weak and diversified powers and scope. Although, it is time to set up a strong monopolies and merger commission with required legal and operational powers, no positive steps have been take by the Government. There are some sectoral regulatory bodies also such as National Transport Commission, Telecommunications Regulatory Authority which are not effective enough to fully control the particular sectors due to lack of powers and political influences.

The widely used privatization model was to sell 51 per cent to 60 per cent of shares to corporate investor through open tender and competitive bidding and 30 per cent shares to public at par value and 10 per cent to employees according to the length of service. By this method the government aimed to realize three objectives at the same time. With the majority of shares government expected investors to transfer technology and invest productive capital in order to make entities more productive. The 30 per cent public share offering was done to develop a more vibrant capital market among the middle class of the country. The 10 per cent employee share offer (ESOP) was to win trade unions and reduce resistance against privatization.

In addition to above standard method some asset reductions, employee buy-outs, gifting 50 per cent of shares to workers and negotiated sale of shares also were used according to particular cases.

Pitfalls in the Restructuring Process

Not Realizing Expected Outcomes

The government had three major objectives in privatizing SOEs.

(a) *Economic*: Repay a part of government debts from the money earned by shares sold, Reduce burden of budgetary transfers to SOEs and thereby reduce public sector borrowing requirement, Earn an income from government shares and collect taxes when the firm is profitable after privatization.

(b) *Management Efficiency*: Thinking that private sector is better than public sector in managing.

(c) *Ideology*: Thought of government failure and market is better than state.

But the Government of Sri Lanka was not able to realize any of the above objectives successfully. Following Figs. 6.8 and 6.9 show the trend of government debts and budgetary transfers to SOEs.

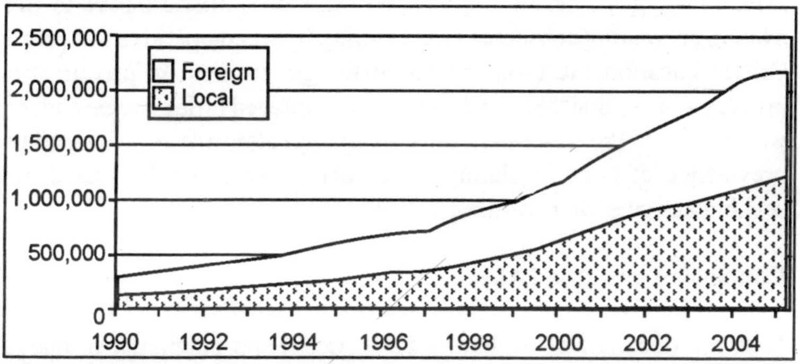

Source: Balasooriya, Alam, & Coghill, 2008.

Fig. 6.8: Government debt (local and foreign) from 1990 to 2005 (SLRs millions)

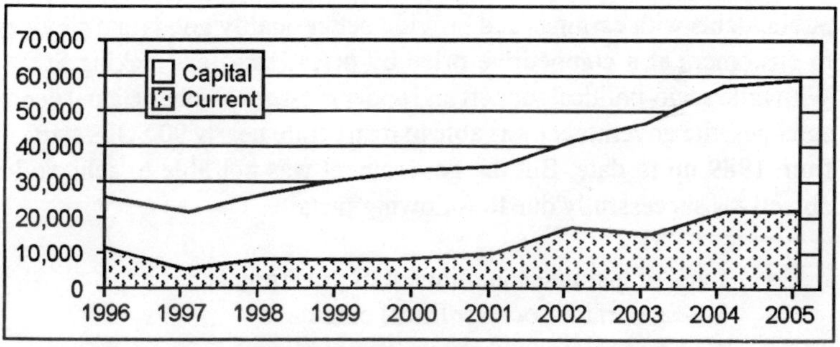

Source: Balasooriya, Alam, & Coghill, 2008.

Fig. 6.9: Government fund transfers to public corporations and institutions from 1996 to 2005—SLRs millions

Figures 6.8 and show 6.9 that government debt burden or fund transfers to SOEs have not gone down during that period due to privatization.

Distribution Impact

The economic and social benefits from restructuring or divestiture of

SOEs should distribute among all the layers of the population equally. Successive governments have not done enough to maximize distributional gains or minimize distributional losses that result from privatization. Overall, the relatively poor have had little or no access to privatization's gains, while the well-connected (both local and foreign), who usually fall into higher income groups, have benefited from increased rent-seeking opportunities under a non-transparent divestiture process" Even after privatizing, government has granted the monopolistic power to new owners preventing consumer's opportunity to get competitive low prices. Critics question the commitment of the government in privatization process and say that "the government has displayed little genuine concern with regard to the lack of effective regulation after privatization and the prevalence of poor regulatory governance, which has facilitated rent seeking activities in privatized entities."

Conclusion and Road Ahead

With the downfall of 'welfare state' concept and popularity of market liberalization, restructuring of state owned enterprises became a key component in the liberalizations process. It was expected to improve economic efficiency, reduce financial burden of state and repay some public debts with earnings and provide better quality goods and services to customers at a competitive price by privatizing loss making SOEs. With little socio-political support and under pressure of international donor agencies, the government was able to restructure nearly 90 SOEs starting from 1989 up to date. But the government was not able to achieve its objectives successfully due to following facts:

- Lack of genuine commitment of government
- Un-favourable socio-political climate
- Non-transparent ambiguous transactions
- Poor legal, institutional and regulatory framework
- Lack of vibrant stock exchange and wide private sector
- Rent seeking behaviour of involved parties
- Resistance of general public due to lack of knowledge and negative past experience
- Politicization of process and institutions
- Lack of required technical competencies
- Absence of a high income middle class
- Not having an independent financial market

- Powerful trade unions
- Extended civil war

It is very clear that if Sri Lanka really wants to achieve an economic development by restructuring its loss making and unproductive SOEs, the past experience provide a lot of valuable lessons. It is necessary to take careful consideration of the country specific socio-political climate and devise reform measures accordingly.

7
Action Plan

This chapter begins with a general framework, in the form of steps, for developing an Action Plan for restructuring. The applicability of the framework is then demonstrated for both sectoral and enterprise restructuring.

Steps

1. The strarting point is essentially the classificaion of the enterprise as a strategic or non-strategic one.

2. The performance of the enterprise is to be then analyzed as an interplay of four level factors:

- MEGA
- MACRO
- MESO
- MICRO

3. The Mega and Macro analysis would lend an insight into the external threats and opportunities and the Meso and Micro would reveal the internal strengths and weaknesses.

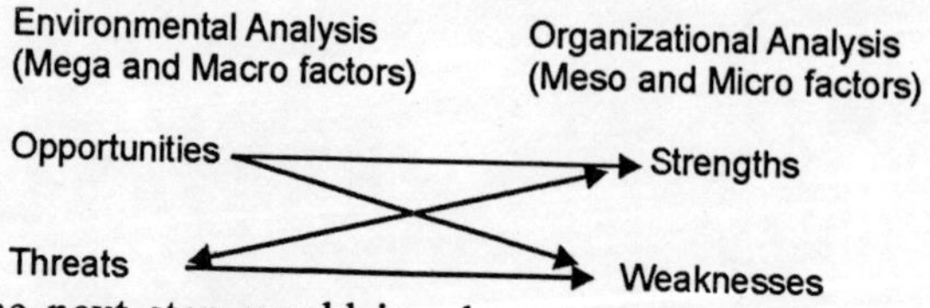

4. The next step would involve conducting an organizational diagnosis. This would encompass:

- Analysis of the causes and symptoms of decline

- Valuation of Business
- Development of Business Plan

The above steps would facilitate an understanding about the viability of the enterprises.

5. Possible application of restructuring strategies and the sequencing of the same.

- Asset Reduction
- Cost Reduction
- Revenue Generation
- Labour Redundancy
- Debt Restructuring
- Financial Restructuring
- Strategic Restructuring
- Cultural Restructuring
- Legal Restructuring
- Physical Restructuring
- Organizational Restructuring

6. Finally, Privatization options should be considered for Government/State owned enterprise/Public enterprise/Parastatal.

- Public Offering of Shares
- Private sale of shares
- Sale of Assets
- New Private investment in the enterprise
- Reorganization into component parts
- Management employee buyout
- Leasing and Management Contract
- Combination of basic methods

Action Plan for Restructuring the Health Sector in the Philippines

Inroduction

Good health for all Filipinos is a vision of the Philippine Government. It means Filipinos leading progressive and healthy lives, people being able to benefit from health services and people contributing towards the economic productivity of the country.

The Philippine health sector covers a wide array of promotive, preventive, curative and rehabilitative services. These include maternal and child care services, nutrition and family planning, control and cure of prevalent diseases, sanitation and environment-related diseases, and prevention programmes for chronic and infectious diseases. Currently, there are three major players in the health sector as follows:

Government Sector: The Government sector is composed of the Department of Health (DOH) and the local government units. The DOH is the principal agency mandated by the Local Government Code in 1991, it has direct authority over municipality, city, provincial health services. With the implementation of the Local Government Code, the municipal and city health services were placed directly under municipal and city governments while the provincial health services under the provincial governments. It retained the regional offices and some specialized hospitals and medical centres under its control.

Private Sector: The private sector in health consists of both commercial and business organizations and non-commercial organizations. Most prominent among the members of the private business sector are practitioners and private institutions such as hospitals, health maintenance organizations, and medical/allied medical schools.

Non-Governmental Organization: Health NGOs are those that are directly involved in health care and in reforming the present healthcare delivery system. Some of them have pioneered alternative approaches in health as exemplified by community-based primary healthcare programmes and promoting and developing indigenous and traditional medicine.

Health services are delivered through health facilities operated by these organizations. These include hospitals, health centres, health stations, clinics and laboratories.

Hospitals: Hospitals are either government or private-owned. Currently, there are 1,809 hospitals in the Philippines of which 587 are operated by the Government and 1,222 are operated by the private sector. Most of the Government hospitals were used to be operated by the DOH. However, with the implementation of the Local Government Code, 534 were devolved to the local government units and 53 consisting of medical centres, special and regional hospitals were retained by the DOH.

Health Centres and Barangay Health Stations: These types of health facilities are government-owned and are primarily responsible for the delivery of basic health services. In the rural areas, these facilities are often the first point of contact between the majority of the poor people and the health system.

Private Clinics and Laboratories. These facilities provide service to a significant proportion of the population particularly those belonging to the middle and upper income classes. Most of the facilities are concentrated in urban centres where they are highly in demand.

Sectoral Diagnosis

Strategic and Non-viable Sector

The health sector can be classified as a strategic sector given the important role it plays in socio-economic development of the country. A healthy populace is a prerequisite to national productivity. To this end, the Philippine Government in cooperation with other sectors of the society should ensure that quality health services are available to all Filipinos. Currently, however, there are inadequate health facilities to provide the needed health services. In addition, the quality of services are not comparable to international standards and the goal of equity has not been achieved so far. With the implementation of the Local Government Code, a number of issues has cropped-up such as the technical and financial capacity and capability of the local government units to take on the devolved health services. Other issues cover financing sources for the sector as well as private sector involvement.

The sector is not a viable sector requiring Government subsidies. Health is a fundamental human right and the Government is responsible for making available adequate, quality and affordable health service to the populace. Taxes account for the bulk of health financing. Because of highly regressive tax rates, public provision of health services tended to be highly inequitable. With the devolution, the poorer local government units find it very difficult to fully meet their responsibilities while the richer ones are able to provide better services. Private health expenditures, meanwhile, are supported from user payments, private insurance and health management organizations. However, in view of the slow growth of household incomes and continued high poverty rates, households have a reduced capacity to finance health expenditure. In addition, the government and the families give low priority to the health sector and as such resources allocated to health services are always at a minimum.

The collection of user charges in public hospitals is based on paying capacity of patients. Cost recovery is low and has in fact been declining despite the same level of usage by both the highest and low-income groups. On the other hand, the local government units with the national government (in the case of poorer local government units) fully subsidize the services provided by the health centres.

Causes and Symptoms of Decline

Despite indications of a modest improvement in health status and decline in mortality rate, a lot of issues still need to be addressed in the sector. For one, regional disparities in infant mortality still persist. Infectious diseases continue to account for most illnesses and deaths particularly among mothers and children. Malnutrition remains pervasive among school children. All these do not contribute towards the building and maintenance of a high quality labour force that could ultimately propel the country towards greater economic growth.

Generally, health services are still inaccessible to many of the population. A recent survey showed that only 40 per cent of total deaths in the country were medically attended. It also showed that the rate of individuals not receiving medical attention before death is higher for members of the low income group. Similarly, around 60 per cent of individuals who had health complaints were unable to seek treatment from any health professionals and resorted instead to home-based health care services.

The above issues are mainly caused by the following factors:

- *Poor distribution and insufficient health facilities*: In general, health facilities are insufficient, inadequately supported, poorly distributed and located. More facilities are located in the more developed and affluent regions. Equipment and physical facilities are lacking and their maintenance is not provided for.
- *Health Human Resource Imbalance*: Some categories of health human resource are in surplus, some are inadequate. There are issues of quality, competence, motivation and commitment, efficiency, distribution and relevance to the needs of the human population. There is no effective mechanism for health human resource planning and production, no commensurate conditions of employment and conductive working situation. There is a mismatch of knowledge of skills of health workers on the administration, management and delivery of health services.
- *Lacking and Unclear Systems and Procedures*: Some hospital operating systems are not well-organized. There are no written policies and procedures in the form of manuals and

administrative issuance. Quality assurance and improvement, and risk management are still at its infancy. Procedures in government agencies need to be further improved to effect faster service and reduce corruption.

- *Weak Organization and Management*: The organization and management of the healthcare delivery system is weak due to poor collaboration and networking among players in the health sector. Further, there is inadequacy of managerial capability, motivation and sense of commitment in the health sector. Weak management is also caused by the devolution of basic health service without adequately building the necessary capability of the local government units to absorb and manage them.
- *Lack of updated and accurate information to use in programme planning*: Only a few health facilities maintain information systems that could be used for future planning. Further, there exist a predominant belief among the population that health services are only needed when a person is seriously sick. As such, some of the information gathered is also inaccurate and incomplete.
- *Unaffordable and rising cost of healthcare*: The rising and unaffordable cost of health care services especially those requiring hospitalization and expensive medicines, and diagnostic examinations have denied access of many poor households to quality healthcare. The cost is threatened further as modern and sophisticated technology is further integrated into the system.
- *Lack of financing*: The budget and other resources awarded to health by the Government and the family is low since health is not among the top priorities and is viewed solely as consumption rather than an investment to the individual and overall development. As a consequence, public health services, which rely mainly on taxes, has suffered. The problem has been made more difficult due to the devolution given the lack of financial capabilities of local government units. Private third party payment schemes (i.e. insurance and Medicare) and health management organizations also have very limited coverage.
- *Poor Policy Formulation and Implementation*: There are some major policies which are not effectively implemented and there are important technical areas for which policy need to be formulated i.e., generic drugs, involvement of the private sector and implementation of insurance schemes.

- *Lack of people's participation in healthcare*: There is an inadequate knowledge and information of the public to make appropriate decisions regarding health care and to make home-based services more efficient and effective. Some segments of the population hold certain socio-cultural values and belief systems that prevent acceptance and utilization of appropriate and effective health services. The mind-set of people regarding decisions about healthcare is to just participate minimally or not at all.
- *Inaccessibility of Health Services*: Geographical location and difficulties of transport, road infrastructure and communication hamper delivery of primary health care services.

Four-Level Framework Analysis

Mega Factors. Trade agreements, global environment issues, and science and technology are three of the global factors which affects the health sector. The operationalization of regional and global trade agreements will install an open market economy, dismantle labour market barriers and increase trade and labour activities. These developments will call for intensified efforts for higher quality health services, closer monitoring of compliance with existing health regulations, and intensified formulation and implementation of new regulatory measures. Global environmental issues may bring about other and even new health risks to the population. Health care facilities should also incorporate appropriate new technologies and methodologies in order to deliver quality health services.

Macro Factors include the growth of the economy (GNP), population growth, rate of urbanization and industrialization, local environment as well as the state of technology in the country.

The level of growth in the economy determines the allocation and use of resources for the health sector. During the 80s, the growth of the Philippine economy was not able to provide such support to the health sector given the political instability, natural disasters and the debt obligations of the country. From 1991-1997, allocation of resources have improved as a consequence of continued economic growth.

While there may be more financial resources for health sector in the future, there will also be more demands for services as a result of a much bigger and better informed and educated population. Currently, the population of the Philippines is pegged at 65 million. This is projected to increase by 1.5 per cent annually up to the year 2020. The increasing population implies more people to serve, especially in terms of health and other essential social services, putting a strain on existing scarce resources of the country.

Industrialization and urbanization will cause a rapid centripetal movement of population towards designated growth and urban areas overwhelming the government's capability to make available the needed social infrastructure and services. The immediate impact would be the generation of industrial hazards and toxic wastes, and work-related/ occupational health problems resulting to more people joining the labour force.

The backlog in terms of safe drinking water supply and sanitation remain serious problems. Consequences of continued environmental depletion and degradation compromises the health and nutritional status of the people.

The science and technology situation in the country is often deplored for its lack of vigour. Scientists have left abroad while much of the technology is simply imported. The suitability, necessity, acceptability and affordability of some of the technologies that are available only in a few areas mostly in Metro Manila. There are basic ones which are not available and some which cannot be applied due to lack of manpower and logistical support.

Meso Factors: The primary healthcare strategy is the overall strategy that the Government is pursuing for the health sector. Primary health care as an approach emphasizes equity and justice and calls for improved efficiency in health service delivery, inter-sectoral (government, private sector and non-government) collaboration and community involvement.

The primary healthcare strategy has been under implementation since 1981.

However, continuing large disparities in health status and health allocation among different geographic areas still persists. One reason is the inadequacy of financing for the sector as a result of lack of funds and the low priority the Government accords the sector. While a Social Reform Agenda was implemented in 1995 in order to put more emphasis on the social aspects of development, the Philippines is still far from attaining its goal of health for all Filipinos.

The health sector has been heavily affected by the devolution in 1991 mandating the transfer of most of the health responsibilities from the national government to the local government units. The transfer of responsibilities was not accompanied by an adjustment period of the local government units that lack the financial, technical and managerial capacity in delivering health services.

Micro Factors: Local government (provincial, city) hospitals will be taken as cases in order to assess and illustrate the relevant factors at the enterprise level. Some of these factors also apply to the national government and private-owned hospitals to a certain extent.

In terms of production potential, local government hospitals have very limited capacity due to outdated and insufficient facilities and equipment and lack of personnel. Only the basic technologies/equipment can be found in local government hospitals.

Health services provided are mainly curative and rehabilitative and user charges are based on the capacity to pay. Users of local government hospitals are the poorer sectors of the society. Marketing and promotion are not done to promote healthcare among the constituents. Further, no budget is provided for research and development, thus, they are mainly dependent on the national government and private sector.

Basic purchasing system is used given the meagre budget they have for supplies and equipment. Procurement is also a problem given the bureaucratic and lengthy procedures of the Government. Despite rigid and strict guidelines, some cases of corruption still exist. Supplies are also provided by the national government and donor agencies through national health projects being implemented.

Local government hospitals are usually located in the city and provincial capitals. Rural people have difficulty in accessing the services of local government hospitals due to inefficiencies in transportation and communication. Only in times of emergency and serious illness are they willing to put up with the cost of going to the capital and city to take health services from local government hospitals. Most often they go to municipal and barangay health centres or undertake health care themselves in their homes.

The costs of undertaking healthcare services have been increasing due to the increasing cost of supplies and equipment, new technologies required and efficiencies in the operations of the hospitals that leads to high overhead costs.

Financing of local government hospitals pose one of the major problems in the sector. Profitability of the hospitals is very low inasmuch as they cater to the poorest members of the society and user charges are based on the capacity to pay. They rely mainly on subsidies from the local government, national government and donor assistance.

Whatever incomes the hospitals generate are not kept with the hospitals to sustain their operations. Instead these are remitted and pooled with other incomes of the local government at the end of the year. The local government allocates budget and resources for the succeeding year from its total income and the internal revenue allotment that they receive from the national government. A problem with the system is that local government views health as a low priority and as such allocates minimum resources to the sector. Local politicians prefer to use their resources mostly for infrastructure projects where there are tangible benefits that they can use as campaign material for the next election.

Local government hospitals are inadequately staffed. Local government hospitals do not provide conducive working conditions as well as competitive salary. As such, they are not able to attract highly qualified medical professionals and support staff to operate the hospitals efficiently. There is a high turnover rate and staff remaining with them are typical and inefficient government bureaucrats. The motivation is low and they take their frustrations out with the patients.

In general, there is poor organization and management of local government hospitals. Hospital administrators do not have the skills and training to plan and administer hospital operations. They do not implement information system to guide them in planning and managing the organization. The hospitals' standard and procedures are very bureaucratic hindering them from delivering proactive and efficient services to their clients. Local government hospitals image and reputation with the people are very low. The poor sectors of society go to the hospitals because they do not have any choice due to their poverty situation.

SWOT Analysis

Using the results of the analysis of the symptoms and causes of decline as well as the four-level framework, the following SWOT analysis has been arrived at:

Strengths

- Improving economic growth of the country.
- Participation of private sector and non-governmental organizations.

Weaknesses

- Insufficient and inadequate health facilities.
- Human resource imbalance.

- Weak organization and management capabilities.
- Poor planning, policy formulation and implementation of programmes.
- Lack of financing.
- Lack of people participation.
- Inaccessibility of health facilities.

Opportunities

- Improving economic growth of the country.
- Improvements in technology.
- Trade Agreements.

Threats

- Industrialization and urbanization.
- Population growth.
- Environmental degradation and depletion.

RESTRUCTURING/PRIVATIZATION STRATEGIES

In order to create a responsive, efficient, effective and affordable health care delivery system in the Philippines, the following restructuring strategies are proposed:

Strengthened Health Organization and Management

The roles and relationship of the national and local governments, private sector, non- governmental organizations, and the communities in the health sector should be clearly defined to be used as a framework for collaboration. They should perform their roles with mutual respect and cooperation, complementing and supporting each other. The government should promote and encourage collaboration and provide the needed incentives and favourable environment for the efficient and effective discharge of functions of its partners.

- The national government, through the Department of Health, should continue to fulfil its mandate of protecting and promoting the right to health and ensuring that health services is made available to the people at an affordable cost. It should be responsible for national health planning and policy making to provide directions to local government units and other partners in health care delivery. Technical assistance and critical resources should be extended to local government units to complete the adjustment process and enable them to perform their newly assumed roles. Standards, licensing and regulations should be strictly implemented by the DOH and closely monitored to ensure that the operations of the private and other sectors are within acceptable standards and beneficial to the people. It should also continue its primary task of creating awareness and consciousness among the populace and the local government units about the importance of the health sector in national development and mobilize all sectors in health development.

- Local government units should continue to be responsible for health planning and promotion at the local level, health service delivery and ensure that adequate, accessible, acceptable and affordable healthcare is made available to all its constituents. More priority and resources should be accorded to the health sector. Further, they should encourage the participation of the private sector, NGOs, and the communities in the local health development. Improving the capabilities of local executives and healthcare providers to manage and administer devolved health services should be a primary goal.
- The role of the private sector should be expanded to cover direct healthcare delivery, inputs provision such as supplies and equipment, health financing, health human resource development and other support activities such as research, project monitoring and evaluation, development of IEC materials. Their increasing participation in healthcare will have to be monitored and coordinated with the Government to ensure complementary activities as well as compliance with set standards and regulations.
- Aside from direct health service delivery to target communities or areas, the role of non-governmental organizations in health should be expanded to health human resource development, research and policy analysis.
- The key to the success of the national health movement is to allow people participation in the sector, as they are the beneficiaries of the sector. Every individual has the responsibility to ensure the family's optimum state of health, nutrition, welfare

and productivity. Health and information and education should be a major strategy of the government to empower the people with knowledge and information to adopt better health practices, demand quality health services, utilize health services, practice a healthier lifestyle, improving their living conditions and most of all take the responsibility for promoting health and preventing disease and disability. Their increased knowledge will eventually influence them to participate not only in simple health activities but also in actual planning and implementation of health care in their respective communities.

Health Facility Development

Health facilities include hospitals, city/municipal health centres and barangay health stations, clinics and laboratories and other entities where health services are provided.

Local government units should continue to manage, fund and expand local health centres and stations to ensure accessibility of health services by the majority of the population. Health services provided in the health centres are currently for free. To sustain operations, cost recovery mechanisms should be instituted by charging user fees to clients. Standard costs should be developed based on the capacity to pay by the clients.

Both private and government-owned (local or national) hospitals involve inefficiencies in their operations leading to high cost of delivery of services. Such inefficiencies could be addressed by implementing cost-reduction strategies.

The systems and procedures of hospital units should be streamlined to enable faster, more pro-active and cost-effective delivery of health services. Use of supplies and equipment should be optimized. Generic drugs that involve lesser cost should be promoted. Technologies proven effective and suitable to local conditions should be used. Expenses on sophisticated technology could be limited by achieving economies of scale through the implementation of an efficient referral system or through mergers between hospitals. To reduce labour and overhead costs, training programmes for healthcare providers and administrators shall be provided. In this way, their productivity increases and service delivery is made more efficient. Hospital information system should be designed and implemented to aid in business planning and operations of the hospitals.

The increasing cost of health services has affected the profitability and performance of private and government hospitals. To sustain hospital operations and improve profitability, cost recovery mechanisms should be instituted such as expanding services of the hospitals to cover promotive and preventive services aside from the traditional curative and rehabilitative services that they are currently focusing on. Further, private hospitals also have the option to diversify into related business such as medical schools/colleges and pharmacy. Government hospitals should be converted into government-owned and operated corporations and should be given autonomy in its operations and allowed to retain earnings for future operations.

Government hospitals are usually undercapitalized which is the main reason why they are not able to provide adequate and quality health services. To raise additional capital for these hospitals, private sector investment should be promoted to improve their facilities and operations, and raise their services to acceptable standards. To address the poor management of government facilities, management contracts may also be entered into between the private sector and the government to improve the operations of the hospital and prepare it for future privatization.

It is a known fact that private ownership provides a more conducive environment for efficiency. If the proposed restructuring strategies will be implemented and proven successful such that the viability of hospitals will be truly improved, privatization schemes may be implemented by the national and local government through private sale of shares. The Philippine Government currently has a well-working pre-qualification and bidding procedures that will work against possible corrupt practices in the privatization process. Private sale of shares is best appropriate for strategic and non-viable enterprises. While government hospitals could be transformed to viable ones, this may not reach a point that will create much public awareness and interest on the enterprise that is needed for a successful public offering at the stock market.

HealthCare Financing

The existing Medicare Programme (which is only benefiting the organized sector of the population) should be expanded into a national health insurance scheme to support healthcare expense of even the poorest families. To implement the programme, however, there is a need to raise and sustain awareness of people about the value of collective savings as a means of protecting members from the catastrophic cost of an unpredictable illness.

Private health insurance and health maintenance organizations should be encouraged to further participate and provide healthcare financing focusing on the middle and upper income class. Partnerships between the private and the government should be initiated taking into consideration mutual responsibilities, risks and rewards to all parties.

Private sector involvement in healthcare financing can also include employer financing for healthcare. With more and more labour force shifting to the manufacturing/industrial sector, employer financing for healthcare will assume increasing significance.

Conclusion and Recommendations

The Philippines is still far from achieving its goal of health for all Filipinos. Restructuring of the health sector needs to be undertaken to improve health sector management and organization, improve and further establish health facilities as well as ensure accessibility of quality health services even to the poorest sector of the society through a working and effective national health insurance system.

Health is a right of every Filipino and the Philippine Government should ensure that this right is provided by giving the necessary policy directions, implementing and monitoring compliance to regulations and standards in the health sector, and mobilizing all other partners for health development. The private sector and the non-governmental organizations are expected to share in this endeavour by providing quality and affordable direct health services.

To ensure successful restructuring of the health sector, health facilities (specifically hospitals) should also be restructured for more efficient, quality and cost-effective services. To do this, cost reduction and revenue-generating strategies are proposed to be implemented such as streamlining operations, improved management of hospitals, optimal use of resources as well as expanding services and diversifying into related businesses. Privatization options for government hospitals could be pursued at a later stage when the viability has improved in order to raise more interest for private sector participation. By privatizing the government hospitals, it is hoped that efficiency in the use of resources is achieved. Access of private health services by the poor sector of society shall be addressed by implementing the national health insurance system.

Restructuring Action Plan for Uganda Commercial Bank

The Government of Uganda decided to privatise most of its public enterprises. Those that were to be retained because of their strategic nature were to be restructured and made more efficient and effective. Public Enterprise Restructuring and Divestiture (PERD) a World Bank funded project under the Ministry of Finance and Economic Planning is charged with this responsibility. Public Industrial Enterprise Secretariat (PIES), also a World Bank funded UNIDO Cooperative is charged with the responsibility of preparing public enterprises in the manufacturing sector investment. PIES has assisted public enterprises in bringing their books of accounts up to date, setting appropriate accounting and reporting systems, organising short term courses, seminars and workshops for top management teams and Board of Directors etc.

The Government of Uganda recognised the need to undertake comprehensive reform programme of public enterprises so as to reduce financial and administrative burden upon government. There is a large number of PESs with huge financial losses and poor performance in general. The government therefore adopted the basic policy objectives which are:

(a) To reduce the direct role of government in the Uganda economy and to promote a correspondingly greater role for the private sector.

(b) To improve the efficiency and overall performance of those PES for the shorter or longer term, which will remain under government ownership, possession and control.

The government has classified PESs into five categories for the purpose of restructuring and divestiture. These classes are:

(1) Those enterprises which the government would retain 100 per cent shareholding. The total number is 14 out of which 3 are in the manufacturing sector.

(2) Enterprises where government would retain majority shareholding. They are 24 in number and 13 of them are in the manufacturing sector.

(3) Those enterprises where government would retain minority shareholding, they are 10 out of which 7 are in the manufacturing sector.

(4) Those enterprises where government would fully divest from. They are 46 and 19 are in the manufacturing sector.

(5) Those enterprises where government would consider disposing of through the sales of their assets in order to wind up their

operations as they not economically viable, are defunct and non-performing. They are 16 and 1 in the manufacturing sector and 11 are defunct.

Quite a number of enterprises have successfully been privatised using different methods. For example, Shell (U) Ltd was divested in a debt equity swap, while East African Distilleries and Lake Victoria Bottling Company were divested through outright sale of government share holding in PESs. Another good example is where government now holds 49 per cent shares in Nile Hotel and African Continental Hotels 51 per cent while under the management contract by Tahar Fourati Hotels. However, there are controversies as regards the rewarding system because the hotel was valued at 19 bn shillings while payment for five years contract requires payment of 27bn shillings.

By the end of 1995, 48 PE's had been divested. The revised projections of the privatisation process indicate that by 2010, 100 per cent target of privatisation would have been achieved especially now that there are more instruments for privatisation that are available to implement the programme including trade sales, auction and public floatations. The process of capacity building for professionals to implement this has been enhanced. There is increased awareness to both the PES and the public of the nature and benefits of the privatisation through public relations exercises, seminars and workshops.

Uganda's strong economic growth is attributed to stronger stabilization and reform efforts. For Africa, the volume of imports have drastically increased and this supports the fast rate of economic growth. However, the private capital flows to Africa has declined. The debt burden for developing countries in general is high and despite some improvement, debt and debt servicing are still of great concern especially in Sub-Saharan Africa, as debt servicing ratios are very low.

(a) Product Range and Substitutes

The world banking industry has been changing rapidly since the1970's. The industry in developing countries of the world experienced a substantial change in competitive conditions. The industry has tended to go international with the opening up of capital markets as well as diversification of operators. This has, therefore, made the global banking industry more complex in the range of services offered.

The banking industry is characterized by regulatory constraints by a growing number of non-banks as being especially attractive corporations with potential operating advantages in specific areas of activity.

A good example is the automobile companies such as General Motors, which extends leasing and credit finance business to non General Motors customers. Travel card companies like American Express offer a variety of financial services to existing account holders at little additional cost.

(b) Technology

Technology has very much affected the banking industry globally, most notably in retail banking. Thus retail banking was faced with mounting tide of paper and administrative costs. Banks have now turned to plastic cards and electronic machinery in an effort to maintain their ability to handle an increase in transaction volume while controlling costs.

Furthermore, the need to increased service especially outside working hours has led to increased use of Automated teller machines. The continued threat of fast changing technology as well as substitute products has threatened the traditional mode of banking operations universally. The emergence of e-business has opened up new avenues for the banking industry.

(c) Interest Rates

Interest rates do affect the operations of a bank substantially. Globally, when the world economy is in recession, the volume of bank transactions decrease. This is so because the lending rates increase while customers don't make much money as profit, due to low purchasing power.

Similarly in this kind of situation, the interest rates given on deposits is low and customers prefer to keep investing and trading with their cash instead of dealing with the bank.

(d) Exchange Rates

World exchange rates continue to fluctuate mainly because of increases in oil prices. The past year has witnessed a sharp price movement in world commodity markets but with more erratic movements in oil prices.

Prices of non-oil raw materials have risen significantly with particularly high price hikes in a few commodities like coffee. This has built up inflationary pressures. For example in Japan, economic activity was slow under the influence of the strong Yen and the uncertainties resulting from mounting problems in the financial sector.

When exchange rates keep fluctuating, the bank business is affected and as such most business people prefer to do barter trade instead of dealing in cash.

(e) Strategic Alliances

Strategic alliances are on the increase in the world business today. There are quite a number of advantages offered and as such most banks like other industries have gone into strategic alliances in order to increase their competitive advantage. Factors like reducing costs, gaining experience, minimising risks, entering new markets, competition, are some of the many reasons for strategic alliances. Big companies like Boeing has formed an alliance with Douglas Macdonel and many others which have been successful.

(f) Debt

The debt burden for developing countries in general declined slightly in 2014 compared to the previous year. The ratio of external debt to GDP reduced from 32 per cent of GDP to about 30.8 per cent in 2014. However, in Sub-Saharan Africa, despite some improvement, debt and debt service are still a cause of concern.

(g) World Commodity Markets

Prices of all major categories of primary commodities continue to rise in US dollar terms although most of the increases reflect weaknesses of the US currency. In real terms, commodity prices are falling. In normal terms, prices of non fuel prices continue to increase. According to IMF World Economic report, commodity prices are expected to decline in US dollar terms and this is likely to put pressure on the current account balance of those countries whose major source of foreign exchange is the export of primary commodities.

(h) Regional Economic Cooperation

Significant progress has been made towards cross border initiative. Also significant progress has been made toward tariff harmonization to facilitate intra regional trade. The developments and evolution of world economy has underlined the importance of this. Good examples are NAFTA,

ASEAN, EU and the East African Community. These initiatives are of great importance because they combine the dismantling of barriers to the cross border movement of goods, persons and capital between countries with the promotion of overall liberalization.

The Macro-National Environment .

(a) The Adjustment Effort

In developing its economic recovery programme, the government has recognised the need to undertake a comprehensive reform of the public enterprises in Uganda with a view to reducing the financial and administrative burden upon government on account of—

(i) The large number of public enterprises.
(ii) The financial losses and poor performance in general.

The principal objectives of Economic recovery programmes have been economic stabilization and growth, restoring internal financial stability and achieving lower inflation, reducing imbalances in the external accounts, particularly through increases in the volume and diversity of exports. This programme has been supported by two economic recovery credits and a structural adjustment credit from IDA, structural adjustment credit from IMF and other assistance from both multilateral and bilateral donors.

(b) Exchange Rates

There are strong pressures arising from a large inflow of coffee that threaten the export sector. Coffee is the main foreign exchange earner of Uganda. The inter bank rates as well as the average bureau rates continue to depreciate. The strength of the Uganda shilling is mainly attributed to the following factors:

(a) The growing confidence in the Uganda shilling as a store of value as inflation continues to be maintained at low levels.
(b) The large inflow of private transfers.
(c) The strong performance of the coffee receipts arising out of increased export volumes despite the sharp drop in world prices.

This has positively affected the nature of the banking industry in Uganda.

The government has liberalised the foreign exchange and this has given rise to a foreign exchange bureau market along side the traditional commercial banking. The exchange rate of the Uganda shilling is therefore determined by market forces and has made the currency more convertible.

(c) Fiscal and Credit Policies

Overall, the main goal of economic recovery programme has been to reduce the level of inflation pressure arising from excessive monetary expansion.

However, the government continues to maintain a strict control over its fiscal policy. With the level of inflation already under control, Uganda is able to lend comfortably with stable interest rates.

The Bank of Uganda has continued to purse a prudent monitory policy with a tight fiscal policy.

(d) Public Finance

Government expenditure goes towards financing of the Deposit Insurance Fund, Non-performing assets recovery trust and Capital Markets Authority.

The revenues collected have continued to increase due to the efficiency of The Uganda Revenue Authority, while non-tax revenue is derived from fees and licenses, national lottery and others.

Uganda's main export is coffee and the recent coffee boom, has increased peoples incomes and as a result the import sector has grown tremendously.

Control in government expenditure has resulted in low inflation rates and a stable exchange rate despite the fact that Uganda still has a weak financial sector.

(e) Export-Import Liberalization

The import and export procedures in Uganda have been liberalised. This was done by replacing licensing by an automatic certificate system. Goods are classified under negative and positive lists. Those on specified negative lists are the ones whose import and export is prohibited by environmental, diplomatic, international conventions or other reasons. Any good that does not appear on the negative list can be imported by the holder of the certificate. This has tremendously increased the import and export business in Uganda Commercial Bank as it has been highly involved in international transfer of funds, like opening up letters of credit, telegraphic transfers to mention a few.

The number of items for export and import has increased substantially over the last few years.

(f) Internal Regulations and Incentives

Commercial banking is regulated by the financial institutions statute 1993 and the Bank of Uganda policy regulations. The Bank of Uganda has however announced licensing of new banks pending restructuring of the weak institutions. The Bank of Uganda has stated its willingness to approve financial institutions which promote new products like mortgage finance, merchant banking and leasing finance. This is, therefore, anticipated to affect UCB due to the fact that it still offers mainly traditional banking services due to lack of capital (under capitalization). Bank of Uganda will also approve well-known multinational banks despite the moratorium. Incentives offered to these investors include a tax holiday of 3-6 years depending on the level of investment. This tax holiday covers the corporation tax, tax on dividends as well as the withholding tax. However, the certificate does not provide an exemption on VAT.

(g) Liberalisation or Deregulation

The removal of market entry restrictions is intended to increase the role of competition. The NRM government has scored highly in this and has allowed the private sector to complete side by side with the government in activities like banking, operation of forex bureau, export of coffee to mention but a few.

(h) The External Sector

The country's balance of payments has continued to improve with an overall surplus of $170 million. As a result of this, Uganda's foreign exchange reserves increased and this has helped in the management of foreign debt. The increase in strength of balance of payments comes from both increased inflow of foreign exchange for investment and export of coffee together with other non-traditional crops. There is an increase in imports of goods and services but the country's trade deficit continues to widen.

The diversification of exports has been in line with the government's policy of liberalization as well as abolition of export taxes. Uganda's exports are mainly agricultural products.

(i) Interest Rate Policy

The Bank of Uganda has recently liberalised the interest rates and allowed commercial banks to fix own interest rates for both deposits and lending. The Bank of Uganda only announces indicative interest rates based on treasury bills auction market.

(j) Protection of State owned Enterprises.

The Government of Uganda protects State owned enterprises more especially against competition.

Uganda Commercial Bank (UCB) is a state owned enterprise and it is the biggest commercial bank with branches spread all over the country. The bank has really enjoyed state protection in a way that all government parastatals, ministries deal with UCB. The state has at the same time continued to recapitalise it due to huge outstanding loans now classified as non-performing assets.

(k) Enterprise Autonomy

Although UCB is supposed to be an autonomous enterprise, in real sense it is not. Government has continued to influence some of the decisions like areas of investment and also the granting of loans.

Most of the loans have been issued without collateral but purely on government orders which have turned out to be bad ones. Investing in non viable projects on government orders has also contributed to huge financial losses incurred by the bank. Most of these investments are either based on political grounds or even mere social justification.

(l) Infrastructure

Uganda faces a lot of challenges, which require special attention, as infrastructure remains inadequate. Posts and Telecommunications and other forms of the infrastructure need expansion in order to foster both foreign and local investment in productive capacities. Rural areas which account for 50 per cent of economic activity require much investment particularly feeder roads. Infrastructure investment is typically government's responsibility.

The Meso Environment

The Ugandan Meso environment consists of very important sectors, which compose the whole economy. These consist of Agricultural, Manufacturing, the financial sector, energy, transport and communication, mining, tourism, education and health.

(a) Agricultural Sector

The agriculture sector is a very important one because it is the backbone of Uganda's economy. About 90 per cent of the population of Uganda lives in rural areas where agriculture is the main economic activity, although it is mainly on a subsistence level. Agriculture is the main contributing factor to GDP and coffee is the main export. The liberalization of the coffee industry in 1990 has brought about further changes in the sector. The Kampala coffee retention plan agreed upon by coffee producing countries in October 1993 has helped to improve coffee prices. There has been improvement in the quality of coffee exported as a result of better surveillance during export certification, intensive extension services, good crop husbandry, and regular factory visits and good weather.

Other cash crops include Tea, Cotton, Tobacco, Vanilla, Simsim, Banana's and fruits.

The Cotton industry is now fully liberalised and has greatly influenced the local cotton business as cash transactions gain prominence. The availability of a ready market has restored farmers' confidence and many ginneries have extended credit to farmers for purchase of inputs and payment for labour expenses.

(b) Manufacturing Sector

The Uganda manufacturing sector has continued to grow over the years. This growth is attributed to the macro economic stability and economic liberalization which have been conductive for investment. The investment climate was further made favourable by a significant reduction in corporate tax rates in addition to the incentives provided under the Uganda investment code. Government has taken further measures in privatizing most of its major manufacturing firms. The main manufacturing firms include food processing, drinks and tobacco, leather and footwear, textile and clothing. Other products include cement, chemicals and selected prototype industrial equipments.

(c) Mining Sector

The countries minerals include, gold, tin, tungsten, salt, beryllium and others in small deposits which include limestone, clay and iron ore. The government has commissioned a number of projects for mining.

Financial Sector

The financial system in Uganda consists of the Bank of Uganda which is the Central Bank, 15 Commercial Banks, 8 Non-bank financial institutions, 12 Insurance companies, 10 Building societies, a post office savings bank, a few pension funds, 2 Investment companies and a Cooperative Savings and Credit Union.

The Commercial Banks dominate the financial sector, accounting for over 90 per cent of the assets and therefore have a strong monetary basis for the financial transactions.

The Commercial Bank sub-sector include Uganda Commercial Bank (UCB), The Co-operative Bank (CB), five joint venture foreign managed banks which are Barclays Bank (U) Ltd, Bank of Baroda, Stanbic, Standard Chartered and Tropical Bank. There are also eight Private banks, which are Gold Trust Bank, Nile Bank, Sembule, Greenland, Orient, Centenary Development Bank, International Credit Bank Ltd and Kigezi Bank of Commerce.

The development Financial Institutions include Uganda Development Bank, East African Development Bank, The Development Finance Company of Uganda Ltd. Other principal non-bank financial institutions are Diamond Trust Uganda Ltd, Housing Finance Company of Uganda, Mercantile Credit Bank, Insurance Companies as well Co-operative Credit Unions.

Uganda Commercial Bank has got the largest network spread all over the country. Private and forcign banks are mostly located and concentrated in the metropolitan areas of Kampala city.

From the above, it is clear that there is a high concentration of the banking system in terms of volume of business operations and coverage mainly in Kampala and other urban centres.

(1) *Overall performance of the financial sector*: During the 1970's, the size and diversity of the sector declined with the exodus of expatriates and increased control of the banking sector by the government. The financial intermediation during this period was limited mainly to public sector operations. Thus there has been no development of capital markets or merchants banks. The inter bank money market is also absent and most of the financial transactions in the economy have since been conducted using a few monetary instruments such as cash, demand deposits and overdrafts. Demand deposit dominates the deposit structure of all the major commercial banks.

(2) *Financial Liberalisation and Sector Reform*: The Ugandan financial sector has been constrained by a number of institutional and operational problems evolving for quite a number of years.

The World Bank financial sector review identified a number of key issues, which are affecting the banking system in the country.

(a) *Government ownership and control*: UCB which is the largest Commercial Bank in the country is fully owned by the government. The Co-operative Bank though owned by the Co-operative movement also depends on the government support. In case of foreign banks Except Standard Bank, government controls 49 per cent of the total shares. Thus the Government is a major player in the banking sector.

(b) *Lack of Competition and Efficiency*: Lack of competition has reduced incentives to minimise costs and improve efficiency which contribute to high financial intermediation costs. Only foreign banks and private banks at present operate profitably.

(c) *Weaknesses in the authority and capacity of the Central Bank*: The Central Bank does not effectively design, implement and enforce monetary policy, banking supervision and other policies. There has also been inadequate prudential regulation and this has affected the depth of the financial system.

(d) *Financial distress in banks*: The factors which are a distress to the financial sector in Uganda are lack of public confidence in the overall financial system, short maturity and instability of deposits, inadequacy of capital as most of the banks are undercapitalized and inflationary erosion of the capital base, inadequacy of the clearing system and doubtful debts.

The Micro Environment

(a) Introduction to UCB

Uganda Commercial Bank was established by the act of parliament in 1965. By this act, the bank took over all the assets, liabilities, staff and contracts of Uganda credit and savings with a view of making it a full-fledged commercial bank owned by the state.

The bank is fully owned by the government of the Republic of Uganda and operates under the ministry of finance, planning and economic planning. The administration of the bank is entrusted to the board of directors with its chairman being the Managing Director appointed by the president, while the board of directors is mostly members of parliament appointed by the minister of finance.

As any financial intermediary, the bank was established to provide banking services and make profit. As a state bank, the mission is to spear head national development efforts by addressing the task of resource mobilization and optimizing resource allocation for national development. In addition, the bank is expected to facilitate the execution of public policies. Thus for over the years, the mission has been to reach all parts of the country, ensure expansion, diversification and automation for improved efficiency and effectiveness

The major objectives of the bank from its inception are:

(1) Mobilisation of deposits.
(2) High quality lending and credit administration.
(3) Marketing of bank services.
(4) Budgetary control.

However, the major strategies, goals and objectives at the moment are:

(1) Increased return on investment and profit maximization.
(2) Enhancing deposit mobilization through improved customer service and branch expansion with emphasis on rural areas.

(3) Expansion and diversification of lending activities.
(4) Mobilization of both foreign and local resources for development finance.
(5) Improved organizational effectiveness.
(6) Staff development and improved staff welfare.

All the functional groups of the bank are set to achieve these set objectives, goals and strategies in light of the corporate mission.

(b) Products

The products and services offered by the bank include mobilization of funds, that is deposits from customers, credit loan facilities to customers, maintaining different categories of accounts such as current accounts, savings accounts, fixed deposit accounts, education savings scheme accounts. Other services offered include trust services, which offer executorship and administration of estates, clearing of bank instruments on behalf of customers, as well as transfer of funds.

The major markets of the bank include all government ministries and parastatals for example, The Uganda Revenue Authority, Civil Aviation Authority, Oil companies to mention but a few. Besides, a big part of the market is composed of rural farmers who constitute 90 per cent of Uganda's population with agriculture being the main source of income. UCB had a market share of about 50 per cent for the last few years but of recent it has dropped to 40 per cent of the total banking industry in Uganda.

Uganda Commercial Bank's (UCB's) main competitors include Uganda Co-operative Bank, which is also owned by the government, other foreign banks, which include mainly Barclays Bank, Standard Chartered Bank, Stanbic Bank, Cairo International Bank and many privately, owned banks by indigenous Ugandans.

(c) Sales

The bank's sales organization is obviously set up in such a manner that it is organized according to responsibility centres. This is typical of service organizations more especially banks where cost centres and profit centres have to be distinguished. However, as regards the bank, one can say that sales are organized through the number of branches that are spread countrywide.

UCB has a branch network of 83 branches. It has a kind of divisionalised form of set up geographically. The sales centres match expenses with revenues and are expected to make profit at the end of the day following the budget. This is not normally the case as most branches are rural based and there isn't much economic activity there. In this case therefore, such branches incur only high operating costs without making any profit.

The marketing within the bank is mainly done through the Public relations department which is based at head office and does not have branches elsewhere. The bank has got radio programmes over weekends.

(d) Location

Branches are widely spread and as such one can say that the location has no specific pattern. This is mainly due to government policies that were clearly stipulated right at inception of UCB. Its main purpose was to spear head development by bringing services to rural areas, which is the base of Uganda's economy. The location of branches is not according to proximity to either inputs or any outputs in respect to banking services. All parts of the country have at least a UCB branch and that is why in Uganda, when you talk of commercial bank people think it is UCB, It is a household name.

However, the infrastructure is not well developed like in most developing countries more especially the road networks as well as telecommunication systems.

(e) Costs

General and administrative costs in UCB are very high. Operating costs are very high and this has brought about hiking of interest rates for lending. The bank tries to overcome these costs by paying low rates on deposits while at the same time, increasing the lending rates. The bank is insolvent mainly due to undercapitalisation on non-performing loan portfolio. Intermediation costs are very high even by developing countries standards. It is estimated that head office expenses account for 60 per cent of total operating costs and the bank has a very low asset/staff ratio (shs.19.9m per staff). This is compounded by a large number of loss making branches, a whole range of non-banking activities and an oversize of head office.

(f) Personnel

The bank's personnel are such that it has got a large number of employees in relation to other banks in the country. It employs more than 50 per cent of the total workers within the industry.

The bank has got both semi-skilled and skilled personnel. The semi-skilled group include those subordinate staff who are employed as cleaners, messengers as well as banking assistants. The skilled level consists of the rest of the levels right from Trainee banking officers to Executive General Managers. These are University graduates as well as those holding other qualifications like ACCA, CIMA, CPA to mention but a few. There is emphasis on early retirement for staff aged between 50 years and the mandatory retirement age of 55.

The staff turnover is comparatively high compared to the nature of available jobs in Uganda. The middle management level is mainly affected due to low motivation and as such staff continue to go away in search of greener pastures.

(g) Management

The banks administration is entrusted to the board of directors with the five levels of management. The Chairman of the board until 2005 had been The Managing Director as it is a political post and the appointment is made by The President. He takes final decisions in consultation with The Minister of Finance. The board of directors are apparently members of parliament appointed by the Minister of Finance.

There are seven divisions and each division is headed by an Executive General Manager. The General Manager carries out divisional functions in co-ordination Assistant General Manager.

The divisions are as follows: Administration, Branch Banking, Corporate Banking, Credit and Collections, Financial Services, International Banking as well as Inspection and Audit. There are 15 main staff ranks ranging from Executive General Manager to Banking Assistant.

Although there is decentralization, at unit level, all major decisions are taken up by head office and therefore there is a problem of red tape due to bureaucratic nature of the organization. Rewards and punishment are prescribed in a code of conduct and human resource manuals. Rewards are normally in form of promotions and punishments range from warning letters to dismissals or even imprisonment where there are serious frauds.

Although there is performance appraisal, this is not normally the basis of promotions and as such staff morale is very low.

The bank used to conduct bank courses like basic banking, advanced banking as well as credit analysis together with basic resource management. However, of late these have stopped due to lack of funds and the manpower development centre now has less activity.

The banks decision-making process is done by the strategic apex at head office while branch managers have autonomy, although major decisions are made after consultation with the head office.

(h) Financial Performance

UCB like most financial institutions in Uganda has been greatly hit by the liquidity problem. The main reasons that brought about this has been due to huge losses made as a result of bad debts characterized as non-performing assets. At the same time this has brought about the dilemma of capital inadequacy.

Losses continue to increase due to high operating costs. However, the government has continued to inject more money. With such a magnitude of capital deficiency and with little earnings the bank has not been able to put in place a good technological system like the Automatic Teller Machines (ATM), credit cards as well as swift code systems for quick transfer of money.

From the above Mega, Macro, Meso and Micro environments affecting the operations of Uganda Commercial Bank, one can derive the strengths, weaknesses, opportunities and threats.

Strengths

(a) Market Share

As a government bank put up to spear head economic development, UCB has managed to acquire the biggest market share since it is spread all over the country. However, this has declined because it used to be above 50 per cent but for over the last few years, it has declined to about 40 per cent.

(b) Range of Products

UCB has got a range of products that it can offer to its customers, unlike most banks in Uganda which are mainly in retail banking. The bank offers many development schemes for the alleviation of poverty and as such has become a household name in Uganda. The large branch network spread all over the country is a competitive advantage as it takes services nearer to the majority of its customers.

(c) Competition

Being an indigenous bank, UCB is at a great advantage more especially over foreign banks in a way that most natives shy away from these other banks and at the same time has got the monopoly of the government. All government parastatals, Ministries and departments bank with UCB.

(d) Government Support

Being a government parastatal, UCB has been fully supported more especially as regards recapitalisation. As already seen the bank's financial position is not healthy at all. In this regard therefore, the government continues to support the bank more especially where working capital is concerned and this is a very strong source of funding. Otherwise it has really reached the verge of collapsc.

(e) Excellent Facilities

The bank has had at least excellent buildings where it conducts its business. This is far much better compared to other banks more especially in towns and at least this has attracted customers to some extent.

Weaknesses

(a) Government Interference

The government continues to interfere in the operations of the bank. This is clearly amplified by the way it takes sensitive decisions more especially in investment. The bank is supposed to be autonomous, like in granting of loans, investment and in other areas. However, the government for example has always instructed the bank to open up branches in very remote areas of the country that lack infrastructure as well as economic activities simply for political reasons. All these branches have failed due to lack of business and continue to make losses. More to that, most loans have been issued on political grounds without collateral and have never been repaid. At the moment, the total bad loans amount to about 4 billion Uganda shillings. These have been classified as non-performing assets. Another good example is where the rural farmers scheme was introduced. This is a kind of credit facility whereby farmers are given credit in form of agricultural inputs. These inputs are given without collateral and at the same time climate cannot be predicted. In this case, most farmers have failed to reap expected yields and pay off loans.

(b) Mission

Uganda Commercial Bank's (UCB's) mission is too broad and really very conflicting. As in the beginning the mission was to spearhead development and at the same time, like all financial institutions has to make profit. It is in this respect that one can say that the mission, objectives as well as strategies are conflicting and, therefore, there has been lack of focus. UCB is supposed to operate under the Ministry of Finance but with a high degree of autonomy. The bank is supposed also to fulfil the expectations of all its stakeholders but this has not been focused in relation to the mission of the organization. This is a great weakness in that it has for a long time lacked direction.

(c) Credit Management

The major weakness that UCB has faced is bad credit management as well as administration. This has brought about its downfall. Credit management in UCB has been very much subject to social, economic as well as technological changes. The evaluation of an individual applicant's ability to repay the loan is not done effectively besides the implementation and monitoring processes. What is being done in UCB is the traditional financial analysis.

(d) Organisation Set-Up

The bank's organization set-up is such that it has many levels of hierarchy. This is a weakness in that there is much red tape in respect to decision-making. Take for instance a branch, it takes weeks to get a feed back from head office to many decisions in respect to customers and in such a manner, the bank has lost many of its customers to competitors.

The other reason is the empowerment of employees. Staff is not involved in most of the decision taken and this demoralizes as most of them don't feel as if they are part of the system. On the whole, one can therefore say that staff has no dynamism that is essential for today's banking sector.

(e) Reward System

The reward system within UCB is not so attractive and adequate enough. That is why there is a high turnover especially with the middle management level. This level is composed of staff that has skills and can be employed easily by other organizations.

(f) Appointment of Top Executives

One can categorically state that the appointments of UCB's top executives has not been properly done. The Chairman/MD is appointed by the government of the day. Members of the board are also politicians who are full time engaged in other pressing state duties. Most of these board members have no experience in banking and therefore policies set have not been in line with the desired objectives.

(g) Inadequate Training

There is need for continuous training but unfortunately this has not been the case with UCB. As mentioned earlier, when the bank started making losses, the manpower development centre became inactive due to lack of operating funds. However, most of UCB's competitors are actively training their staff, especially the foreign banks with a high level of innovations. It is very essential for any organization to have a continuous learning process which is not the case with UCB.

(h) Inadequate Information Technology

UCB does not have adequate information technology; this is what is important for an organization to add value to its products for its customers. Most customers have always complained of delays in bank services as well the general quality of the whole system. Due to the fact that the bank lacks funds, very few branches have been computerized and the manual workload is still very high. The bank does not have automatic teller machines, swift code transfers to mention but a few.

(i) Lack of Customer Focus

Due to the fact that the bank has all the time been supported by the government, there have been customers exclusively for only UCB and not any other bank. As such there has been lack of customer focus as a way of competing. The interest rates charged on lending are high while those on deposits are low in order to cover the high operating costs. With the recent government policies on interest rates, other banks have an advantage as they charge low rates than UCB.

(j) Delay in Returns

Due to a high branch network, there is late compilation of returns and, therefore, delays in preparation of financial statements. Most of the rural branches lack the logistics and therefore delay in submitting their returns to head office. This has affected the daily operations more especially where budgeting is concerned as no proper budgeting can be done without knowing the actual performance.

Opportunities

(a) Rapid Technological Change

This is an opportunity in a way that it has eased work in financial institutions. It has reduced the volume of work with less costs more especially in retail banking. It has also helped in delivering customer services within the few computerized branches in the required manner.

(b) Liberalisation

Through liberalization of imports and exports, the volume of trade in Uganda has increased so much so that there have been substantial increases of foreign transactions in financial institutions mainly through opening up of letters of credit and telegraphic transfers of money. Through this liberalization of the economy the bank is likely to gain access to low cost capital especially through foreign investors.

(c) Rate of Growth of the Economy

With Uganda's rate of growth at 8.5 per cent, there is a promising growth in financial institutions.

(d) Economic and Political Stability

Uganda is a country that is at the moment enjoying economic stability due to the successful economic reforms that have taken place, at the same time the political stability ushered in by the National Resistance Movement.

With these reasons coupled together, The Uganda Investment Authority has been able to attract quite a number of substantial investors both foreign and local. This has created a changing dynamic environment for the banking industry. Uganda is the 15th fastest growing economy in the world.

(e) Educated Population

Uganda is one of the countries that can at the moment boast of an educated population. This has increased awareness to the people of the need for banking services, and has therefore increased UCB's business. As already mentioned above, UCB is a bank that is widely spread within the country and has therefore become a household name in Uganda.

(f) Government Support

Being a government parastatal, UCB has continued to enjoy all the benefits from government especially in acquiring big customers. All the foreign aid and grants to the government for most of the structural adjustment projects is channeled through UCB. A good example is the PERD which operates a very big account sponsored by the World Bank. At the same time all the proceeds from sale of government parastatals are channeled through UCB.

As stated already, all Government Ministries Bank with UCB. More to government support, is the issue of recapitalisation. As the bank continues to make losses, the government also continues to recapitalise so as to keep the bank operational.

(g) Regional Co-operation

Uganda enjoys good relationship with its neighbours and therefore being located in the heart of Africa, it has become a member of many regional bodies. The defunct East African community was revived in 1994 and this is co-operation between the three East African states of Uganda, Kenya and Tanzania.

The COMESA/PTA include Eastern, Central as well as Southern African countries which are 22 in number. These provide good market opportunities for a wide range of agricultural produce from Uganda. Market entry regulations are less demanding.

Threats

(a) Competition

As already seen from above, there is a very big threat in respect to banking competition in the Uganda banking industry. First of all, many banks have come up and obviously the level of UCB's customers has dropped. The market share has tremendously gone down from 50 per cent to 40 per cent. Big threats come from foreign banks like Standard Chartered, Stanbic as well as Barclays Bank. This is mainly due to the fact that they have the expertise and new technology as well as enough operating capital.

There are also threats coming up from banks owned by the indigenous Ugandans. A good example is The Greenland Bank which has become very successful within a short period of time. It operates seven days of the week and at the same time closes very late at around 9 p.m. in the night mainly receiving deposits from businesses which close late. Greenland Bank has expanded to other countries in the neighbourhood like Kenya and Tanzania and is doing very well.

There is also competition from other non-bank financial institutions coming up like the housing finances, which offer housing loans to the population on a long-term basis like the Development finance company of Uganda ltd.

(b) Future Plans for Privatisation

Like all government parastatals, UCB has also got to be privatised considering the fact that it is continuously making losses. The staff reduction exercises have already been implemented and most staff have been laid off in order to reduce operating costs. This has created an atmosphere of punic as well as less trust in customers as they wonder who the next owner will be. Staff have become demoralized and are engaged in malpractices of frauds and forgery.

(c) Fluctuation in Dollar Rates

Like other businesses, the fluctuation in the dollar rate continue to affect the banking business as this automatically affects the levels of businesses within the country. As levels of Imports and Exports fall. banking business is also affected.

(d) Technological Changes

Besides being an advantage, the level of technological development can at the same time be a disadvantage in the operations of the bank. This is because as mentioned, the bank does not have enough resources for keeping pace with the rapid technological development. This is a great threat that is inevitable as regards the operations of a banking organization.

(e) Macro Economic Pressures

There is a threat of macro economic pressures emanating from the economic situation within the country. The government has embarked on an economic recovery programme and this to some extent has affected the operations of the bank.

The Central Bank's tight mcnetary policies like that of reducing the interest rate continue to conflict with the operating costs of the bank.

(f) Loosing Government Support

There is a likelihood of loosing government support as long as the bank continues to make losses. In the long run, supporting bodies like the World Bank will put pressure on government to stop supporting some of these organizations that are not economically viable. After all, these funds can be invested in other better productive areas within the country's economy.

Causes and Symptoms of Decline

Causes

(a) Poor Management

Uganda Commercial Bank (UCB) has greatly suffered from lack of better management. This has been the case where there has been a one-man rule. The posts of Chairman to the board as well as Managing Director has all along been entrusted to just a single person. In this case therefore, it is as if the bank is ruled by just one person since he is only answerable to the Minister but still with a high degree of autonomy. This means that for quite a long time, there has been no checks on the CEO's operations.

The ineffective board of directors have brought about poor management of the bank. As already indicated, these are inexperienced politicians who have continued to set conflicting policies and at the same time are not all the time readily available to check on the operations of the bank. There has been lack of management depth as there hasn't been any proper strategic thinking. The fact that the bank does not have a clear stated mission statement signifies that there is no clear vision that is supposed to set direction to the organization. And as such, there has been slow decision-making bearing in mind the many levels of management.

(b) Inadequate Financial Control

There are many loopholes within the financial control system of the bank.

A good example is where the top management have given themselves loans amounting to huge sums of money and yet payment is so small and poor in terms of instalments. Most of these loans will never be paid because the money has been used to purchase luxurious cars and build huge mansions.

Another way where the bank has been loosing money is because of bank frauds and forgeries. This has been mainly done by the bank staff that has not got any incentive.

Costs also are not carefully controlled and have been escalating. Most times, expenses have exceeded budgets. In UCB, there is no cash flow forecasting since the trend is unpredictable. The costing system in the bank is mainly concerned with charges of fees, interest rates etc. The budgetary control is there but it is not very effective. The three systems do exist in the bank but they are not integrated with the management information systems. Another good example of inadequate financial control is where the expenditures have continued to exceed the income causing losses.

(c) Competition

Competition in Uganda's banking industry has increased. This is due to the fact with Uganda's policy of encouraging investors both foreign and domestic, many banks as well as non-banking financial institutions have opened up in offering a wide range of services. Most of these services are of high quality and at low cost. Some of these institutions have highly developed financial management which enables them to no longer base themselves on narrow bank customer relations.

(d) Inability to Collect Credit

The most significant indigenous factor of the bank's decline is the continued inability to collect credit and interest thereon.

(e) Lack of Marketing

The Bank's marketing system is so poor. There is only the public relations department that is charged with this and its performance is below standard. This department does not even have any other branch. Advertising is only done on the radio and only once a week.

(f) Poorly Motivated Workforce

The inadequate reward system has brought about staff being demoralized. Staff work without any interest or their organization at heart and this causes lack of customer focus. This is a great problem in UCB as it has brought about loss of many customers due to poor handling. Poor motivated staff have also become involved in frauds and forgeries.

(g) Lack of Market Segmentation

The bank has got a wide range of services offered. However, all of them are not very sufficiently offered. This is a problem in that it has failed to satisfy any particular segment or even create a market niche. There could have been some kind of market segmentation.

Symptoms of Decline

(a) Decreasing Profitability

The bank's profitability continues to decrease year after year.

(b) Decrease in Deposits

In a bank when deposits start decreasing it means that there is loss of business. The trend in UCB's deposits has continued to go down.

(c) Increase in Debt

UCB's reserve account with the central bank is ever withdrawn due to lack of working capital for over a number of years. This becomes very acute during the peak seasons when almost all the customers are withdrawing cash. The account becomes more overdrawn and in a service industry, this would signify an increase in debt.

(d) Decrease in Liquidity

All the above reasons in the bank would definitely mean a decrease in liquidity. The current ratio as for the financial year 2010 was 0.80. This is a very low situation when compared to other profitable organizations that are doing well. The main cause has been poor loan recovery, high operating costs and failure of earning interest on investments.

(e) Dividend Policy

Due to the fact that UCB has not been making any profits, it has therefore, not been able to declare dividends to the treasury for a period of time.

(f) Management Turnover

There is a high turnover especially among the middle management level that possess the expertise.

(g) Declining Market Share

The decline in market share can be attributed to loss of customers and at the same time to stiff competition.

(h) Lack of Strategic Planning

The mission, objectives as already seen are very conflicting, therefore, there has been lack of strategic planning.

Prediction of Enterprise Failure

A comprehensive quantitative indicator used to predict failure is the Altiman Z-score. It is based on a weighted sum of financial ratios. The Z-score model has three general outcomes like bankruptcy, unlikely bankruptcy and gray area. It is about 90 per cent accurate in forecasting business failure one year in the future and 80 per cent accurate in forecasting it two years in the future.

Score	probability of failure.
1.8 or less	very high.
1.81- 2.7	high.
2.8 – 2.9	possible
3.0 or greater	not likely

UCB's Z-score.

$$Z = 1.2\,X_1 + 1.4X_2 + 3.3X_3 + 0.6X_4 + 1.0X_5.$$

where

Z = Index.
X_1 = Working Capital/Total Assets.
X_2 = Retained Earnings/Total Assets.
X_3 = Earnings Before Interest and Tax/Total Assets.
X_4 = Market Value of Equity and Preferred Stock/Total Liabilities.
X_5 = Sales/Total Assets.

Liabilities

X_1 = WC/TA
= (CA–CL)/TA
= (117,915 M –203,163 M)/146,558 M
= –85,248M/146,558 M
= –0.582M.
X_2 = –123,287M/146,558M
= –0.841M.
X_3 = –2,723M/146,558M = –0.019M.
X_4 = 0.
X_5 = 11,913M + 9,744M + 2,029M/146,558M
= 0.162M

$$Z = 1.2\,(-0.582) + 1.4\,(-0.841) + 3.3\,(-0.019) + 0.6\,(0) + 1.0\,(0.162)$$
$$= -0.6984 - 101774 - 0.0627 + 0 + 0.0162.$$
$$= -1.7765$$

The bank situation is very alarming, as the Z-score is negative.

(i) Generic Strategy

The bank can adopt a product identitity strategy. In a service organization it can be achieved by merely creating a good image through customer services and providing a high back up for quality customer service. UCB can recognize its corporate customers, offer special services like collecting deposits from business premises.

Restructuring Strategies

(a) Change Top Management

The Top Management of the Bank is to be changed in order to have a full turnaround of the organization. Most of the Top Management have worked for quite a number of years, are only familiar with the traditional banking and have gone to the top levels through experience. The banking they practice is that of the 70's whereas, the banking industry is a fast changing one. In this respect, Top Management has to be changed so as to allow in new and well-qualified top managers who possess the expertise and at the same time have a clear vision of the organization.

(b) Asset Reduction Strategy

Reduction of assets will mean selling those assets that are not productive. However, since there is no way branches which are making losses can be divested individually, the best way will be to close them and sell off all the buildings in rural areas that these branches have been operating from. The premises of the bank that are rented out should strictly be on commercialized basis and payments done promptly.

The bank has got a lot of vehicles which most of them are being misused more especially by the top management. This is simply because the maintenance costs are high. Still on the issue of vehicles, the bank can create a pool so as to avail transport according to the needs, and also to closely monitor the expenses on fuel, repairs and maintenance. The bank policy should also be clear as to who qualifies for transport in order to avoid conflicts and misuse of these vehicles.

Typewriters, old counting machines also have to be sold off so that at least the bank earns some revenue from them.

In its bid to reduce assets, the bank must reduce its debtors and not to keep on lending when the deposit lending ratio is high as this reduces the working capital.

(c) Revenue Generation Strategy

The bank should increase its collection on commission and fees, as there is a big short fall between the actual and the budgeted. New areas such as consultancy should be critically analyzed and whenever possible carried out. Consultancy can be given in areas of training, budgeting, costing, pricing, credit control, cash flow, stock control as well as management and financial accounting. Other areas like the safe custody still lacks publicity for the public to appreciate their purpose. Otherwise, the earning is still very low. Foreign exchange dealings are among the most profitable avenues the bank can invest in.

Improvement of credit pricing is very essential so that at least the interest charged is able to cover all the costs.

The bank can at the same time charge library fees. The manpower development centre has got a good library which is able to attract many people from outside. In this case, a fee could be levied on library use and opened to whoever wishes to utilize it irrespective of whether he is staff or not.

The bank can also consider selling the economic publications published by the research division. Advertising in the publication can also be considered. Besides it can also improve on the quality of publications.

More to increasing revenue, the bank can intensify wooing nationals living abroad to remit their funds through the bank. The bank can either invest it in projects instructed by the remitters or offer a good return on them and use it in other investments. On both, the bank will be able to earn commission.

(d) Install Control Systems

The bank has to install a good control system as a turnaround strategy. There has to be a system in terms of cash flow management and all responsibility centres will have to submit returns especially as regards expenses every week. Costs will have to be controlled as well as ensuring good working capital management. Emphasis will have to be put on profit margins more especially with branches, which are doing retail banking as well as forex bureaux.

(e) Improve Marketing Efficiency

Marketing within the bank will have to be improved more especially now that the competition is becoming very stiff. A lot of awareness to customers has got to be emphasized as well as explaining the services offered in detail. More ways of promotion apart from the radio will have to be implemented. Use of the television, magazines, social media promoting some sports are some of the ways that the bank can use to improve the marketing efficiency.

Also in its bid to improve efficiency, the bank will have to change prices more especially the fees that are charged, also the interest rates have to be revised.

Much improvement has to be done with the staff that deals with the customers. Cashiers need refresher courses; they also need skills in customer handling as well as public relations. Receptionists will also need to be trained on how to handle visitors whether they are customers or not as this will help in improving the bank's image.

(f) Financial Reorganization

UCB will have to reorganize its financial status by first of all writing off all the bad loans so that they do not appear on its balance sheet and give an image that the bank has got assets when actually they are non-performing assets.

There is also need of infusing more capital as already done by the government.

The bank will have to restructure the existing debts for some of the customers by either stopping charging interest and also at least endeavouring to recover the principle paid or even rescheduling most of these loans and giving customers more time for repayment.

(g) Redundancy Programmes

As part of turnaround strategies, UCB will have to implement some labour redundancy programmes.

First of all, the organization of the planning effort will be undertaken by a small *ad hoc* group from management. This will be composed of General Manager Board Secretary and Administration. He will be working with the Assistant General Manager human resources. The Chief Managers from all departments will have to be involved since this is an exercise that is going to affect the whole organization.

No replacement is tc be done in case of any retrenchment but only in cases of dismissals. The labour union will be consulted just only as a way of informing them the number of employees who have been declared redundant. Since UCB has already undergone this exercise, the number of staff to be declared redundant is going to be less.

The administration will have to take into consideration possibilities of strikes more especially by unionized staff who are ever seeking salary increments through the industrial court.

Staff performance appraisals have to be very much emphasized so as to help selecting those staff that are to be laid off. The take away package has to be reasonable.

Finally, there is a need for preparation of a master statement so as to inform all the stakeholders about the programmes in place. The success of this whole exercise will depend upon how the bank will be able to put forward the importance of the need for a redundancy programme to all the concerned parties.

Privatisation Options

UCB is categorized as being strategic and non-viable. It is strategic in the sense that it employs a large number of people, it covers the whole country but most important of all it is meant to boost rural farmers' agricultural production for economic development. Agriculture contributes about 90 per cent of the total GDP. It is non-viable because its fair market value is a negative figure due to huge amounts of non-performing assets. There is need to have a pre-privatization restructuring action project.

Option 1

New Private Investment

There is no need for the government to dispose of its equity but rather to have dilution of its own equity. This is a good method for dealing with an undercapitalized enterprise like UCB. Most of the banks have got a healthy financial standing and can therefore, invest in this as a way of merging. Besides, since there is much investment going on both foreign and local, any other foreign bank that qualifies can still have a joint venture with the government. The proposal is for the government to retain 49 per cent and sell off 51 per cent to private owners. Since UCB has gross lack of capital, there is great need for capital for its long-term operations.

Option 2

Management Employee buyout.

This is a best way of providing incentives to insiders so as to increase the efficiency. Once employees know that the bank belongs to them, the output will increase. However, since both management and employees do not have resources, the establishment of ESOP is very necessary. This is based on the concept of a pension plan. However, the government will still retain 49 per cent and sell off 51 per cent. The government has to retain these shares simply because of the objective of spearheading national development and can still cater for the masses. Should the bank prove successful, and then the government can divest it fully so as to have more and even better returns.

Conclusion

UCB is a wholly government owned parastatal that requires privatisation, but a lot needs to be done prior to this which calls for much effort from the employees, government as well as funding agencies. It is an enterprise which will be very successful if turnaround strategies are carefully implemented and due to lack of capital, the option of either New private investment or Management employee buy out is recommended.

Current Status

In 2001, the Bank was privatised and merged into Satbic Bank (Uganda) Ltd. The Bank is the largest Commercial Bank in the country, by assets with an estimated asset valuation of over US$ 1.26 Billion accounting for 20 per cent of the total Bank assets in Uganda as of December 2014.

8

Case Studies and Review Questions

CASE STUDIES

Case 1: AIP – Bulak Tobacco Company—Kyrgyztan

At present there are currently four tobacco processing plants in Kyrgyztan. Two tobacco processing plants are set up in each of the districts of Osh Oblast and Jalal-Abad Oblast. Aip Bulak Tobacco Company is the second largest after Kizil Kim Tobacco Company, situated in Osh Oblast which has a capacity of 22000 tonnes. Aip Bulak Company, in the good old days, had about 350 workers with a theoretical capacity of about 14000 tonnes, processing on an average off 6500 tonnes. Aip Bulak had also processed upto 10000 tonnes atleast during one season.

The company would pay local farmers a 25 per cent deposit on the crops at planting time in the early spring and would pay the balance at harvest time. Tobacco processing would then take place and 70 per cent of the processed tobacco would be sold to 15 Russian cigarette factories, 20 per cent to factories in Ukraine, Belorus and Moldovia, a negligible quantity to the Baltic Republics and 10 per cent to Bishkek. Table 8.1 summarises the amount of tobacco produced and sold from the years 1990 through 1996.

Aip Bulak was converted into a joint stock company in 1992. The workers collective was offered 20 per cent, but actually bought only 12 per cent. Mr. Rumantsev, a Russian from St. Petersburg bought 24 per cent of the Government's holding. The State Property Fund of Kyrgyztan has a holding of 64 per cent.

The Tobacco Blend is used in cigarette manufacture in Russia. There seems to be a strong Russian interest in the factory. Yaroslavl Company from Russia has envisaged interest even in a 100 per cent buy out. The

Table 8.1: Tobacco Sales and Purchased

Year	*Amount produced*	*Amount sold/ Payment received*
1990-91	10000 tonnes	Sold to 15 large Russian factories-full payment received.
1991-92	9000 tonnes	70 per cent unsold
1992-93	6500 tonnes	Unsold production of previous year and part of current year's production sold to the Ministry of Trade and Industry (Min Torg). The Russian Ministry of Trade and Industry, finally affected the sale. The Kyrgyz Ministry of Trade and Industry paid Aip Bulak after almost one year. The remaining production (50%) was sold to small private wholesalers half of whom have not paid till date. The amount outstanding is 10 million.
1993-94	5000 tonnes	Sold through Min Torg
1994-95	3000 tonnes	No direct sales were effected. Aip Bulak fermented the tobacco and returned to farmer owners for 18 per cent payments in kind.
1995-96	1850 tonnes	Same as above till date

Source: USAID Bankruptcy Project, 1996.

Russian cigarette manufacturers have not so far switched over to other suppliers like from Moldovia or elsewhere. Mr. Aitachunov is quite confident that the processed tobacco can be sold to Russians if the company can be restructured and direct contacts established with the Cigarette factories, instead of having to go through the Ministry of Trade and Industry. According to Mr. Aitachunov about 20 new small entrepreneurs have sprung up in Osh oblast and Jalal Abad Oblast who quite often use Aip Bulak's name and imitate their labels. However, the small entrepreneurs do not have the equipment to produce quality fermented tobacco since expensive equipment is required for the same. There are eleven chambers where the tobacco is cured in for about one week each. Each such chamber has a different temperature and humidity control. Aip Bulak has a rail line that comes right into the factory to pick up the cured tobacco. Mr. Aitachunov supplies out of Jalal Abad this year informally, by adapting illegal means. All these facts further prove the point that there is a great demand for Kyrgyz tobacco from the Russians.

Mr. Aitachunov has made some rough calculations and believes that the break even production is 5000 tonnes. If Aip Bulak is able to sign contracts with just 5, the major credit facilities for Aip Bulak is extended by bank. Currently 11 million soms has been advanced by AKB Bank. Small local wholesalers owe the company 10 million soms. According to the Chief Engineer of Aip Bulak, Mr. Aitachunov, there has been of late a breakdown of relationship with the Russian factories primarily due to the cost of transportation and the transit time involved because of the crossing of borders in Uzbekistan, Kazakhstan and Russia. Added to these are the problems of tariff and bribes involved in passing through the three countries. According to Mr. Aitachunov, currently there is an acute shortage of working capital and the company is not in a position to effect purchases of tobacco crops. Thus, the main activity involves providing the mundane service of processing tobacco for the farmers and getting a return in kind and sometimes in cash. From 350 workers during good times, the workforce has shrunk to 35. This will be further reduced to a skeleton crew of 5, after the processing season is over in October. To tide over the difficulties AKB Bank had extended a credit of 5 million soms at the interest rate of 150 per cent. Aip Bulak could neither repay the Principal nor the interest and the repayment period was extended by one more year at 520 per cent interest. The company till this date has paid 28 million soms and still has a debt of 11 million soms.

There is a history of doing business with Kyrgyz Tobacco growers by Russian cigarette manufacturers. The tobacco from Kyrgyz region constitutes a given percentage of Russian factories for supply of one ton of tobacco each, and the company will be back in business. It may be mentioned that negotiations are still going on with Yarslavl company for 1000 tonnes for next year.

The current business plan of Aip Bulak stated the following strategic objectives:

1. to gain better access to Russian and International markets.
2. to increase the quality of existing tobacco.
3. to obtain new machinery and equipment for the processing of high quality tobacco.
4. to introduce modern management techniques in the production and marketing of tobacco.

Mr. Aitachunov has come to the conclusion that these developmental objectives are attainable only through a strategic alliance with one of the big international tobacco and cigarette manufacturers. Setting up a joint venture was considered to be the best way to provide for the long-term prosperity of the company.

The State Property Fund has considered other possible privatization techniques such as a management and employee buy out complemented by a public offering of shares. In its search for potential strategic partners, the State Property Fund is focusing on two potential investors that have expressed strong interest in purchasing the company—Reemtsma from Germany (in alliance with French Sieta) and Yarslavl Company from Russia. The staff of the State Property Fund essentially served as consultants in preparing the Privatization plan, designing tendering procedures, analyzing the offers and negotiating the deal with the winning bidder. At the end of the negotiation, the State Property Fund will sign the contract with the foreign partner.

Mr. Aitachunov realized the advantages of the active involvement of the SPF, not only in providing professional support, but also in minimising the danger of speculation that a transaction was structured "under the table" to benefit the existing management. Foreign investors were also pleased to work with the SPF, because they had confidence that all steps, being in compliance with legal requirements, would minimise the problems of getting necessary approvals and guarantees.

Both of the bidders are being given the opportunity to have their financial and technical advisors analyse the company thoroughly. The advisors currently are in Jalal Abad Oblast. The developmental objectives for Aip Bulak are being carefully explained to foreign investors by the management. Both bidders are using International Accounting and auditing companies to appraise the value of the company. Both potential investors will be given a formal invitation to submit their offers and explain the financial and commercial arrangements through which they would take a stake in the company. They will be asked to prepare a detailed programme on how they could contribute to fulfil the developmental objectives of Aip Bulak by developing new products, modernizing technology, developing marketing strategies, introducing changes in internal organization, developing human resources and stabilizing local supplies of raw materials. They have been told that price would be important, but not necessarily the main criteria for deciding on the preferred bidder. It has been announced to both of them that in evaluating proposals, future prospects of the company and the overall implications for the Kyrgyztan republic would be taken into account as well.

Case Questions

1. As a foreign buyer, would you prefer an asset purchase or a share purchase? Give reasons
2. The State Property Fund seeks your advice regarding
   (a) the appropriate mode of divesting its holding in Aip Bulak.

   (b) A choice between the Yarslavl Company from Russia and Reemtsma of Germany.
3. What steps would you initiate to ensure transparency in the privatization process?
4. How relevant is the process of business valuation for the privatization of Aip Bulak?
5. Foreign buyers insist that special privileges be granted to them by the Governments as part of the deal. Give your views.
6. What debt restructuring measures would you advocate, for Aip Bulak?

Case 2: SHUMKAR – Bazar Kuron Rayon—Kyrgyztan

The economy of Kyrgyz Republic is primarily agricultural, including animal husbandry. Most of the country's territory lies at altitudes in excess of 1000 meters above sea level and only 7 per cent of the land is arable, of which about three-fourths is irrigated. The primary crops and agricultural commodities are cotton, tobacco, fruits and berries, grains, meat and wool. Areas under sugar beet and oil crops are being expanded. In recent years the agricultural sector accounted for 40 to 45 per cent of net material product and 33 to 35 per cent of total employment. There has always been a sizable private agricultural sector producing between one-third and one-half of some important crops, such as vegetables and fruits. In 1995, gross output worth 9563 million soms was produced by all kinds of farms which was 98 per cent of 1994's production.

Shumkar Company is in the business of supplying chemical, organic fertilizers and various types of pesticides to local farms. The enterprise besides selling the fertilizers, rendered the service of spreading the same in the farms by using its own specialised tractors. 1992 was the last normal year of its operation, when it had employed workers totaling 100. The staff were extremely well trained in spraying pesticides also. Besides, it had a well equipped laboratory.

The state owned enterprise was privatised partially on Oct. 29, 1993. The statutory capital was fixed at 267,000 soms. Initially the Workers collective were given a holding of 35 per cent and the State Property Fund had 65 per cent. However, the workers collective did not buy out its portion having failed to pay the commission within the stipulated date. At present the Workers Council has a total of 23 per cent holding and 70 per cent is with the State Property Fund. Seven per cent was sold at coupon auction to outsiders during May 1995.

The year 1993 marked the beginning of downfall of the enterprise with practically no work during 1995 and 1996. The scope of services being provided is substantially reduced. The enterprise owns twelve trucks of which six are specialised ones, fleet of cars, one bus and twenty-three tractors. Most of the vehicles are currently not being put to effective use. Atleast six tractors have been leased to its own workers. These tractors are in turn rented out by the workers to the local farmers for tilling the soil. There is currently about 13000 hectares under production in the region, but only 1000 hectares were chemically fertilized in 1995. Availability and price of fertilizer are major constraints. Also there is gross lack of any substantial capital among the farmers to buy the fertilizers. The number of employees on role with the enterprise is 58, with only 20 actually working. The management category consists of 5 and the workers 15. There is a large administrative building, parking area for motor vehicles, specialised building for storing chemicals. The assets also include four fuel storage tanks.

During the year 1987, the enterprise had built a well equipped laboratory. However, in 1995 the Local Government by a decree transferred the laboratory to the town for being used as a school. During February 1996, the enterprise's statutory capital was reduced by 20,576 soms to reflect the transfer of this asset. However, based on the general re-evaluation of the asset, this was equivalent to 760000 soms. The enterprise contends that 760000 soms be credited against their Government debts. Local government is reluctant to carry out this, at present.

Additional information is provided in Table 8.2 and Table 8.3.

Table 8.2: Information for 1992-95

	1992	*1993*	*1994*	*1995*
Chemical fertilizer	1500 tonnes		3400 tonnes	150 tonnes
Organic fertilizer	60000 tonnes			5000 tonnes
Pesticides	3-5 tonnes			1-2 tonnes
Hectares chemically fertilized		8000	5000	1000

Table 8.3: Financial Data

Total debt Soms	800000
Taxes	400000
Social fund	76000
Jalal abad Selhozchemia	196000
Debtors somes	500000 (owned by local farming concerns)

Case Questions

1. Would you recommend a liquidation of the enterprise? What are the issues to be considered before recommending such an action?
2. What are the pre privatization restructuring measures you would like to recommend for Shumkar?
3. How would you ensure that the restructuring measures recommended by you are properly implemented?
4. How would you resolve the debt issue of Shumkar and the local Government's tough stand regarding the laboratory?
5. Can the enterprise be sold as a going concern to the Workers collective, or to the Management, or to both? If so, arrive at a rough fair market value for Shumkar.

Case 3: Mailuu Suu Sewing Factory—Kyrgyztan

Mailuu Suu Sewing Factory used to be under the administrative control of the Ministry of Light Industry, till 1989. A lease agreement was entered into by the Workers Collective during that year according to which 100 per cent of the profit of the enterprise would belong to the collective itself. The enterprise was transferred as a Government enterprise to the State Property Fund in the year 1992. Also during that year, the Ministry of Light Industry was merged with the Ministry of Trade and Industry. Intensive discussions took place between the Ministry of Trade and Industry, Oblast Level State Property Fund and the Republican State Property Fund with regard to the privatization of Mailuu Suu Sewing Factory. However, no consensus was reached, and till this date the enterprise exclusively belongs to the State.

The Sewing Factory till 1992 had twenty Russian Suppliers of clothes. This accounted for almost 50 per cent of the supplies. There were, two suppliers from Kazakhstan, who accounted for 30 per cent of the supplies and three local suppliers, which accounted for 20 per cent of the supply. Till 1992 the production was as much as one million pairs of men's and children's pants per year. At present the production is just 10 per cent of the 1992 volume. The pattern of production is also different now. The factory produces Slacks (50%), bathrobes (25%), and the rest of the production is for bed sheets, work uniforms and children's clothes. At present the factory is working at 25 per cent capacity. The marketing of the finished product was exclusively carried out in Kyrgyztan in the past.

The position is the same at present, however, the supply also is only from Kyrgyztan.

There is a general decline in demand for new clothes. Thus there is a substantial loss of market. The present market includes Bishkek ZUM, Children's World, House of trade Bishkek and the Jalal abad Univermag. There is plenty of cheap Chinese and Indian goods in the market.

Added to this, is the problem of landslide in the area where the factory is located. There was a major landslide during 1992, as a result of which the area surrounding the factory was cut off for a period of four months. It is expected that more such landslides will occur in the near future and a geological survey is to be carried out soon.

Recently, there has been a visit from Japanese company, which has expressed a strong desire in investing in the company.

The current management has expressed a strong desire for a Management buy out. The management realizes that three things had to be done towards this objective:

1. Cancellation of the company's debt.
2. The financing plan and the labour redundancy plan.
3. Search for a practical method for making the buy out feasible.

Cancellation of Debts

The total debt is of the order of 2.2 million soms. The Ministry of Industry and Trade was used as a clearing house and the debt owed to them is 933400 soms. They owe to the suppliers a total of 1135500 soms. Other liabilities include—Wages 21500 soms, Social Fund 100000 soms. The planning calculations of the Management show that the Factory could survive only if it was relieved of the burden of debts.

The Financing Plan and the Labour Redundancy Plan

The Management team realises that the restructuring plan will be successful in the long-term only if the enterprise had enough capital. A proposal has been worked out by them according to which some of the machineries will be sold off and the money spent on training of key staff members in the areas of marketing and pricing. Labour has been substantially reduced from 470 during the normal year of 1991 to about 70 as on today. The positive development in marketing and investment depended on the management working efficiently so as to implement the restructuring strategies and make them a success. This means winning over the workforce to the new duties involved. Personnel changes, notably a reduction of the workforce to one sixth of the original figure, were inevitable if any jobs at all were to be saved for the future. The enterprise is only in a position to run economically if it has a staff of about 100 employees. The management very recently conceived a new corporate philosophy of its own. It is based on the idea that restructuring from the plan to the market has not only to do with the introduction of economic thinking, of business know how and techniques, but also calls for the development of a new system of value entailing major learning processes at the factory in question. This entails specific steps by the Management in all fields of its activities:

- *Marketing and sales*: Development of marketable products and new distribution channels,
- *Production and costs*: Increase in productivity, steps to reduce costs,
- *Personnel and Organization*: Personnel development and organizational reforms.

Apart from efforts on sales markets, cost reduction strategies are essential to earn sufficient profits through efficient production patterns. The Management requested the Japanese team to carry out a short productivity study, during their visit to the factory. This study revealed shortcomings in production. The rationalization efforts which ensued have brought considerable improvements, but the efforts must be continued in the future.

Search for a Practical Method for Privatization

Privatization is always a particularly difficult matter given the situation in Kyrgyztan. Favourable conditions are just being initiated to encourage privatization by Management buy-out. A successful MBO requires thorough preparation and detailed discussions on the part of all parties involved.

There is no single model for the takeover. Three possibilities exist for the Sewing factory.

(i) The SPF makes arrangements for the enterprise by providing capital as if it were already privatized.

(ii) The enterprise is taken over by an equity investment company. This would offer a way of obtaining venture capital.

(iii) The existing management buys-out.

Case Questions

1. The Mailuu Suu Sewing factory has been facing a crisis for some years now. Explain the reasons for this crisis.
2. Explain what steps the Management took to restructure the enterprise. What were the conditions dictated by the Market, and what did the Management do to satisfy them?
3. Support from the State Property Fund would no doubt play a major role in the restructuring of the enterprise. What in your view should the SPF be doing in this regard?
4. Would you suggest a Management Buy-Out or acquisition by the Japanese?
5. Suppose you are the future Manager in an identical factory which is in the stage of transition from the plan to the market. Work out the following:
   - a Corporate strategy
   - steps towards restructuring
   - a new sales organization

   Explain the major differences between your restructuring strategy and that of Mailuu Suu Sewing factory. What extra help would you require to successfully restructure your enterprise?

The above three cases for Kyrgyztan were prepared by the author during his mission at the Bishkek International School of Management, sponsored by the United Nations Development Programme.

KarlaGallardo (Mexico), Gabriel Ramos (Peru), Satish Ganga Ram Pandey (Suriname), Kezang Wangmo (Bhutan), Arjun Welaratne (Sri Lanka), Judith Lungu (Zambia), Abdul Iddrisu (Ghana) provided valuable inputs for the country cases.

Case 4: Farsons Group of Companies—Malta

The origin of the Farsons Group of Companies dates back to the year 1880. At the end of the nineteenth century, H&G Simonds, brewers of Reading, England, established a branch in Malta with stores at Pinto Wharf, Marsa and offices in Palazzo Ferreria, Valletta. In 1928, L. Farrugia

& Sons, with a brewery in Hamrun, launched their first beer, the first ever beer brewed in Malta. During that same year, another company, The Malta Export Brewery launched another competitive beer.

The following year L. Farrugia & Sons and H&G Simonds merged to form a new company called Simonds Farsons Ltd. which started operating on 1 March 1929. During 1947, the merger of the two breweries, namely Simonds Farsons Ltd and The Malta Export Brewery, was finalised. The new company was called Simonds Farsons Cisk Ltd.

Due to the ever-increasing market demand for the company's products, the company embarked on an expansion project and established a new brewery and beverage production plant in Mriehel, which is to-date the existing premises. This new brewery was officially inaugurated by June 1950.

During the consequent years Simonds Farsons Cisk Ltd was to be entrusted as a franchiser for various international brands, including Pepsi, Carlsberg, and Sunkist. In addition to this excellent international product portfolio, the company still believed in local produce and invested largely in products created exclusively by the company. Today the company boasts some exceptional locally produced quality products namely Cisk, a hallmark in local beer, and Kinnie, an exceptional non-alcoholic beverage.

In 1980, the Farsons Group started taking shape. The wines and spirits division was separated, and a new company, Wands Ltd was established. Later on, the group also diversified its strategy and established Food Chain Holdings Ltd, which runs a number of outlets throughout Malta under licence by some of the leading global fast food franchises, including Pizza Hut, Burger King and Kentucky Fried Chicken. The strategy was carried on further by establishing joint ventures with other major local companies, namely in shopping and entertainment centres, and in the operation of a new franchise, the TGI Fridays.

Simonds Farsons Cisk plc operates in what can be broadly termed as the beverage and catering trade. The market conditions are of a highly competitive nature both on a global market environment, and on a local scenario. The organisation faces tough competition and demanding market conditions in most of the sectors.

As in all other sectors of the business, the beverage industry is in a fast, ever changing, highly competitive environment. All companies that want to survive must always keep abreast of all international happenings and keep up-to-date in terms of efficiencies, technology and working methods.

All international factors directly or indirectly affect the way things are done within the company. Upcoming and new methods of quality assurance are a major example. Over the years companies have tried to evolve a methodology by which quality is maximised and maintained while cost is minimised.

Over the past years, the company has embarked on a very important quality assurance programme, the HACCP project. As with any other sector of the Food and Beverage industry, HACCP (Hazard Analysis Critical Control) is becoming the recognised acceptable quality assurance system approach. By initially carrying out hazard analysis the master brewer must identify the areas/points within his process which if not controlled properly, could lead to a hazardous situation for the consumer. Safe limits must be identified for the Control Point and procedures for monitoring and taking corrective action should be documented. Records should be maintained for all monitoring of Critical Control Points. 'Probably' the most important Critical Control Point for any HACCP Plan is the monitoring of raw materials; the suppliers of hops and barley should provide reassurance of the use of acceptable pesticides or fungicides on crops, and that supplies are free from foreign bodies. Unfortunately, the cost of testing for pesticides and other organic materials is expensive and for most micro-breweries the only economic method to monitor supplies is to obtain certificates of conformance from the suppliers on a regular basis. The process also looks into the monitoring of the water conditions, the purchase of materials from certified suppliers, and the training of staff into good manufacturing procedures i.e. hygiene training, cleaning, handling glass breakage, documentation, aseptic techniques, processing procedures, corrective action, and procedures for monitoring critical control points.

Another important factor is interest rates. Changing levels of interest rates, highly affect investment patterns. The company tends to utilise times of low interest rates to increase its investment programmes. Thus fluctuations in interest rates directly contribute to the growth of the organisation.

On the other hand, exchange rates influence directly the operations of the business. Since most of the company's raw and packaging materials are imported, exchange rates contribute to the final cost of producing the products.

From the early years of its existence, Simonds Farsons Cisk plc has always formed strategic alliances, and franchises, with international companies. The underlying concept was that of sharing the expertise with international companies, whilst adding local flavour to the products being produced. Strategic partners provided the company with invaluable knowledge relating to work practices, the products, production methods, and manufacturing technologies. Overseas and local training was also provided from such international companies, which finally resulted in benefits to both the company and the employees. The company is convinced that there is sound potential for developing the business further and, on a strategic level, the company has prioritised the development of new opportunities and alliances that will enable the future success of the company. *"As with any large business organisation, opportunities continually arise and each one is analysed in the context of strategic synergies and how these could benefit the long-term interest of the group." Louis A. Farrugia—Managing Director—Farsons Group—Annual Report 2000.*

The established status of the company today, provides an effective tool for gaining favourable terms of trade with foreign and local suppliers. The alliances with foreign strategic alliances also help in this area, in that special trading agreements, payment terms, deliveries and other functions of the terms of trade can be better negotiated.

In light of Malta's bid to join the European Union, the company has embarked on a series of projects over the last 10 years, to improve and upgrade its working practices and procedures, in order to bring them in line with the current European requirements. Some of these programmes are the HACCP programme and the ISO 9000 certification.

> "We await the challenges that Malta's future membership to the European Union and an open market will create, confident in the knowledge that the Farsons Group of Companies is organisationally both well resourced to compete effectively, and capable of expanding its presence within the wider market." Louis A. Farrugia—Managing Director, Farsons Group—Annual Report 1994.

Farsons has also become a member of the European Bottled Water Association, headquartered in Brussels. This association promotes the interests of companies operating in this market sector. Membership demands a thorough inspection and audit of the bottling plant, carried out by an accredited auditor—NSF International. The plant passed with a 94 per cent sanitary compliance rating.

As stated earlier, the long-term success of the local beverage industry depends on achieving greater efficiencies and increasing export markets. The group operates in a highly competitive and to-date price regulated environment. For a long number of years therefore, the beverage industry in particular had to operate in the absence of a mechanism to compensate for cost increases. The move towards liberalised local markets has begun and the end of 2002 will accomplish the complete removal of tariff protection for many products.

This industry is generally sensitive to the fluctuations in disposable income and during the summer period, it is heavily influenced by tourist arrivals. In addition, particularly in the beverage sector, the organisation also has to contend with the random whims of weather during the crucial summer months.

With regard to innovation and investment, the Company has been very active in this area. The organisation has a dynamic product innovation strategy and every year the company has introduced new or repackaged products. On the other hand, investment has always been a major strategic factor, which the company believed in for most of its years in existence. Louis A. Farrugia states, "*our primary aim behind the Master Plan's budgeted Lm 14 million capital spend is to place Simonds Farsons Cisk plc at the forefront of international brewing quality.*"

The major investment areas can be highlighted as:

(a) Ongoing investment (e.g. offices, computer, equipment, infrastructure)
(b) Upgrades to current plant
(c) Market driven investment
(d) Brewery redevelopment programme

The company has always taken a long-term view of its capital investment, in spite of the short-term implications.

A strong belief in the quality of the local brands, such as Kinnie, and in the international standard of the Farsons Beers, has long been a driving force behind the company's intention to strengthen its presence abroad. At the same time as the Group's brand portfolio was displaying so much vigour at home, decisive and determined efforts to expand overseas operations manifested a parallel dynamism. The company's commitment is to fully develop the export business potential. This activity represents a central element within the Farsons Group's corporate development programme, a programme that envisages Malta strengthening its commercial ties with a wider European Community and its neighbouring countries. The company believes that a major long-term success factor is the expansion of the markets, which in this case can only relate to foreign and international markets.

Led by a strong entrepreneurial spirit and a determination to move forward, Simonds Farsons Cisk plc possesses unveiled capabilities and resources in technical, human and marketing areas.

Simonds Farsons Cisk plc has always been a 'living' company. Throughout the years, the company has evolved both in working practices, and in management styles, in order to be able to face the challenges of the evolving business world. A major restructuring effort started way back in 1990. The process, which was the result of a two-year programme, involved a fundamental reappraisal of the company's core businesses and their respective activities. It enables management to clearly focus upon the Group's market and operational strengths and, through the creation of the business units, to implement an efficient and highly co-ordinated development strategy.

> "This restructuring has been an important element of the Group's medium-range master plan, which has involved significant investment in modernising the entire range of Farsons' beverage packaging and production processes."—Louis A. Farrugia – Managing Director, Farsons Group – Annual Report 1992.

The result was the formal restructuring of the corporate activities and the creation of a number of business units, namely Beers, Soft Drinks, Marketing, Exports, Distribution, Technical Services, Financial Services, Management Services, and Human Resources.

Simonds Farsons Cisk plc is a quality conscious company. It is considering ISO 9000 certification as part of a Total Quality Management programme. In addition a Performance Improvement Programme has been launched company-wide with the help of a specialised foreign consultant.

Customer Service is perceived to be an important competitive element. Apart from product quality and product image, customers can be won by providing excellent service tc clients with regard to product availability, delivery reliability and delivery speed. The key factor was in providing quality products with increased customer service. The distribution function of the company's products was restructured towards the beginning of 1999. To ensure better and faster communication and to improve the quality and timeliness of the service, the company reinforced the direct links to its customers, both on premise and the take-home trade. The entire system of warehousing, credit control and inventory management need to be continuously upgraded and improved. The system definitely helped Farsons come closer to its customers.

Of growing concern in all activities of the company are the labour conditions of the company's employees. Increased mechanisation and automation is perceived to be necessary to be able to improve labour conditions.

Organisation Structure

Throughout the years, the company structure has been changed, reorganised and restructured to ensure that the company was effective in responding to ever changing market requirements. The structure evolved from that of a family owned business early in the 20th century, to a more public oriented organisation. Today 20 per cent of the company's shareholding is owned by public bodies, whilst the rest still remains within the family.

Merger talks that started early in 1999, with another local beverage giant on the island tried to restructure this situation creating 5 equal shareholding units with stakes of 20 per cent each. The first attempt failed, but the company is still attentive to other opportunities for strategic alliances.

The restructuring of the company's corporate activities in 1992 brought about another important milestone in the company's history. This reflected the outcome of an earlier fundamental appraisal of the core businesses and their respective activities. The aim behind this ongoing process of change is to augur greater operational independence and accountability within an organisation structure that is ready to sustain and benefit from such an action.

The psychological intent in this change has been facilitated by the significant infrastructure investment in information technology already undertaken. Each business unit has its own Management Board, the composition of which will be the representative of all disciplines that a business normally needs, namely Finance, Human Resources, Operations and Sales. Additionally to retain the group-wide relationship, and to ensure that good communication exists across each of the business units, each unit will have on its respective board, General Managers from other business units. This allows for cross-fertilisation of ideas and a full appreciation of the objectives, both immediate and long-term, of the respective businesses within the Group.

The immediate and apparent benefits derived from these changes centre on the flat management structure employed within each business unit, whereby previous multi-tier structures have now been replaced with a single level.

The company believes that the greatest benefit emanating from this restructuring is to relate to the individual worker, and his input relative to the profitability of the group as a whole. This will benefit employees through greater productivity and job security, shareholders through increased profits, and ultimately the Maltese economy as a whole.

None of this would be possible without the professional capabilities of the management and senior management, which is strong as any leading management team within the European marketplace, and the commitment of the workforce as a whole.

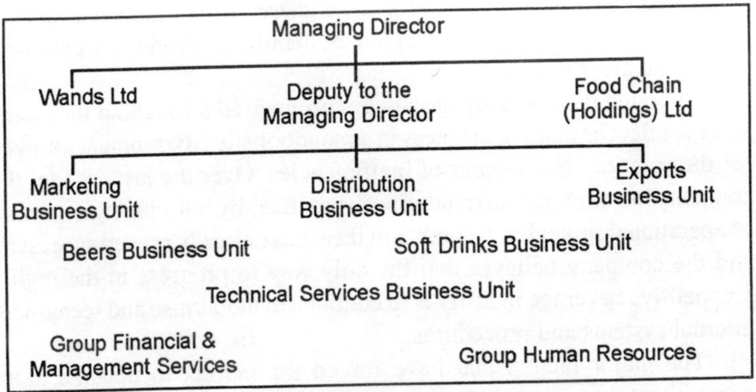

Fig. 8.1: Simonds Farsons Cisk plc – Business Units Layout

The Mission Statement

The mission of the company is to satisfy consumers' needs in the beverage and leisure market sectors, thereby maximising shareholder value and rewarding employees. The company identified five main areas on which to consolidate it corporate mission.

- *Customer Satisfaction* – by always listening to customers, the company is able to deliver service levels that are recognised as being superior to those of competitors.

- *Product Quality* – the company ensures that its products are always the very best available, by continuously improving standards in all its operations.
- *Brand Strength* – understanding consumer needs, the company ensures that its brands are continuously growing in popularity, both locally and internationally.
- *Human Resources* – by selecting and training the very best people, the organisation ensures the high levels of performance and ethical standards required to compete in today's global economy.
- *Future Investments* – investing in proven systems and technology and in the development of our people, the company will be continuously building its competitive edge.

For a long number of years Simonds Farsons Cisk plc operated in a monopolistic environment. Competition was at a minimum and Farsons controlled and had most of the market share. Today the situation has changed dramatically and external forces, mainly, are driving the company to become more effective.

Although the company has always progressed throughout the years, still the effect of making business in a monopolistic environment allowed for the creation of a number of inefficiencies. Over the last decade, the company has struggled to remove such practices by introducing a number of operational strategies. A number of them have already proved successful and the company believes that the only way to progress in the highly competitive beverage industry is to continue to modernise and reengineer internal systems and procedures.

The major factors that have forced the market to become more competitive are:

- Malta's application to join the European Union
- The establishing of a new brewery producing Lowenbrau
- The removal of protectionism—such as tariffs, levies and duties

The organisation always believed in change and changing practices and cultures, thus the whole programme could be implemented much easier than expected.

The major problem areas that were faced are as follows:

- The introduction of business units, as explained earlier on, removed complete ranks of excessive management that hindered efficiency. The company became more efficient to respond to the market demands, in terms that the system became less bureaucratic and was more efficient. Business units restructuring also brought about a decentralisation effort and an organisational and cultural change.
- Again the major benefit came from the business unit system development. Units became more conscious of their costs and thus worked more focused on their area to resolve wastage and inefficiencies. The decentralisation effort resulted in better cost management. In addition financial control was also being controlled throughout the group function by setting up a Group Financial Services unit, that audited working practices and spending requirements in conjunction with the units concerned.
- Business units brought about a more efficient way to manage resources. Production planning was introduced for the specialised productions rather than for the whole company, and responsibility to produce at lower costs now had become accountable. Inefficiencies within the production flow were identified easily due to more decentralised functions.
- The company was creating new products every year, and was seeking strategic alliances more often. The company believed in branding and making consumers aware that the brand was linked to quality. This was a driving force in enhancing the marketing function. To enhance the competitive force on the market, the company enriched its product portfolio, reduced costs of production and improved its marketing strategy by making this more focused on the market segments identified.

SWOT ANALYSIS

The SWOT analysis was carried out in conjunction to each respective business unit, with the intention to highlight furthermore the external opportunities and threats, the operational strengths and weaknesses relating to every line of business.

The Distribution, Marketing and Selling Functions

Strengths	*Weaknesses*
• good sales force, and qualified management team • effective integration of the marketing and selling functions • reliable distribution function • rigid credit control system • effective stock control system	• ineffective communication of marketing plans • insufficient product innovation • information leaks
Opportunities	***Threats***
• improve exports and franchising activities • new strategic alliances • expansion of the product range, and exploiting of niches	• losing key staff players to other competitive companies • liberalisation of importation and removal of protectionism • loss of franchises due to uncontrollable factors

The Production Departments

Strengths	*Weaknesses*
• good brewing and beverage makers tradition • strong relations with brewers and beverage suppliers overseas • highly qualified personnel • effective training strategies with overseas franchisers • good quality products • quality standards always being upgraded • serious response to customer complaints	• production is carried out within two separate sites, thus increasing costs • at times there is lack of effective communication • inefficient use of human resources

Opportunities	*Threats*
• improvement of the quality standards to minimise cost of damages, and provide a better product • since the introduction of the distribution function it would be ideal to link the short term market requirements through the sales ordering process, to issue a short-term production plan, thus reducing stock obsolescence • more effective communications between the units involved • improvement of material resource planning and better inventory management • improve quality consciousness among all employees	• other breweries and beverage production companies setting up in the country • loss of franchise function for major brands, like Pepsi, or Carlsberg • possibility of stock-outs

The Purchasing and Shipping Departments

Strengths	*Weaknesses*
• well balanced and experienced team • clear definition of operations • synergy between purchasing and shipping departments • shipping is controlled centrally	• no formal insurance skills or formal insurance training • weak stock management control

Opportunities	*Threats*
• achieve economies by consolidating purchases on the basis of more extensive forecasts • more open to supply resources • reduction of freight costs • more effective resource and inventory management and ordering to reduce the risk of stock outs • more electronic and flexible system	• risk of inefficient buying due to some unplanned production plans • risk of saturation in seeking new suppliers

The Human Resources Department

Strengths	*Weaknesses*
• high incentives for training • training is an ongoing system provided by the unit • flexible team • credibility with unions and staff • creation of the suggestion scheme system	• ineffective communication to other units on the developments taking place • lack of social activities

Opportunities	*Threats*
• improve staff appraisal procedures • improve training media and keep abreast with all new technologies relating to training	• possible unions strikes and mishaps • loss of key personnel when the country joins the European Union

The Finance and Management Systems Department

Strengths	*Weaknesses*
• team of highly qualified personnel • knowledge of the working environment of the company, and the ability to overview a wide cross-section of the company – highly exposed to all areas of the business • highly computer literate	• some staff lack flexibility skills • high degree of pressure, can result in employee fatigue

Opportunities	*Threats*
• improve communications through better networking and utilisation of electronic mailing systems • more paperless environment • more timely and accurate reporting	• computer viruses • information leaks • loss of key staff due to quick development of employees capabilities

Case Questions

1. Suggest appropriate restructuring strategies for Simonds Farsons Cisk plc.
2. In what ways the suggested measures would differ for an identical Company in your own country?

Case 5: PEMEX—Mexico

Petroleos Mexicanos—PEMEX is Mexico's state owned oil company since 1938. PEMEX became the largest Latin American oil exporter company after the former Mexican President Mr. Lazaro Cardenas had nationalized the existing 17 foreign oil companies and merged under one entity. One of the most notorious times in the PEMEX's 70 years life is the period between 1970's and 1980s when the discovery of new oil wells led to a high national spending, and to large borrowings. Crude oil production tripled in Mexico but the country went virtually bankrupt after 1981 when the price of oil collapsed and former President Lopez Portillo raised Mexican oil prices.

The Labour Union of PEMEX established since 1942 has a powerful voice that the company tries to align with harmony by aligning mutual benefits through open and transparent communication under standards of trust, justice and teamwork. PEMEX strives to preserve this compromise in order to achieve efficiency across the organization.

In 1992 a new law was issued that restructured PEMEX into one corporation with four subsidiaries—(1) PEMEX Exploring and Production (PEP), (2) PEMEX Refining (PXR), (3) PEMEX Basic Petrochemical and Gas (PGPB), (4) PEMEX Petrochemical (PPQ).

PEMEX has four different stages in the history of the Mexican oil industry. The first stage relates to the origins of the Mexican oil industry between 1884 and 1938 through foreign companies. The second stage relates to the internal market development by the Mexican oil industry through its consolidation in 1939 to 1970. The third and fourth stages refer to the period between 1971 and 1996, and then from 1997 to 2008 characterized by the export orientation of PEMEX, and a period of growth and stability followed by a second stage of development.

Today PEMEX accounts for around 40 per cent of the Mexico's total economic revenues and 7 per cent of Mexico's export earnings. The company operations range from exploration and production to refining and petrochemicals. Oil reserves were estimated to be 14 billion barrels in 2010. According to PEMEX in the year 2006 the average production was around 3.25 million barrels per day.

PEMEX International trading operation is managed by a subsidiary called PEMEX's P.M.I Comercio Internacional. The company's products and services are marketed within Mexico and abroad. Most of the plants throughout Mexico are engaged in the areas of production, commercialization, conveyance, safety, supply, accounting, cost, planning and financing.

PEMEX's four subsidiaries are in charge of different market segments. PEMEX Exploring and Production (PEP), activities are mainly related to Oil and Natural Gas exploration and exploitation; conveyance, storage in the terminals and for first hand commercialization. PEP is ranked as third in the world for crude production. PEMEX Basic Petrochemical and Gas (PGPB) is the subsidiary in charge of managing the division dealing with natural gas, liquid hydrocarbons and basic petrochemical products such as ethane, sulphur and natural gasoline. PEMEX Petrochemical—PPQ's main activity is non-basic processes of petrochemical, derived from the first transformation of PEMEX Natural Gas, Methane, Propane and Naphtha. PPQ is in charge of production, commercialization, and distribution of High, and Low Lineal Density Polyethylene, Ethylene

Oxide, Glycol, Vinyl Chloride, Ethylene, Ammonia, Methanol, Styrene, Benzene, Toluene, Xylem, Paraxylene, Propylene, Orthoxylene and Acrylonitrile in the national market and international market. PEMEX, P.M.I. manages the imports and exports of crude oil and refined products to several international markets. Main activities of PEMEX Refining are industrial processes refining, management, storage and distribution of the manufacturing of oil products and derived from oil.

In November 14, 2008 Mexican President Felipe Calderón announced a modification of the Federal Law of Budget and Fiscal Accountability that made PEMEX PIDIREGAS debt to be included in PEMEX's balance sheet in accordance with government standards applicable to Mexican public sector entities. Petróleos Mexicanos became primary debt obligator to all payment obligations for PIDIREGAS financings as of December 31, 2009. Further, it has been decided starting from 2009, investment on PEMEX will be excluded from the annual goals of the Mexican Government's budget.

Based on the company's financial reports from 2005 to 2009, PEMEX reported profits only in 2006. Losses are reported in 2005 at $7 6.3, then profit of $ 45.3 in 2006, and then back to three consecutive years of losses of $ 18.3, $112.1, and $ 94.7 respectively

PEMEX has four main mechanisms to finance its debt:

- Publicly traded peso denominated notes—CEBURES, a kind of domestic issue of bonds.
- International issues of bonds
- Bank credits
- Export credit agencies

Table 8.4: PEMEX Debt Structure

Composition of Petroleos Mexicanos Debt		
Founding Source	*% Captered Debt in 2010*	
	Range Proposed in 2010 (%)	*Range Estimated in December 2010 (%)*
International Capital Market	30-65	33.60%
Domestic Capital Market (CEBURES)	8-35	15.50%
Bank Credits (bilateral and syndicated)	8-35	21.50%
Export credit agencies	10-25	19.60%
Others	2-5	9.90%

Source: PEMEX.

In 2009 PEMEX had the lowest cost of exploration at USD$ 4.85 compared to international competitors like Exxon USD$ 7.5, Shell USD$9.5 and Total USD$ 6.1.

The findings of the four level framework of Mega, Macro, Meso and Micro, coupled with the external threats and opportunities and the internal strengths and weaknesses, can be summarized as follows:

Strengths	*Weaknesses*
• Low cost of exploration and production • Dominant market position (Monopoly)	• Lack of advance technology • Excess of regulations • Lack of infrastructure to diversify the market • Heavy tax burden • Have capital constraint
Opportunities	***Threats***
• Recovery of United States and increase its demand. • Internalization of PEMEX activities. • Diversification of new markets. • Growing demand for natural gas. • Strategic alliances and partnership for investments.	• Price volatility • Diminish of reserves • Regulatory policies

As part of the organizational diagnosis, the causes and symptoms of decline of PEMEX were identified. Also a detailed business valuation, Operating cash cycle, were carried out.

1. **Inadequate financial control:** PEMEX had a heavy tax burden and high financial leverage which hinders its access to sources of financing on competitive terms.
   Moody's Rating Agency stated that PEMEX still remains constrained in terms of capital despite the benefits derived from recent fiscal and energy reform. This does not allow the company to attract foreign capital and technology.

Table 8.5: Financial Highlights

	2009 (Jan.-Sep.)	*2010 (Jan.-Sep.) Figures in Billion Pesos*
Total Revenue from sales and services	779	939
Operating Income	358	414
Income before Taxes and Duties	360	463
Net income (loss)	(30)	(21)

Source: PEMEX.

PEMEX has a negative income due to the tax pressure. The Company has high operating income that could be used to invest further on their expansion to enhance their competitiveness, but the retention of high taxes reduces that opportunity. Mexico Government has a programme called Pidiregas (public works) which is for contributing to budget for building public infrastructure. Mexican government under the "Federal Law of Budget and Fiscal Accountability" made PEMEX PIDIREGAS debt to be included in PEMEX balance sheet which they also made applicable standards for all the Mexican public sector entities

PEMEX thus needed external source of finance to cover its negative financial performance. PEMEX's debt obligations showed sizable increases from 2002-2006, and due to higher pricing and cash flow in 2007 the debt had declined. In 2009 the total gross debt had increased to $50.6 billion after an increment of $7.6 billion. Moreover, PEMEX had sizeable pension obligations.

Declining Production

PEMEX has downward trends in reserves and production. The company requires more capital in order to increase its production. Moreover, PEMEX needs to make infrastructure investment in upstream and downstream activities because another constraint which is hindering its growth is its obsolete technology. Moreover, with this investment on infrastructure the company can meet the increasing demand. Oil production requires high capital investment. However, the financial policy of the Company does not allow making important investments such as advance technology.

The company needs to improve its efficiency, productivity and technological competencies to keep its competitive position in the market.

Poor Marketing Effort

The company has low flexibility to compete. PEMEX has to necessarily follow the price regulation and natural gas regulatory policy. The company does not have a customer focus. Because of its limited resources the Company did not invest on customer oriented programmes in order to increase customer awareness and satisfaction. Moreover, the Company is monopolistic in nature, so its incentives to focus on customer care is very low. The company needs to reduce its logistics cost as well as improve efficiency to become more competitive and fulfil the delivery lead time. This is a hard task for the company because of its obsolete infrastructure.

An insight into the operating cash cycle for PEMEX revealed something interesting. One can conclude that the company does not have problem in collecting its receivable accounts (21 days). Also inventory turnover of 20 days does not pose a problem. However, the OCC shows that PEMEX has problems in order to pay on time to its suppliers (301 days). This makes sense as most of these suppliers of PEMEX are the divisions of the same company and have no incentive to maintain healthy finances because they are also the part of the government's agencies.

Operating Cash Cycle

$$\frac{(\text{Initial Inventory} + \text{Close inventory})/2}{\text{Cost of sales}} * 365 + \frac{\text{Accounts Receivable}}{\text{Credit Sales}} * 365 - \frac{\text{Accounts Payable}}{\text{Purchases}} * 365$$

A Strategic Development Questionnaire was administered on PEMEX, which indicated that strategic decisions are primarily political and enforced-choice led. PEMEX is an organization where negotiations and power are highly determined by control of resources. Enforced choice highly influences the organization strategy given that PEMEX is a government owned company.

Operating Cash Cycle Calculation	
Initial Inventory	$ 31,874,174
Close inventory	$ 38,037,560
Cost of sales	$ 632,290,416
Average Inventory Holding Period	**20**
Accounts Receivable	$ 74,810,631
Credit Sales	$ 1,282,064,310
Average settlement by debtors	**21**
Accounts Payable	$ 53,076,654
Purchases	$ 63,277,711
Average payment period to creditors	**306**
OCC	**–265**

Thus, the main problems of PEMEX were: (a) low incomes and cash flow that do not allow the company to address its technological obsolescence, (b) heavy tax burden, (c) low efficiency and reliability of business process, (d) high labour liabilities such as the pension debt, (e) a lack of economic vision caused by the limited results oriented culture.

The company employs more workers than other large oil companies in the industry. This is in part due to the labour union that is part of the board of PEMEX and has great power in the decision of labour redundancy.

Business Valuation of PEMEX

Fair market value as part of the business valuation process for PEMEX was determined, using the financial figures provided in the Annexure. The forecast of the operating cash flows of 2011, 2012 and 2013 were estimated based on the assumption that the company will perform in the same way, as at present. Thus, the values were adjusted to the inflation target forecasted by the Mexican Central Bank (4%).

	2008	2009	2010	2011	2012	2013
Net cash flows from operating activities	115,260,616$	204,207,071$	160,118,126$	166,522,851$	173,183,765$	180,111,116$

Note: * 2011, 2012 and 2013 are forecast values.
* All data is in thousands of Mexican pesos.

In order to estimate PEMEX's range of values, discounted cash flow method was used, with a discount rate range from 4 per cent to 6 per cent. The lower limit was assumed, base on the free risk rate determined by the government bonds. And the upper limit was assumed base on the commercial interest rate (6%).

After calculating the net present value of the future cash flows as well as the terminal value, the PEMEX'S range value is from US$ 235,994,648.43 to $ 319,176,175.23 US dollars.

Lower Limit		*Upper Limit*	
Discount Rate	4.50%	Discount Rate	6.00%
Net Present Value	519,753,413 $	Net Present Value	519,732,590 $
Residual Value	4,002,469,237 $	Residual Value	3,001,851,928 $
Terminal Value's Present Value	3,830,114,103 $	Terminal Value's Present Value	2,831,935,781 $
FMV (In thousands Mexican Pesos)	3,830,114,103 $	FMV (In thousands Mexican Pesos)	2,831,935,781 $
FMV (In thousands American Dollars)	**319,176,175.23 $**	**FMV (In thousands American Dollars)**	**235,994,648.43 $**
Average FMV (In thousands American Dollars	**277,585,411.83 $**		

Notes:

* 2011, 2012 and 2013 are forecast values.

* All data is in thousands of Mexican pesos.

The following assumptions were made to arrive at the range of fair market value.

1. The future company's cash flows are estimated based on the current values actualized to the Mexican inflation forecasted by the Mexican Central Bank.
2. The inflation rate utilized was 4 per cent
3. The discount rate utilized to calculate the net present value as

well as the residual value was 4.5 per cent. This figure represents the free risk rate stated by the government bonds (CETES).

4. The currency exchange rate have been utilized to transform the result in US dollars was 12 MPX = 1 US$. This figure was obtained from the Mexican Central Bank as of June 30, 2011.
5. The valuation method utilized was the discounted cash flow method.

From the above description it is evident that though PEMEX is a strategic firm for Mexico, it can be categorized as a non-viable entity. Based on these two facts and with the aim to close the gap between the PEMEX's current performance and the industry benchmark, the following restructuring strategies are recommended:

Labour redundancy: PEMEX operates under the influence of a strong labour union that generates huge cost to the company, and contributes to the inefficient operation of the company. Government has to come up with a reform plan to reduce the unwanted and unskilled labour force rather than take a political advantage by allowing this labour union to influence the overall operation of the company. Unfortunately, the aforementioned union has significant power which is backed up by number of politicians therefore, it seems difficult for the government to remove or reduce their involvement in decision-making.

Debt restructuring: In 2009 the total gross debt increased by 7.7 per cent. Moreover, PEMEX has sizeable pension obligations that have been increasing. The actual PEMEX's debt structure must be restructured otherwise in near future company's overall sustainability would be compromised

Strategic restructuring: The main need of this strategy is to generate a long-term vision besides the political interest of the company's top management as well as the government in charge. Government should focus more on long-term strategic goals rather than make this company a victim of political compulsions. In addition government should bring the changes in overall business plan which will give PEMEX a competitive edge.

Legal restructuring: PEMEX operates under a legal framework that does not allow this company to get adjusted to the ever changing dynamic business environment. Therefore, a restructuring in this field is required to give PEMEX the opportunity to perform in a competitive way in the global arena.

PEMEX's authorities must consider reorganizing into component parts through breaking up the company into different legal entities. This strategy could allow the Mexican government to maintain the ownership of the company and give concessions on some of the activities to strategic partners. Their main objective for doing this should be aimed towards developing and modernizing the company's infrastructure, enhancing distribution, logistical operation and marketing activities. Beside that, government can bring prudent industry specialists through management contract that can help the company to turn-around while keeping the overall strategic goals intact.

PEMEX thus faces lot of challenges to become a viable enterprise. These challenges are:

- The regulatory framework that the Mexican government uses to manage PEMEX.
- Technological obsolescence
- The necessity of investing in a better distribution network as well as in exploration projects.
- High labour liabilities
- Move forward to a market oriented operations rather than remain a bureaucratic one.

Case Questions

1. PEMEX, needs to upgrade technology and substantial investment would be required. Suggest a plan for physical restructuring and the sequencing of such a strategy?
2. What are the measures advocated by you for improving the operating cash cycle for PEMEX?
3. Outline the details for carrying out a debt restructuring for PEMEX?
4. What forms of organizational restructuring would you like to recommend for PEMEX?
5. Comment on other restructuring measures to be adopted by PEMEX?
6. Consider a similar large petroleum corporation in your own country and prepare an action plan for restructuring the same?

Annexure

Consolidated results	Financial Summary				
	2005	2006	2007	2008	2009
Assumptions					
Mexican mix price (US$/b)	42.71	53.04	61.63	84.35	57.42
Natural gas (US$/Btu)	7.77	6.68	6.91	8.42	3.79
FX (Ps/US$)	10.78	10.88	10.87	13.54	13.07
Income Statement (Ps. MMM, except change data)					
Total sales	908.4	1,062.5	1,136.0	1,329.0	1,089.9
Change	26.4%	17.0%	*6.9%*	*17.0%*	*-18.0%*
Exports of crude & condensates	378.9	463.2	483.4	562.1	410.4
Domestic sales of natural gas	81.1	78.0	82.3	106.8	59.9
Domestic sales of petroleum products	382.0	446.0	486.0	543.0	515.7
Operating income	498.8	581.3	590.4	571.1	428.3
Comprehensive financing result	(4.5)	(23.0)	(20.0)	(107.5)	(15.3)
Taxes and duties	580.6	582.9	677.3	771.7	546.6
Taxes and duties/Sales	63.9%	54.9%	59.6%	58.1%	50.2%
Taxes and duties/ Operating income	116.4%	100.3%	114.7%	135.1%	127.6%
Net income	**(76.3)**	**45.3**	**(18.3)**	**(112.1)**	**(94.7)**
EBITDA	595.7	786.2	833.7	969.6	649.8
EBITDA / Financial cost	11.3	17.7	14.4	13.0	8.3
Balance Sheet (Ps. MMM, except growth data)					
Total assets	1,042.6	1,204.7	1,330.3	1,236.8	1,332.0
Cash and cash equivalents	120.8	188.7	171.0	114.2	128.2
Total debt	**537.7**	**569.3**	**500.9**	**586.7**	**631.9**
Change	**9.4%**	**5.9%**	**-12.0%**	**17.1%**	**7.7%**
Net debt	416.9	380.6	329.9	472.5	503.7
Reserve for employee benefits	375.7	454.6	528.2	495.1	576.2
Equity	(26.9)	40.0	49.9	26.9	(66.8)

Case 6: ZESCO—Zambia

ZESCO is the electricity supply company in the Republic of Zambia. It is wholly owned by the Government of the Republic of Zambia (GRZ) and operates under the Ministry of Energy and Water Development. There are many institutions in the energy sector and the liberalising of the economy led to the setting up of the Energy Regulation Board in 1997.

> Zesco limited is a parastatal that was established in 1970 and its governance has evolved overtime. The first initiative to coordinate power generation was taken in the early 1950s when at least four stations with a combined capacity were connected to a central switching station in Kitwe. The most significant development in the electricity supply situation took place when the Kariba Dam and consequently the Kariba South Power Station were constructed. It was owned and operated by Central Africa Power Corporation (CAPCO) which was jointly owned by the governments of Southern and Northern Rhodesia (now Zimbabwe and Zambia). The construction of Kafue Gorge Power Station to be an alternative to the Kariba scheme was the next major step in making hydro-electric power potential abundant in Central Africa. After Zambia gained independence in 1964, the government revived the project and preliminary work began in July1967. The first generating unit was commissioned in 1971 and the project was completed in 1973.

ZESCOs vision and mission statement are about embracing technology and innovation so as to be the main distributor of electricity to all. ZESCO is committed to use technology and innovation in the generation, transmission, distribution and supply of safe, reliable, quality and competitively priced electricity for the sustainable development of Zambia and beyond, thereby facilitating the creation of wealth and improving the quality of life for all. Its vision is to be a leading electricity service provider in Africa through a highly innovative, motivated and dedicated team driven by a passion for excellence

ZESCO is a strategic enterprise as it contributes to the national development. Without electricity most industries in the country will not operate as they depend on electricity. Power is crucial for dynamic economic growth. Zambia's major export is copper, making it a mining country that has an abundance of minerals. Therefore, electricity does play a big role though some mines can source electricity from other places.

ZESCO has been performing poorly in the last few years. Most of the services it offers are highly subsidized, with no net returns to be ploughed back into the company. About 93 per cent of domestic electricity and bulk sales to the mines are subsidized and only 20 per cent of the marginal costs can be recovered.

Mega

On a global environment, South Africa's national utility is the seventh largest in the world and it overshadows all other regional utilities. The company has not fully utilised its hydro capacity as it only uses 1700MW of the 6000MW available. The trading of the exchange rates on the international scene affect ZESCO as its majority customer, the mines have access to international finance which they use to pay for their services. If there are any downward trend on the operations of the mines as happened during the crisis when copper prices went down. ZESCO is affected through the loss of customers when the mines reduce operations or shut down and retrench their workers.

ZESCO has been accessing funding from various financial institutions including its shareholder the government but they have failed to repay the Power Rehabilitation Project (PRP) loans. This has attracted high interest on the cost of repayment hence their recent suggestion that government converts the loan to their share capital in the company.

The company has a significant currency exchange risk that must be carefully managed. The financial revenues of the company come from their largest customer Copperbelt Energy Corporation (CEC). This is paid in US dollars and accounts for at least 50 per cent of its revenue. ZESCO posts exchange gains on current operations when the Kwacha depreciates against the dollar, but exchange losses when the Kwacha appreciates.

ZESCO has not entered into any strategic alliances with any company. Hence, the necessity that it be unbundled as there are views that interested investors would want to invest in specific activities that the company deals in and not in totality as is the situation at present.

ZESCOs financial performance from 2002 to date has been of a downward spiral. The company began to lose money from operations in 2002 i.e. K 24.5 billion (24.5 Zambian Kwacha). The company also experiences increasing trade payables, as a result they have not been able to pay their suppliers on time and this sometimes leads to increased load shedding when the suppliers do not deliver.

Macro

The macro factors include the inflation rate, interest rates, exchange rates, capacity utilization and employment rates. Following the previous down turn of the economy in the sixties and seventies, the country did not prepare for an increase in demand for power during the recovery hence ZESCO has been experiencing challenges in meeting demands as most of its infrastructure had been left to rundown.

Other challenges aggravated by the changing macroeconomic conditions, are the negative effects of inflation, depreciation of the Kwacha and rising interest rates.

As a parastatal, ZESCO is highly dependent on capital injection from the fiscals. The government under the Ministry of Energy and Water development subsidises the company for some costs that it incurs.

The existing Zambian electricity industry is characterized by three main players:

- ZESCO, which is a vertically integrated state-owned utility,
- The Copperbelt Energy Corporation (CEC), a privately owned Transmission and Distribution Company, and
- Lunsemfwa Hydro Power Company (LHPC).

ZESCO faces no competition from the other companies locally as it is the main supplier of electricity to the mines and even sells some to (CEC) which also later sells to the mines.

ZESCO has been benefiting a lot from subsidises from the government as its tariffs are the second lowest in Africa after Zimbabwe. Its under-pricing of customers has meant that it is not able to generate enough revenue to meet all of its costs. Therefore, the government has to meet the deficit. This is coupled with the fact that it has a high cost structure of staff costs that accounts for about 50 per cent of its costs.

As previously mentioned, investors are reluctant to form joint ventures with the company in its totality as they are specifically interested in investing in different activities of the company. The delay in unbundling of the company is therefore, a constraint on the company's ability to attract foreign investment. The low tariffs have also been identified as one of the factors that have made it unattractive for the private sector to invest into new power generation projects.

The energy sector being a vital part in the economic development of the country deserves to be protected by the government. The viability of the company has to be sustained in order to meet the demands of the existing customers and also the new industries that are opening up due to the economic growth. The expected developments to be undertaken imply that the government has to secure some finance that the company may use to meet the increase in the need for electricity.

The distorted tariff structures used by ZESCO results in poor economic efficiency and low returns on investment. Hence, the request for reforms by the World Bank. The company has to adjust its prices to competitive rates that are being offered in other southern African countries if it is to revamp its financial position.

Meso

Electricity is a major subsector in the economy as it contributes a major share towards industrial output in the country. The sector needs restructuring as its underperformance and financial problems are affecting the country's attractiveness to potential investors.

The unsustainable financial situation at the company is affecting the views that the international lenders have of the government. The World Bank is known for urging the government to consider reforms so that the company can be viable. Government decided to consider commercialisation of the company instead of privatisation and this has assisted in reducing debt owed from government. All sectors of the economy are highly dependent on the efficient performance of the power sector.

Micro

ZESCO is a vertically integrated unit that has a board of directors and management with experience and qualifications to oversee the operations of the company.

Fig. 8.2: ZESCO Management

The appointees for the Board of Directors have to be nominated from various independent bodies in the country among them the Law Association of Zambia (LAZ) and Zambia National Farmers Union (ZNFU). This is in line with the road map towards commercialization that involves the appointment of a board of director's independent from government interference. The Board of Directors has the power to appoint and remove the managing director. The managing director is the head of the corporation and he is assisted by nine different directors from the functional departments as shown in Figure 8.2.

Operational Challenges

The inadequate investment in generation and transmission infrastructure over the last 20-30 years has negatively affected company infrastructure. This was further made worse during the debate of whether to privatise and/or restructure, when government took away generation projects from the company and did not permit them to invest in new projects. The dilapidated infrastructure badly affected the operations as there were massive load shedding being experienced as the company tried to maintain the balance between increasing supply and demand during the peak hours. The under capitalization of the company also poses some challenges in its operations.

The costs that ZESCO incurs as it maintains its existence include; general payroll and operation costs like employees' salaries and stationery. Other related costs are internet and telephone service. About 50 per cent of the staff costs opt for pensions, gratuities and Group life assurance. Temporary employee payments are on the high side as the numbers of such workforce keeps increasing. Maintenance costs, interest, fuel and insurance are all part of the overhead costs.

Thus, the causes and symptoms of ZESCOs decline can be summed up as follows:

Causes

- High cost structure
- Weak Financial controls
- Bloated work force
- Low tariffs leading to poor revenue generation

Symptoms

- Dependence on the government to service their debts
- Dilapidated equipment causing constant load shedding

- Lack of planning leading to inability to meet increased demand due to insufficient capacity
- Inability to pay their loans and remit taxes to the Zambia Revenue Authority

The four level framework (Mega, Macro, Meso, Micro) for analysing ZESCO, coupled with the internal and external analysis can be summarised as follows:

Strengths	***Weaknesses***
• Has governments full support • Major supplier of electricity in the country • Has the infrastructure already established therefore they just need to maintain and upgrade it	• Company has not adopted business practices • Bloated workforce • Not able to meet target of metering 100 per cent of all its customers (i.e. about one third are not metered) • Under-pricing of major customers • High staff costs

Opportunities	***Threats***
• Substantial efficiency gains due to low customer per employee ration • Endeavour to properly price the mining load since it represents 50 per cent of total consumption • Should enter into contracts with new mining loads that will reflect proper prices • New mining companies being established and others expanding • Growth in other sectors such as industry, commerce, agriculture and housing, • Country electrification programmes – rural and urban	• Domestic clients may resort to using generators as alternatives due to persistent load shedding • Poor infrastructure due to lack of funding contributes to increase in load shedding • Dependency of about 50 per cent on one customer is dangerous as the customer has more power over the company

The company has revalued its property, plant and equipment as a result of the ongoing rehabilitation of assets under the Zambia Power Rehabilitation Project. The company appears to be profitable but it is heavily influenced by 'non-operating' profits reported each year. Adjustments for net exchange gains in 2004 improved performance by K 140 billion. Thus the Net Asset method was used for business valuation purposes.

Restructuring Strategies

Asset Reduction Strategies

The company has assets in excess of US$ 3 billion from its three sections:

(i) *Generation*: Kafue Gorge, Kariba North bank, Victoria falls, and other small holdings
(ii) *Transmission*: high voltage substations are 25, national control centre 01 and three regional centres
(iii) *Distribution assets*: 6 diesel power stations, in excess of 5,000 substations

The solution that would be recommended is to unbundle the three sections so that they can be operating independently. This may bring about proper accounting and handling of costs of operations for the divisions.

Cost Reduction

There are some critical areas that the company can target as they consider cost reductions in their restructuring efforts:

(i) Reducing the high staff cost they currently are facing. This can be done by re-evaluating the whole company structure. This will ensure that a clear picture is obtained of which sections need what employees and which employees can be redeployed or laid off. It will also highlight on exactly which employees can be kept on temporary basis as this figure keeps increasing over the years.
(ii) Increasing domestic customer base as only about 20 per cent of the population has access to electricity. Bringing in more customers will mean that the company has to improve on service delivery through rehabilitation of infrastructure.

(iii) Increase revenue generated by setting up proper pricing rates. At the moment the company is under-pricing the mining companies. With the mines expanding and other new mines being established the company should seriously work on their pricing framework.

(iv) Reducing bloated workforce through retrenchments.

(v) Encourage users to use energy efficient strategies so that the company does not face deficit and in the process shut down some areas.

(vi) Business process re-engineering: The fundamental radical redesign of activities to create an output that is of value to the customer. Re-engineering of ZESCO would involve abandoning existing assumptions, breaking tules and coming up with new way of doing things.

(vii) Total quality management:The company may use a company that is in a similar industry as a benchmark on where they want to be. In ZESCOs case, ESKOM of South Africa, which is the largest power company in Africa, may be used as a benchmark. Getting an outside certification that may compare their service quality to that of ESKOM will help them get good reviews from the public and their customers. Above all quality improvement will improve the level of service to the customers and in the process reduce costs of the business.

Revenue Generation

The plans that ZESCO may consider in order to generate more revenue for needed investments in expanded generation, transmission and distribution capacity:

- Increase generation capacity by building new plant so that the remaining 4300 MW hydro-power potential can be utilised.
- Improve on demand side management so that deficit can be managed.
- Complete roll out of prepaid meter installation so that more customers can be brought on board.
- Adjust tariffs and make them cost effective according to regional standards.
- Quick implementation of the regional interconnections to share

regional generation capacity for example between Zambia-Tanzania-Kenya.

- The company needs to make its tariff system cost effective if they are to improve the revenue generation. Engaging the mines must be the first step especially that 60 per cent of ZESCO's sales to the copper mines are at subsidised rates. If allowed to continue in its present state, the financial situation will undermine its commercialisation efforts and the viability of the power sector.

Labour Redundancy

The company has to address the ever increasing number of staff on temporary contracts. The numbers of staff under temporary i.e. skilled workers and casual workers i.e. unskilled workers needs to be looked into. Activities that are not the core of the business should be outsourced for example, security. Permanent employee numbers also should be reduced to fit the activities. Arrangements should be made to involve the government and union representatives to come to an agreement on the best way to implement this plan.

Debt Restructuring

ZESCOs' financial position is partially weak because of the high debt levels it has had to undertake to invest in its infrastructure. The US$ 250 million Power Rehabilitation Project (PRP) loans from the government to the company may be converted into government's share capital in the company.

Cultural Restructuring

An organisations culture plays a pivotal role in how the employees approach their work. Being a state owned enterprise, ZESCO is affected by the attitudes that emanate from such institutions. It is more service oriented than profit oriented and this affects its way of doing business. The top positions are usually political appointments and hence they avoid making decisions not supported by the government even if the decisions may be good for the company

Legal Restructuring

Government has set up positive and progressive steps to revamp the energy sector. The enactment of the National Energy Policy in 1994 and the repeal of the Zambia Electricity Supply Act in 1995 had given ZESCO monopoly in the electricity sector. In addition, setting-up of the Energy Regulation Board (ERB) to license and monitor operators created a level playing field for all actors in the sector.

Table 8.3: Lagislation that Government Improve the Energy Sector

Electricity Act No. 15 of 1995 was passed in 1995 (Chapter 433 of the Laws of Zambia) (Electricity Act)	Legislative framework for ESI reforms, including competition
Energy Regulation Act No. 16 of 1995 (Chapter 436 of the Laws of Zambia) (Energy Regulation Act)	Establishes the Energy Regulation Board (ERB) as the regulator for the country's energy sector, including the ESI. Although published on 28 April 1995, it only came into effect on 17 January 1997. Amendments were introduced in 2003 to strengthen ERB to ensure that it had sufficient authority to 49 carry out its mandate by ensuring enforcement capabilities
Electricity Regulations	Technical supply regulations

Table 8.3 shows the legislation that government has put in place to improve the energy sector in the country.

Physical Restructuring

This should be continuously done whether the company is to be sold or not. In ZESCOs case, rehabilitation is an on-going process as letting the infrastructure deteriorate may lead to load shedding. Non-maintenance and repairs lead to system delays and this negatively affects the company.

Organizational Restructuring

Divisionalisation and decentralisation as turnaround strategies will be appropriate as the company looks at achieving efficiency through unbundling its activities.

Investors may come on board after the unbundling as it will make it easier to them, due to the fact that some of them may just be interested in investing in one of the activities, for example distribution.

With its current financial position, it will be a challenge for ZESCO to attract investors due to reasons such as:

- Under capitalization; the utility company owes government and financial institutions loans it took when it embarked on infrastructure rehabilitation
- A weak financial base; the company's financial position has not been good since 2002 and it continues to report operational losses of which staff costs seem to be on the increase
- Its size may also work against its advantage as investors may be more interested in investing in specific activities and not the whole company.

ZESCO should be privatised as it will be the best option for the company. Most utilities in many countries have to decide whether to go in for divestiture, meaning thereby 100 per cent privatisation or privatising in bits and pieces. Partial privatization is possible if the utility is split up into different components and a specific strategy is adopted for each part. However, as the power sector is a strategic sector in society, the government may keep a minority percentage in the company and also sell some shares to the public so that they can feel part of the new company. This will mean that government keeps some checks and balances on the new investors so that they do not neglect the rural areas.

Case Questions

1. Discuss in detail the merits and demerits of the proposed restructuring measures.
2. Would you advocate a divestiture of ZESCO or a partial privatization?
3. What restructuring measures do you suggest for eliminating/minimising the distribution losses?
4. If there is a compulsion on ZESCO, because of Government policies, such as rural electrification etc, should incentives be provided for the utility to be viable in the long run?
   What regulatory mechanisms do you recommend?
5. Work out an action plan for restructuring a water utility/electric utility from your own country.
6. What are the special privileges which the Government can offer to a foreign investor?

REVIEW QUESTIONS

1. (a) Modify the integrated framework for restructuring to suit your country specific requirements.
   (b) Accordingly identify a strategic and non strategic enterprise. Classify the same as a viable or a non viable one.
2. You have recently taken over as a Restructuring Consultant for Farsons group of companies. The Management of the Group furnishes you the Altman Index (Z-score) for three units, arrived at by the Chief Finance officer.

Unit	*Z-score*
A	3.1
B	1.5
C	2.1

   The Management seeks your advice regarding the interpretation of the same, and the appropriate approaches for restructuring measures of the three units.
3. You have been appointed as a Restructuring Consultant for ALFA (Mexico), a Mexican conglomerate consisting of three group of companies. The Management of the Group furnishes you the Altman Index (Z-score) for three units, arrived at by the Chief Finance officer.

Unit	*Z-score*
A	1
B	4
C	2.1

   The Management of ALFA (Mexico) seeks your advice regarding the interpretation of the same, and the appropriate approaches for restructuring measures of the three units under the following assumptions:

Unit	*Assumptions*
A	— Strategic – Viable
A	— Strategic – Non-viable
B	— Non strategic –Viable
C	— Strategic – Non-viable

Comment also on the inconsistencies, if any between the z-score and the assumptions about the viability of the enterprise.

4. Estimate the range of values for the following situations:

		$ billions
(a)	Asset Appraisal	50
	Market Comparison	40
	Earnings Capacity	30
(b)	Asset Appraisal	20
	Market Comparison	30
	Earnings Capacity	35
(c)	Asset Appraisal	15
	Market Comparison	10
	Earnings Capacity	18

5. Generation Ukraine Inc, furnishes the following details from its financial statements for the years 2009 and 2010.

Balance Sheets as of April 1

(Millions of Dollars)

ASSETS	*2009*	*2010*
Current assets:		
Cash	0.26	0.23
Receivables	2.09	2.37
Inventories	2.03	2.27
Other	0.08	0.10
TOTAL CURRENT ASSETS	$4.46	$4.97
Fixed Assets		
Gross	$3.79	$3.94
Less Depreciation	1.35	1.55
TOTAL FIXED ASSETS	2.44	2.39
LIABILITIES AND CAPITAL		
Current liabilities	1.08	1.25
Long Term debt (5.5%)	1.05	0.95
Stockholders equity (600000 shares)		
	4.77	5.16
Earnings per share	0.77	0.73

The shares on an average are quoted in the market at $ 25 and $ 30 respectively for the years 2009 and 2010. The value for reputation of the business is independently fixed at $20M and the earnings capacity value at $1 billion. Fix up a range of values for Generation Ukraine Inc. Make necessary assumptions and state them explicitly.

6. Azerbaijan Cermington Enterprises Ltd, (ACE) has recently carried out an organizational diagnosis and furnishes the following details. The average inventory holding period is 90 days and settlement period by debtors is 75 days while the norm as per the credit policy is 60 days. An age-wise classification of the accounts receivable for the year 2009 follows:

0-30 days	$ 82981
31-60	$ 510,064
61-90	$ 928786
Over 90	$ 82981

Purchases of raw materials by ACE are made on credit basis and payment is made by forty days on an average. ACE seeks your suggestions for restructuring the company through Asset reduction measures. State your assumptions clearly.

7. The Kadota Semanek Corporation formed in the early eighties, is the result of the acquisition by Kadota Film, Image and General Company of Semanek Pharmaceautical Company (SPC). Kadota had $ 2.2 billion in long-term debt outstanding and SPC had $ 208 million in long-term debt and $140 million in short term debt. Interest cost on this outstanding debt was currently $ 216 million a year. Bankers of Kadota included Imperial bank of Commerce, Deutsche Bank, ABN AMRO, and investment banks—Cerebus, Goldman Sachs and Lone Star. Outline the steps involved in debt restructuring of the Corporation

8. There has been a gradual evolution of Information technology applications. (a) Data processing—conversion of huge mass of data into information, (b) Management information systems—Providing information for strategic planning, management control and operational control purposes, (c) Decision support systems—Easy to use software for unstructured, ill defined problems, (d) Business process reengineering—Abandoning existing rules and assumtions to attain quantum leaps in performance in terms of cost, service and speed, (e) E-business—The web and e-commerce are key industry drivers. E-business is the complex fusion of business processes, enterprise applications, and organizational structure necessary to create a

high performance business model. All these applications have a tremendous bearing on the restructuring of enterprises, both private and public.

Develop an action plan highlighting the possible e-support applications for restructuring the enterprise/organization, you work for.

The following are the steps involved in preparing the action plan entailing e-support for restructuring. The same can form the basis for further restructuring efforts:

(a) Analyse the type of e-government transactions in your country
G2C (Government to citizen)
G2B (Government to business)
G2E (Government to enterprise)
G2G (Government to Government)

(b) An analysis of specific restructuring activities in the enterprise/organization.

(c) Consideration of possible application of restructuring strategies along with the sequencing and timing of the application of the following measures:
- Asset reduction
- Cost reduction
- Revenue generation
- Labour redundancy
- Debt restructuring
- Financial restructuring
- Strategic restructuring
- Physical restructuring
- Organizational restructuring

(d) E-support systems for deploying the suggested restructuring measures
- TPS (Transaction processing system)
- MIS (Management information system)
- DSS (Decision support systems)
- BPR (Business process re-engineering)
- E-Business

Bibliography

Ashley Braganza 2001, Radical Process Change: A best practice blueprint: Wiley.

Asian Development Bank 1985, Conference on Privatization Policies, Methods and Procedures. Manilla, Philippines.

Benton, E. Gup 2003, Too big to fail: Policies and practices in Government bailouts: Praeger.

Brian, S. Silverman 2002, Technological resources and the logic of corporate diversification, UK: Routledge.

Central and Eastern European Privatization Network 1992, Preparing Enterprises for privatization: Business valuation Workshop series No. 2 Ljubljana: CEEPN&UNDP.

Champlin, Dell P. and Knoeder Janet T. 1999, "Restructuring by design: Governments complicity in corporate restructuring" *Journal of Economic issues* (Vol.33).

Christopher L. Culp and William A. Niskanen 2003, Corporate Aftershock: The public policy lessons from the collapse of Enron and other major corporations: Wiley.

David Vance 2009, Corporate restructuring: From cause to execution: Springer-Verlag.

David Skeel 2005, Icarus in the Boardroom: The fundamental flaws in corporate America and where they came from: Oxford University Press.

Edward I. Altman and Edith Hotchkiss 2005, Corporate Financial distress and bankruptcy: Predict and avoid bankruptcy, analyze and invest in distressed debt: Wiley.

Fabrizio Barca and Marco Bechi 2002, The Control of Corporate Europe: Oxford University Press.

Frederick M. Zimmerman 1991, Turnaround experience: Real World lessons in revitalizing corporations: McGraw-Hill Inc.

Gilson, Stuart C. 2010, Creating value through Corporate restructuring: Case studies in bankruptcies, buyouts and breakups: John Wiley & Sons.

Gouri Geeta, Jayashankar, R. and Fadahunsi Olu (Eds) 1993, Efficiency through competition in Public utilities-Policies for restructuring, Ljubljana: Commonwealth Secretariat and ICPE.

Harvard Business Review on Turnarounds 2001: Harvard Business School Press.

Harry, G. Broadman (Ed) 1996, Policy options for reform of Chinese State—Owned Enterprises, Washington DC: World Bank.

Ira, W. Lieberman and Daniel J. Kopf (Eds) 2008, Privatization in transition economies- The ongoing story: London Elsevier.

James, B. Shein 2011, Reversing the slide: A Strategic guide to turnarounds and corporate renewal ; Jossey-Bass.

Jayashankar, R. 1993, "Reforming Self-managed enterprises in Slovenia "in Revitalizing socialist enterprises—A race against time John Heath (Ed): UK Routledge.

Jayashankar, R. 1996, "Organisational Diagnostics: A prerequisite for Restructuring" In The challenges of corporate restructuring in the 1990's, El Namaki and Steve Foster (Ed): Maastricht School of Management.

Jayashankar, R. 1993, "Development of Management support systems for Slovene enterprises" in Consultancy on strategic Information planning, Zdravka Pejova and Forest W Horton (Ed): ICPE, Drexel University College of Information Studies.

Kasteele van de A and Stichele van der M. 2005, " update on the banana chain" in The International Banana Conference.

J. Fred Weston, Kwang S. Chung, Susan E. Hoag 1990, Mergers, Restructuring and corporate control: Prentice Hall International.

Jonathan, I. Klein 2000, Corporate failure by design: Why organizations are built to fail: Quorum Books.

Kenneth, P. and Mitchel Lee Marks 2003, Resizing the organization: Managing Layoffs, divestitures and closings: Maximising gain while minimizing pain: Jossey—Bass.

Kevin Danaher and Jason Mark 2003, Insurrection: Citizen challenge to corporate power, UK; Routledge.

Kikeri, S. and Nellis J. 2001, Privatization in competitive sectors: The record so far, Private sector advisory services, Washington DC: World Bank.

Liangrong, Zu 2009, Corporate social responsibility, Corporate restructuring and firm's performance, Berlin Heidelberg: Springer-Verlag.

Michael Pomerleano and William Shaw 2005, Corporate Restructuring, lessons from Experience, Washington DC: World Bank.

Nag and Pathak 2009, "Corporate restructuring a boon for competitive advantage" in Advances in Competitiveness Research, Vol. 17.

Nellis, J. and M. Shirley 1991, Public Enterprise Reform: The Lessons of Experience EDI, Washington DC: World Bank.

Nikolai Rogovsky 2005, Restructuring for Corporate success-A socially sensitive approach: International Labour Organization.

Patrick, A. Gaughan 2011, Mergers, acquisitions and corporate restructuring: Wiley.

Ramanadham, V.V. 1987, Studies in Public Enterprise: From evaluation to privatization: London Croomhelm Ltd.

Ravi Ramamurthy and Raymond Vernon 1991, Privatization and Control of state owned enterprises. EDI development studies, Washington DC: World Bank.

Rathinasamy, R.S., C.R. Krishnaswamy, and Krishna G. Mantripragada 2000, "Capital Structure and Product Market Interaction: An International Perspective," in *Global Business and Finance Review*.

Shannon Praat 1989, valuing a business: The analysis and appraisal of closely held companies: Homewood IL: Business one Irwin.

Shehadi, K. 2002, Lessons in privatization: United Nations Development Programme, Sub regional resource facility.

Shleifer A. and Vishny, R. 1994, "Politician and firms" in The quarterly Journal of Economics, 46.

Simeon Djankov and Peter Murrell 2000, The determinants of Enterprise restructuring in transition, Washington DC: World Bank.

Stuart, St P. Slatter and David Lovett 1999, Corporate Turnaround: Penguin Business.

Sweeney, A.P. 1994, "Debt Covenant violations and managers accounting responses" in *Journal of Accounting and Economics*, 17.

Thomas Laryea 2010, Approaches to corporate debt restructuring in the wake of financial crises; International monetary Fund.

Vuylsteke, C. 1988, Techniques of privatization of State owned enterprises, Vol. 1, Methods and implementation Technical paper No; 88 Washington DC: World Bank.

Index